A CULTURAL HISTORY OF THE HOME

VOLUME 3

A Cultural History of the Home
General Editor: Amanda Flather

Volume 1
A Cultural History of the Home in Antiquity
Edited by Andrew Wallace-Hadrill and Joanne Berry

Volume 2
A Cultural History of the Home in the Medieval Age
Edited by Katherine L. French

Volume 3
A Cultural History of the Home in the Renaissance
Edited by Amanda Flather

Volume 4
A Cultural History of the Home in the Age of Enlightenment
Edited by Clive Edwards

Volume 5
A Cultural History of the Home in the Age of Empire
Edited by Jane Hamlett

Volume 6
A Cultural History of the Home in the Modern Age
Edited by Despina Stratigakos

A CULTURAL HISTORY OF THE HOME
IN THE RENAISSANCE

Edited by Amanda Flather

BLOOMSBURY ACADEMIC
LONDON • NEW YORK • OXFORD • NEW DELHI • SYDNEY

BLOOMSBURY ACADEMIC
Bloomsbury Publishing Plc
50 Bedford Square, London, WC1B 3DP, UK
1385 Broadway, New York, NY 10018, USA
29 Earlsfort Terrace, Dublin 2, Ireland

BLOOMSBURY, BLOOMSBURY ACADEMIC and the Diana logo are trademarks of
Bloomsbury Publishing Plc

First published in Great Britain 2021
This edition published in Great Britain, 2024

Copyright © Bloomsbury Publishing, 2021

Amanda Flatther has asserted her right under the Copyright, Designs and Patents Act, 1988, to
be identified as Editor of this work.

Cover image © Heritage Images /Getty Images

All rights reserved. No part of this publication may be reproduced or transmitted
in any form or by any means, electronic or mechanical, including photocopying,
recording, or any information storage or retrieval system, without prior permission
in writing from the publishers.

Bloomsbury Publishing Plc does not have any control over, or responsibility for, any
third-party websites referred to or in this book. All internet addresses given in this book
were correct at the time of going to press. The author and publisher regret
any inconvenience caused if addresses have changed or sites have ceased to
exist, but can accept no responsibility for any such changes.

Every effort has been made to trace copyright holders and to obtain their permissions
for the use of copyright material. The publisher apologizes for any errors or omissions
and would be grateful if notified of any corrections that should be incorporated in
future reprints or editions of this book.

A catalogue record for this book is available from the British Library.

A catalog record for this book is available from the Library of Congress.

ISBN: HB: 978-1-4725-8423-6
Set: 978-1-4725-8424-3
PB: 978-1-3504-1225-5
Set: 978-1-3504-1235-4

Typeset by RefineCatch Limited, Bungay, Suffolk
Printed and bound in Great Britain

To find out more about our authors and books visit www.bloomsbury.com
and sign up for our newsletters

CONTENTS

LIST OF ILLUSTRATIONS   vii

SERIES PREFACE   ix

Introduction   1
Amanda Flather

1   The Meaning of Home   13
Cynthia Wall

2   Family and Household   35
Joanne Begiato

3   The House   59
Danae Tankard

4   Furniture and Furnishings   83
Catherine Richardson

5   Home and Work   103
Jane Whittle

6   Gender and Home   127
Amanda Flather

7   Hospitality and Home   147
Paula Hohti Erichsen

| 8 | Religion and Home
Tara Hamling | 167 |

NOTES 195
BIBLIOGRAPHY 201
NOTES ON CONTRIBUTORS 227
INDEX 231

ILLUSTRATIONS

CHAPTER 1

1.1	'The Parts of a House', [1658] 1672	19
1.2	Cheapside, City of London, 1585	20
1.3	'Four-Footed Beasts', 1672	27
1.4	Portrait of Henry Wriothesley, 3rd Earl of Southampton, *c.* 1603	28

CHAPTER 2

2.1	*A Family Saying Grace Before the Meal* by Claeissins, 1585	39
2.2	*The Four Conditions of Society: Work* by Jean Bourdichon	44
2.3	*Two Sisters and a Brother of the Artist* by Sofonisba Anguissola, 1570–90	49
2.4	*Jakob Fugger in his office*, 1518	55

CHAPTER 3

3.1	Cutaway plan of Bayleaf, 1978	63
3.2	Plan for a new lobby-entry house at Holbrook, Suffolk, 1577	66
3.3	Cutaway plan of Pendean, 1977	67
3.4	West Smithfield and Cow Lane, 1612	72
3.5	Fenchurch and Billiter Streets, 1612	73
3.6	John Speed's map of Chichester, 1610	77

CHAPTER 4

4.1	Joined and carved oak chest, 1560–1600	90
4.2	Tin-glazed mug, 1632	95
4.3	Dutch majolica bowl, late-sixteenth–early-seventeenth centuries	100

CHAPTER 5

5.1	*The Visit to the Farm* by Pieter Brueghel the Younger, *c.* 1620	104
5.2	Preparing food for the winter, December, from the Golf Book by the workshop of Simon Bening, 1520–30	107
5.3	The holy family at work, from the Hours of Catherine of Cleves, *c.* 1435–60	113
5.4	*The Egg Seller* by Huybrecht Beuckelaer, 1563–84	118
5.5	House plan from Gervase Markham's *English Husbandman*, 1613	122
5.6	*A Woman Spinning* by Adriaen van Ostade, 1652	124

CHAPTER 6

6.1	*The Account Keeper* by Nicolaes Maes, 1656	135
6.2	*The Kitchen Maid* by Wenceslas Hollar, date unknown	139
6.3	*The Prayer Before the Meal* by Jan Steen, 1660	140

CHAPTER 7

7.1	*Marriage Feast at Cana* attributed to Damaskinòs Michele, 1561–70	159
7.2	*The Birth of Caterina Cornaro*, anonymous, sixteenth century	159
7.3	Detail of *A Marriage Fete at Bermondsey* attributed to to Joris Hoefnagel, *c.* 1569	164

CHAPTER 8

8.1	Illustration of the Annunciation accompanying Matins, Book of Hours, *c.* 1530–5	170
8.2	Page from Richard Day, *A Booke of Christian Prayers*, 1578	171
8.3	An Elizabethan 'assembly chapel', Hardwick Hall, Derbyshire, 1590–7	175
8.4	Head of St John the Baptist, carved panel, fifteenth century	178
8.5	Virgin and Child, pipe-clay statuette, fifteenth century	179
8.6	Wall painting with biblical texts, *c.* 1600–17	181
8.7	*The Family of Hans Conrad Bodmer*, attributed to Heinrich Sulzer, 1643	183
8.8	Marriage Feast at Cana, *c.* 1600, stove plate	189
8.9	Section of barrel-vaulted plasterwork ceiling, *c.* 1620	190
8.10	The Spies of Canaan, sixteenth century, brass dish	191
8.11	Cupboard (Beeldenkast), 1622	193

SERIES PREFACE

A Cultural History of the Home is an authoritative, interdisciplinary, six-volume series investigating the changing meaning of home, both as an idea and as a place to live, from ancient times until the present. Each volume follows the same basic structure and begins with an overview of the cultural, social, political and economic factors that shaped ideas and requirements of home in the period under consideration. Experts examine important aspects of the cultural history of home under eight main headings: the meaning of home; house and home; family and home; gender and home; work and home; furniture and furnishings; religion and home; hospitality and home. A single volume can be read to obtain a thorough knowledge of the period or one of the eight themes can be followed through history by reading the relevant chapter in each of the six volumes, providing an understanding of developments over the longer term.

Individual volumes in the series will cover six historical periods:

Volume 1: *A Cultural History of the Home in Antiquity* (500 BC–800 AD)
Volume 2: *A Cultural History of the Home in the Medieval Age* (800–1450)
Volume 3: *A Cultural History of the Home in the Renaissance* (1450–1650)
Volume 4: *A Cultural History of the Home in the Age of Enlightenment* (1650–1800)
Volume 5: *A Cultural History of the Home in the Age of Empire* (1800–1920)
Volume 6: *A Cultural History of the Home in the Modern Age* (1920–2000+)

Amanda Flather

Introduction

AMANDA FLATHER

This volume addresses the relationship between people and their homes in Christian areas of Western Europe in the Renaissance, traced from the late fourteenth century to around 1650. The essays vary in their geographical focus of study and disciplinary approach but taken together they try to uncover how people used, thought and felt about their homes in the sixteenth and seventeenth centuries. They try to understand what home meant – or if home even existed as a concept – for the people and the places they discuss. They also consider ways in which gender, status, age and geography contributed to different meanings of home, both as an idea and as a place to live. The rest of this introduction explores the key factors behind the relationship between people and their homes in the Renaissance, the different methods and approaches to the study of homes in the past and how the essays in this volume contribute to our understanding of these issues.

The meaning of the word 'home' is always more than simply a physical structure even if it carries different ideological freight for different individuals in different periods and places. Twenty-first-century people often see home as a sanctuary, a place of privacy and comfort that is separate from the world of work. Domestic arrangements differed in the Renaissance because the home was not separate from work and the wider economy. Most people in this period, whether small farmers, artisans, merchants or shopkeepers, worked at home. In many households, servants and apprentices unrelated by blood and marriage lived and worked with the family on fairly close and intimate terms and, in some regions, farm animals sometimes also lived side by side with people, under the same roof. As Jane Whittle's essay here shows, the classical meaning of the word 'economy' was management of the household and this meaning was still current between 1450 and 1650. The household was of fundamental economic importance as a place of production, retailing and consumption in this period. It was a business and an economy, and productive and reproductive work were seen as equally necessary for its survival (Gray 2000; Muldrew 1998: 158).

The conception of home as a place of comfort and sanctuary is thought to have its roots in the eighteenth- and nineteenth-century idealization of the home when people began in England, for example, to distinguish between the meanings of the words 'house', 'household' and 'home' (Harvey 2012: 12). But as Cynthia Wall reveals in her essay for this volume, already in the Renaissance, home meant more than a living space or shelter from the elements. An emotional idea of home is evoked by Erasmus' *Convivium Religiosum*, where he idealizes a cosy 'home' with enclosed gardens, fine art and excellent food (Thompson 1965: 46). In Shakespeare's *The Taming of the Shrew*, Katherine imagines the housewife's life as one of lying 'warm at home, secure and safe' (1593: 5.2.155).

The boundary of the Renaissance home was also very important legally, culturally and socially, for the preservation of security. In many regions of Europe, the borders of houses were protected against supernatural threats to the humans and animals within them by bundles of special herbs placed in lintels of doors through which people left the house. Witch-bottles were often also buried under the hearth as a precaution against witches entering the house through the chimney stack. In Germany, the legal principle of *Hausfrieden* granted special protection to the house and those within it up to a symbolic boundary drawn along the line of drops that fell from the eaves when it rained (Rowlands 1999: 34). In Italy, too, the statutes of *Forli* forbade arresting anyone in his home, 'As the house is a most safe refuge and a vessel of repose' (Kuehn 2017: 80). The legal precept in England that no one may enter a home unless by invitation from the owner was established as common law by Sir Edward Coke in 1628. The principle that 'a man's house is his castle, and each man's home is his safest refuge', enshrined into law a popular belief expressed in print by several authors in the late sixteenth century. Henri Éstienne's *The Stage of Popish Toyes*, includes the comment that [The English papists owe it to the Queen that] 'youre house is youre Castell' (Éstienne 1581: 88). Richard Mulcaster, the headmaster of Merchant Taylors' School in London, echoed the idea in his treatise on education, *Positions, which are necessarie for the training up of children*, 'He [the householder] is the appointer of his owne circumstance, and his house is his castle' (1581: 225).

The Renaissance home was regarded by contemporaries as an essential component of political and social order. The locus of patriarchal authority, legally, culturally and socially, was in the home. The household was often described by English social commentators as a 'Little Commonwealth' and everywhere in Europe the maintenance of patriarchal relations between master, mistress, children and servants at home was regarded as vitally important for the maintenance of social and political stability outside it (Flather 2007). It is not by chance that in this period the words 'house' and 'family' were used interchangeably in all major European languages and throughout all strata of society. Indeed, as Amanda Vickery notes, 'homes or the lack of them materialized one's place in the social hierarchy' (2009: 306). Many commentators laid particular stress on the links between women and the home in these contexts. The classical doctrine that order in families and by extension within wider society required adherence to a spatial system that assigned a role outside the house to men and confined women within the domestic sphere was an important Renaissance rhetorical principle. It was based on views about the differences between men and women that were very different from our own. Renaissance ideas about gender difference were derived from classical thought, Christian ideology and contemporary science and medicine. Men and women were thought to inhabit bodies with different physical make-ups and to possess fundamentally different qualities and virtues. Men, as the stronger sex, were thought to be intelligent, courageous and determined. Women, on the other hand, were more governed by their emotions, and their virtues were expected to be chastity, modesty, compassion and piety. Men were thought to be more aggressive; women more passive. These differences were echoed in the faults to which each sex was thought to be prone. Men were prone to violence, obstinacy and selfishness, while women's sins were viewed as the result of their tendency to be ruled by their bodies and their emotions, notably lust and excessive passion. Expectations of male and female conduct derived from these perceived virtues and weaknesses. In marriage, men were expected to rule over their wives, and all property belonged to the husband. Men were meant to be active away from home in the world of work, business and politics, while women were expected to stay within and preside over the management of the home (Wiesner Hanks 2019: 22–60).

Numerous historians of women and gender have pointed out problems with a wider thesis of 'separate spheres' with which these ideas are often allied. Commentators have pointed out that the conceptual distinction between public and private spheres did not come into play until after the end of our period. They have also drawn attention to distortions in twentieth-century histories of women and the family in the Renaissance that sometimes confused gendered ideals in advice literature with actual day-to-day practice (Vickery 1993). The effect was to underestimate women's activities outside the home as well as leaving the male contribution to domestic life unexamined. As the chapters in this volume by Whittle and Flather show, while in the Renaissance period work was frequently gender related and women were closely associated with domestic management, a host of evidence from a variety of regions describes women, both housewives and female servants, performing productive as well as reproductive work inside and outside the house. Examining the significance of home as a place of work also underlines the presence and importance of men and their contribution to the home. Men as well as women often worked at home in craft workshops, agricultural buildings, shops and alehouses that were attached to houses. Shepard (2003) and others have also underlined the crucial role of the home in the formation of masculine identity. Paula Hohti shows in her essay for this volume that the Renaissance home was necessarily open to the outside world for business and for sociability, ensuring that men and women, old and young, worked and socialized alongside one another inside the walls of the house. Of course, this did not mean that everyone experienced and used their houses in the same way. Amanda Flather's essay here shows that spatial control, personal freedom and the ability to limit access contributed to different meanings and lived experiences of 'home' for different individuals according to gender, status, age and 'place'.

In practice, homes contained complex and variable groups of people which, as the chapter by Joanne Begiato shows, were more complicated and more fragile than contemporary descriptions and some modern historians have allowed. Twentieth-century historical demography saw Europe as having had two broad types of household system. To the west and north, there was the zone of nuclear family households, where marriage was late and far from universal, because it was typically linked to the formation of a new household as an independent economic unit. To the east and south of this line, the non-European (Eastern European) pattern prevailed: multigenerational complex families were ubiquitous, and marriage was universal and happened at an early age (Hajnal 1965; Laslett 1965; Laslett and Wall 1972). Driven by micro-historical and anthropological perspectives, more recent research has uncovered a significant degree of variation in household structure within and between regions that cannot be explained simply by a bipartite model, and that calls for a much more complex set of explanations that take into account a wide variety of demographic, socioeconomic and cultural factors. Families were precarious and frequently faced by change brought about by death, desertion, economic disaster and remarriage. At any one time, households could contain a variety of kin and step-kin, such as spouses, widowers, parents, children, siblings, uncles, aunts, grandparents, non-kin (Goldberg 2010: 22–8; Cavallo 2010: 11–12). Moreover, the Renaissance concept of family also included not only the conjugal unit but also servants connected to households through contractual bonds (Tadmor 1996). While the head of the household was usually imagined as male, and married with dependents, exercising a patriarchal authority over wife, children, apprentices and servants, in practice, because of high mortality rates, many households were headed by women, usually widows (Cavallo and Warner 1999).

Early attempts to historicize the emotional tenor of home life argued that in the face of this uncertainty, people in the past withdrew from strong emotional connection to those who they lived with (Stone 1977). These interpretations have largely been discounted as evidence comes to light in court records, letters and diaries, of the full range of emotional relations between men and women, parents and children, even masters and servants. Begiato shows in her chapter in this volume that these emotions played an important part in the formation and shaping of family life and the ability of the household to absorb change and complexity. Renaissance homes were social and cultural units that were formed by and helped form relationships with a wide variety of individuals, not all of whom were related by blood.

To understand what factors were involved in shaping structures and meanings of home in the Renaissance we also need to look beyond the domestic environment to the wider patterns of continuity and change in society, economy and culture that characterized the era. Legacies from the medieval period included a hierarchical and patriarchal structure of society. Women were everywhere subject to men even if within a formal legal and political structure of male domination, some women exercised a great deal of power. Lineage still determined opportunity to a large extent. The nobility formed a tiny proportion of the population but continued to enjoy a disproportionate share of wealth and social and political power. The vast majority of Europeans lived in the countryside and while 'peasant' is too narrow a term to capture the variety of types of tenure, size of landholding and farming methods of the period, it can be usefully applied to the roughly 85–90 percent of the European population who lived in heavily stratified local rural societies, who cultivated a plot of land with the labour resources of the household and who owed various combinations of rents, dues and services to their lords. Religion also continued to play a central role in social, cultural and political life, with regular church attendance and adherence to Christian values expected of everyone (Kümin 2018).

The two centuries after 1450 were, however, also characterized by a cluster of interrelated forces that led to significant changes in the material, social, cultural, economic and political landscape. Religion and culture were fragmented by the Protestant and Catholic Reformations (Brady, Oberman and Tracy 1995). The invention of print triggered an information revolution and the voyages of discovery in the fifteenth century began a process of transatlantic colonial expansion. Politically, rulers embarked on projects of development of their territories beyond their borders and consolidation of power and authority within them through increasing levels of state administration, legalization and taxation. This combination of religious division, dynastic ambition and colonial competition made warfare a frequent feature of life between the late fifteenth and seventeenth centuries (Rogers 1995).

There was also a degree of socioeconomic transformation. The basic engine of change was demographic. Broadly speaking the population of Europe grew rapidly from around 1450 to 1600. There were regional variations in the rate and timing of growth and periodic instances of crisis mortality, however, by 1580, most areas had recovered or surpassed population levels reached before the catastrophic plague epidemic of the Black Death in the fourteenth century. Associated with this demographic expansion was a marked rise in prices. Between 1500 and 1640, the price of foodstuffs increased nearly sevenfold. Industrial prices were more sluggish but they increased threefold. This inflation was largely the result of the failure of production to keep pace with supply. The productive response to demand was not negligible, however. High prices stimulated improvements in agricultural output and the marketing system. There was also some industrial development in rural areas, as in the mines of the Austrian Tyrol and the north-east of England. Processes of growth, specialization and diversification also occurred in manufacturing and a growing number and range of luxury goods such as furniture, jewellery and elaborate ceramics were produced, mostly in towns, in the workshops of specialist craftsmen. Proto-industrial manufacture also took place in rural areas. Textiles were an important part of the economy in many regions and production was organized under the putting-out system, whereby urban merchants bought raw wool or flax and sent out parcels of the material to rural villages, where men women and children worked as spinners and weavers at home (Musgrave 1999).

These economic shifts led to a degree of sociostructural change. The nobility began to be joined by wealthy merchants and bankers who benefited financially from the expansion of the market economy. A 'middling order' also emerged in this period, made up of people with a wide range of occupations. The wealthier yeomen in England, *coq de villages* in France and *Vollbauer*, wealthy tenant farmers with full rights in communal resources in Germany, owned or rented reasonably large landholdings, could increase production and benefit from high prices and thus tended to do well. Merchants, traders and manufacturers also grew in numbers and became more prosperous as demand for goods and services increased. These individuals were influential on a local level, often holding political positions and responsibilities. Moderate levels of increase in income also enabled them to become consumers of a growing range of new colonial imports and luxury items such as porcelain, silk and plate (De Vries 2008; Ogilvie and Cerman 1996).

Regionally, the impact of these general trends varied according to differences of economic and social structure. In Eastern Europe, landowners sought to consolidate their profit and increase production through re-enserfment of their peasant labour force. In the west, landowners tried in various ways to improve income, often through increase in rent. Small tenant farmers could often not afford to pay and were forced to move out. People who were wholly or largely dependent on wages either as agricultural labourers or industrial artisans became worse off as real wage rates declined and unemployment increased as population expansion outran economic growth. The result was an alarming increase in problems of poverty and mobility. Many people, especially the young, moved to towns (Scott 1998).

Urbanization was a marked feature of the period and closely linked to population rise, the growth of market networks and rise in grain prices. Some areas of Europe such as Flanders and northern Italy were already highly urbanized in the fourteenth century. But the sixteenth century saw unparalleled urban growth in North-Western Europe. Towns grew because they were capital cities or centres of royal administration, or because they were ports which expanded in this period as the volume of seaborne trade increased. There was some regional variation. The growing trade in commodities associated with the late-fifteenth-century voyages of discovery benefited, above all, areas and cities along the Atlantic seaboard, with Spain and Portugal at the forefront of trading activities in the sixteenth century and the Dutch and British obtaining pre-eminence from the seventeenth century (Cowan 1998; Nicholas 2003).

Many of these social, economic, religious and cultural developments impacted very directly on homes in the Renaissance. W.G. Hoskins's celebrated essay of 1953 identified 'the rebuilding of rural England' in the sixteenth century, whereby prosperous farmers in the midlands and south-east of England used their growing incomes to rebuild or redesign their homes. Medieval houses had their halls ceiled over, fireplaces installed and windows glazed. Specialist service rooms such as kitchens were also added for the first time. Subsequent research has shown that patterns of change were more complex than Hoskins assumed. The essay by Danae Tankard for this volume shows that while many vernacular houses were built, rebuilt or altered in this period, the pace of change was uneven and construction, size and layout varied according to wealth and to region. Those who lived in cities lived differently from their counterparts in rural areas. The housing conditions of the expanding numbers of labouring poor deteriorated and many people lived in one-roomed tenements or shacks. Nevertheless, broadly speaking, one of the trends across Europe in the Renaissance amongst a variety of social groups in different national contexts was a trend away from single-roomed dwellings based around a multifunctional hall, to houses with more rooms designed for specialized functions such as kitchens for cooking and bedrooms for sleeping upstairs (Sarti 2002).

Home life was also affected directly by developments in manufacture and global trade. Changing consumption practices led to a huge expansion in the number and variety of objects to be found in ordinary households, as well as in the luxury goods of the well-to-do (De Vries 2008). Catherine Richardson's essay in this volume is interested in the role played by non-elite material culture in the construction of status and identity. She traces intense changes in the form, meaning and range of household objects, how the relatively bare interiors of medieval houses gave way to homes filled with household goods. The most valuable piece of furniture was almost invariably the bed belonging to the master and mistress of the house. The most common items were chests for storing valuables, tablecloths and other textiles. During the period, the number of beds, chairs and tables possessed by a household multiplied; cushions, carpets, clocks and looking-glasses were introduced. Eventually, upholstered furniture arrived and, with it, new notions of comfort. Wooden trenchers were replaced by pewter dishes. The coarse pottery of the fifteenth century gave way to stoneware, slipware, tin-glazed earthenware, glass and eventually porcelain (Sarti 2000; Roche 2000; Ogilvie and Cerman 1996).

An older scholarship saw these changes as connected straightforwardly to technological improvements, a universal desire for comfort and a slow advance of physical privacy for the elite (Hoskins 1953; Chartier 1989). However, more recent histories have pointed out that these values are culturally specific and that shifts in house design are closely connected to culture. Most prominent in this regard has been Matthew Johnson, whose thesis of 'closure' argues that architectural changes to houses in the sixteenth and seventeenth centuries reflected and reinforced a reordering of traditional, communal face-to-face social relations in the context of the rise of agrarian capitalism. Wealthier families retreated behind glass windows into more comfortable homes, household life was lived less publicly and neighbourly and parochial interventions diminished. Homes also became increasingly segregated with respect to gender and status as women and servants were ousted from the 'front', 'public' living spaces of the hall and parlour and relegated, marginalized and 'privatised' to the 'back' spaces of the kitchen and service areas around the yard (Johnson 1996: 188).

Other scholars, however, have drawn attention to some complexities within these broad generalizations (McKeon 2006). Interested in the changing divisions and meanings of 'public' and 'private' over time, it has been pointed out that privacy in the modern sense of the word was not something that Renaissance people could easily achieve or something that they particularly desired. To us, privacy means peace and lack of interference but to them it suggested secrecy, suspicion or the 'dishonesty' associated with illicit sex. Lena Orlin has persuasively questioned the assumption that a desire for privacy motivated 'the great rebuilding' in this period, arguing, on the contrary, that prosperous homes belonging to the middling sort were constructed for conspicuous display. Some of the best furniture and decoration was positioned carefully in rooms that were accessible to visitors and that could be admired through windows by passers-by on the street (Orlin 2007: 1–72). Larger homes increasingly offered the possibility of some seclusion through the addition of closets and studies, where men and women could read or pray alone. Even in smaller dwellings, the use of keys and locked boxes suggests a growing sense of possession. But a simple transition from more open living arrangements to greater privacy and segregation is not always supported by what we know about rooms and their furniture (Meldrum 2000: 77). Vernacular houses remained small and crowded. Chairs, rooms and beds were often shared. In these circumstances, segregation was not possible or practical and people had little opportunity to develop a space for themselves.

Homes continued to be rooted in communities. Important developments in the history of gender, work and home in the Renaissance has emphasized the open character of houses, expressed in the way work was organized cooperatively and in the need for connection and collaboration across households (Ågren 2017; Muldrew 1998). As Whittle shows in her essay, the Renaissance economy continued to be a household economy and openness remained crucial to its conduct and survival. Architectural division was taking place within more affluent homes between work spaces and rooms intended for sleep, leisure and socializing (Orlin 1994; Overton, Whittle, Dean and Hann 2004). But to maintain the orderly operation of the household economy, most houses had to be open and accessible most of the time. The hall had a front door entering into the street. Shops were attached to houses on the street frontage and open to serve customers. Kitchens and service rooms at the back of the house were not separate or segregated spaces. They had back doors opening onto the yard, where men and women mingled together even if performing separate tasks. These rooms were also often the first entry point for visiting servants or tradesmen. Men, women, servants and children of both sexes regularly appeared in all the rooms and service areas throughout the period and mixed with customers and neighbours who visited (Flather 2007).

It is also clear that the Renaissance home remained central to religious experience. Change and division associated with the Reformation had a complex impact on the ways in which people engaged with religious beliefs, practices, rituals and objects in their homes. Domestic devotion meant something distinctive for religious minorities, who were often not allowed to observe their religion in church. For them, the home became the safest place to perform religious rituals, as was the case for Catholics in England and Huguenots in France during periods of the sixteenth century (Dolan 2002). But even for those individuals and households who conformed to established religion, the home remained a lively site of domestic devotion. The concept of the holy home was central to early modem Catholicism and historians have charted the increasing numbers of devotional images, relics and furniture that decorated Renaissance houses in Catholic Europe. Sacred objects provided an outward expression of piety, a means to enhance private devotion, and also served additional roles as protective devices (Faini and Meneghin 2018). Research has also begun to dismantle previous historical assumptions about Protestant hostility to Christian materiality (Hamling 2010; Martin and Ryrie 2012; Faini and Meneghin 2018). Tara Hamling's chapter in this volume discusses the newly manufactured everyday devotional objects that filled Protestant homes: the schemes of interior decoration and furnishing – from earthenware pots, plaster ceilings and stove tiles to tapestries, chimney breasts and firebacks – that communicated Protestant moral and spiritual priorities and functioned as symbols of spiritual identity.

METHODS AND APPROACHES

The renaissance home was not then something separate from the world of politics, economics and religion. It was in the home that large impersonal forces were intimately experienced by most of the population; and it is in the home that scholars look to find not only the changing material context in which people lived, but also what patriarchy, gender and social differences meant in practice. Traditionally, historical scholarship has tended to treat the physical setting of the house and its contents as a static backdrop for the study of these wider concerns. More recently, scholars have begun to consider ways in which the architectural form of houses, their layout and contents were an active component in the shaping of social identity and social and gender relations. These preoccupations have been encouraged by the influence of the French sociologist, Pierre Bourdieu, who showed how values and identities were shaped by daily interaction with objects and spaces at home. His concept of *habitus* was founded on the belief that ways of thinking and behaving were closely related to domestic environments. The link between mental and physical space is also important here. Influenced by the French sociologist, Henri Lefebvre, who studied how space is produced conceptually as well as materially and suggested this occurs through three different, yet connected, processes: 'spatial practice' (material or functional space), 'representations of space' (space as codified language) and 'representational space' (the lived everyday experience of space); writers in a variety of fields have shown ways in which the meaning of spaces within and beyond the home can be different, even when they are shared by men or women, old and young, rich and poor, through perception, experience and use. Individual sense of space, and behaviour within it, is influenced by a host of cultural clues that enable people to create 'mental maps' to help them to use spaces and to let them know when spaces might be difficult or dangerous to enter. These different perceptions and experiences are determined in large measure by the different degrees of power wielded by individuals or groups over how the space is accessed, used and given social and cultural meanings (Lefebvre 1991).

These approaches have led to the recognition that to understand the meaning of home in the Renaissance, we need to consider the interaction between ideas, building practices and social experience. As a consequence, the available sources for the study of the home are almost limitless. Material evidence such as objects, plans and inventories are vital tools for the study of the physical structure of houses and changes in lifestyles over time. More traditional aspects of historical research must also be combined with our analysis – social, economic, political – to construct appropriate contextual explanations and interpretations. But to consider the more complex historical questions of meaning, more refined methods and a variety of sources need to be deployed. The study of home has always been interdisciplinary, theoretically as well as historically informed. It is important that this continues to be the case and to work against unhelpful divisions such as the ones this volume aims to bridge. If we do so, then new insights will become available, in part because of a turn to new kinds of evidence or to new strategies for reading evidence that we already have. Conduct literature, sermons, poetry, plays, letters and diaries offer insights into how people thought about and imagined their homes. Legal records also contain very useful evidence about social practice. Some of the most interesting recent work on the Renaissance home has been distinguished by inventive and historically grounded analysis of ballads and plays as well as personal accounts in diaries and letters in relation to material evidence and alongside legal depositions. Court records are not, of course, straightforwardly descriptive – witnesses and litigants were also telling stories, even if they presented them as true. But close attention to the language of these documents reveals emotional resonances as well as day-to-day practices that add depth and complexity to historical understanding of the changing meaning and use of the home in this period (Richardson 2006a–b; Hamling and Richardson 2017).

The essays in this volume draw on these varied approaches. The authors are rooted in a range of disciplines and traditions and use a variety of sources. But, together, they attempt to find some means of understanding not only how people created the homes in which they lived in this period, but also how home shaped individual values and behaviour. They aim to uncover something of the experience of home in the Renaissance and its role in the construction of power, identity and emotion. The volume does not claim to be a comprehensive survey, but rather it offers a series of thematic studies that aim to provide a good indication of current research being undertaken on the Renaissance home. It is hoped that the volume will encourage future research in the field.

CHAPTER ONE

The Meaning of Home

CYNTHIA WALL

> EVERY Mans proper *Mansion* House and *Home*, being the *Theater* of his *Hospitality*, the *Seate* of *Self-fruition*, the *Comfortablest part* of his owne Life . . . [is,] to the Possessors thereof, an *Epitomie* of the whole *World*.
> —Henry Wotton, *Elements of Architecture* (1624: 82)

The philosopher Gaston Bachelard has said that we should all "say how we inhabit our vital space, in accord with all the dialectics of life, how we take root, day after day, in a 'corner of the world.' For our house is our corner of the world" ([1958] 1969: 4). All historians, anthropologists and literary critics are in a sense temporal and spatial travellers who become settlers of a particular place and time and call it an academic home. In this essay, I make a second hop, from eighteenth-century Britain to its Renaissance. I am a visitor, an invited guest in the house of someone I have known long but not intimately. I am looking around, sometimes bumping into unexpected nouns, and trying to clarify the orthography, trying to understand the ways it rhetorically inhabits its corners of the world to make a home. To what extent does the concept of 'home' extend across centuries, countries, languages, classes, genders? In what ways do historical differences emerge? To what extent is the concept cultural, communal or even individual?

'*Houses* are built to Live in, and not to Looke on,' said Francis Bacon ([1625] 1985: 135). Those for whom 'home' means something share with Henry Wotton and Gaston Bachelard the sense of it as microcosm, as its own universe. In one sense, Bachelard suggests, the instinct for home is universal:

> all really inhabited space bears the essence of the notion of home. . . . [T]he imagination functions in this direction whenever the human being has found

> the slightest shelter: we shall see the imagination build 'walls' of impalpable shadows, comfort itself with the illusion of protection[.]
>
> —[1958] 1969: 5

Thus, we think of Robinson Crusoe, making his shelves and pots and umbrellas in his 'Fortress', and cultivating the limes and grapes and goats on his 'country seat'; or Fanny Price, arranging her books and geraniums in her East Room; or the Boffins dividing their parlour down the middle into spaces only for him and others only for her; or Rabbit pragmatically using Pooh's back legs to hold dish towels; or Dorothy in her own backyard. It is, most basically, the 'place where a person or animal dwells', says the first definition in the *Oxford English Dictionary*. 'Looke but upon the poor spider,' says Jack of Newbury, 'the frogge, the flie, and every other silly worme, and you shall see all these observe time to returne to their homes' (Deloney [1597] 1859: 32). 'The bird loves her nest,' nods the proverb (Herbert 1640: A4v). The travel writer J. B. H. Peel is certain that, '[d]imly in their brief and brutish lives[,] the prehistoric cave-dwellers felt more secure – more, as we say, at home – in their own accustomed cavern. The descendants of those cavemen – the nomadic food hunters – felt a similar fondness for the hides and pots that accompanied their travels' (1972: 2). Home, then, is most fundamentally the place where one dwells: a universal premise (or at least impulse) for premises, oblivious of time, place, condition.

And yet, perhaps not. Is it 'home' if one has half a dozen palaces, and travels among them with a retinue of hundreds? Is it 'home' if you do not own it? If you are a servant working and dwelling in its margins? Can a homeless person call her corner of the world in the street or park a home? Peel 'dismiss[es] homes that are not homes, by which we mean caravans, barges, houseboats, and those skyscraping human-hutches ... Many people occupy such places, and some people feel fond of them; but ... they are not truly a home. ... They are merely premises' (1972: 4). The anthropologist Mary Douglas argues, on the other hand, that although 'home is located in space, ... it is not necessarily a fixed space. It does not need bricks and mortar, it can be a wagon, a caravan, a boat, or a tent' (1993: 261). I know people who pay no attention whatsoever to their domestic surroundings, for whom 'home' is simply a place to park a toothbrush. Douglas herself opens her essay referring to the 'tyranny of the home' and its 'inexorable and absurd' routines, its censorship and surveillance, and its capitulation to the lowest common denominator of indifference – implying that home itself, almost by definition, is *unheimlich* (ibid.: 227–8).

This essay, however, takes as its premise that we *do* mean something beyond the first dictionary definition of 'home', and that something is historically and emotionally inflected. Building materials, exterior appearances, interior arrangements, furnishings, household patterns, have all changed dramatically from the medieval period to the Renaissance to the eighteenth century to the present; along each point period shapes concept. The very etymology and proverbial life of 'home' demonstrate its most intuitive meaning: 'with reference to the feelings of belonging, comfort' (*OED* 2b). As the visiting houseguest, I will try to evoke what 'home' could mean in the early modern period, when *domus* became domesticated, changing from a literal to a figurative castle. The proverb, 'A man's house is his castle,' owes its legal foundation to Sir Edward Coke, who, in 1628, inscribed into law a cultural assumption: 'For a man's house is his castle, *et domus sua cuique est tutissimum refugium* [and each man's home is his safest refuge]' ([1628] 1832: 162).[1] '*Home* is home though it be never so homely,' as another proverb goes (Ray 1670 [1678]: 155); although, for some, it might be 'to [too] homely some tyme' (Heywood 1555: Aiiii) – a little *too* familiar, a little *too* close, a little *too* much. My own premise is that the meaning of 'home' depends less on what it is than on how it is inhabited: historically, spatially, psychologically. Fundamentally, 'home' is a verb, the act and actions of dwelling, more than simply living; it is an *alignment*, a way of positioning oneself in one's corner of the world.[2]

'AN ENGLISHMAN'S HOME IS HIS CASTLE'

Although this version of the proverb seems to have evolved in the nineteenth century,[3] it reflects centuries of the English giving themselves first dibs on the concept. Mark Twain observed: 'They say there is no word for "home" in the French language' (1869: 106). 'They' are basically correct: there is no single corresponding word for 'home', as opposed to or separate from 'house', in French, or, indeed, in the Latin or Slavic languages (Rybczynki 2001: 62n). Northern European languages (German, Danish, Swedish, Icelandic, Dutch and English) all have similar sounding terms derived from the old Norse 'heima', 'abode' or 'homestead'.[4] ('Home' as 'abode' extends into strange worlds in Old Icelandic: 'Jøtunheimr' is the abode of giants, and 'Niflheimr' the abode of mist.) These are distinct from 'house', 'haus', 'maison' or 'casa'. To be sure, there are equivalent *phrases* to capture the concept: 'chez Wall' (always used with a personal name or pronoun); 'hogar, dulce hogar' (signifying hearth, the warmth of home; 'foyer' in French). But a phrase takes the long way home, so to speak.[5] A quintessentially English distinction was marked by the eighteenth-century American ambassador, Benjamin Rush, who noted that prominent English families 'have *houses* in London, in which they stay while Parliament sits, and occasionally visit at other seasons; but their *homes* are in the country' (quoted in Peel 1972: 20). And even those great country 'homes', most of which were built between 1500 and 1640 (Airs 1975: vi), however palatial, were not called châteaux or palazzos or even villas, but *houses* (Rybczynski 2001: 106).

A number of the definitions of 'home' imply geographical or national identity. Part of the first (now obsolete) dictionary definition of 'home' is 'a collection of dwellings; a village, a town' (*OED* 1a); related to that are its meanings as 'a landed property; an estate, a manor' (*OED* 1b), including all those living on the estate, and 'a person's own country or native land' (*OED* 5). The author of *A Relation, or Rather a True Account of the Island of England . . . about the year 1500* (attributed to Andrea Trevisano, the Venetian ambassador to the court of Henry VII) remarked on a distinctive national self-identification in the English:

> the English are great lovers of themselves, and of everything belonging to them; they think that there are no other men than themselves, and no other world but England; and whenever they see a handsome foreigner, they say that 'he looks like an Englishman', and that 'it is a great pity that he should not be an Englishman'; and when they partake of any delicacy with a foreigner, they ask him, 'whether such a thing is made in *their* country?'
>
> —[1500] 1847: 20–1

No other world but England. The same sentiment, the same nationalistic satisfaction, is noted a hundred years later by the German lawyer Paul Hentzner, who published his account of his travels in Switzerland, France, England and Italy in 1612: 'If they see a foreigner very well made, or particularly handsome, they will say, *It is a pity he is not an* Englishman! ([1612] 1797: 64)' The land defines its people; as the captain, crew, cousins and aunts of HMS *Pinafore* contentedly sing: 'For he is an Englishman, / And he himself hath said it, / And it's greatly to his credit / That he is an Englishman!' (Gilbert and Sullivan [1878] 2006: 143–4).

The idea of place (country, city, house) as the home of identity plays out frequently in Renaissance literature. In *A Comedy of Errors* (c. 1594), the farce turns on the (mis)recognition of 'home', in terms of both national identity and local habitation. The servant, Dromio of Ephesus, is trying to explain to his mistress, Adriana, that her husband, Antipholus of Ephesus, is 'stark mad' because he would not 'come home to dinner', responding to every line of Dromio's reasoning ('"Tis dinner time'; 'Your meat doth burne'; 'Will you come?') with the dogged repetition of 'My gold' (2.1.60–5).[6] Of course, Dromio of Ephesus has confused Antipholus of Syracuse with his twin brother, Antipholus of Ephesus, and Dromio of Ephesus's own twin brother, Dromio of Syracuse, is the fourth counter in this farce of exchanges. Each identifies himself with his house or inn: the Centaur for the Syracusans and the Phoenix for the Ephesians:

> [*Antipholis Errotis {of Siracusa} to Dromio Siracusia*]
>   How now sir, is your merrie humor alter'd?
>   As you loue stroakes, so iest with me againe:
>   You know no *Centaur?* you receiu'd no gold?
>   Your Mistresse sent to haue me home to dinner?
>   My house was at the *Phoenix?* Wast thou mad,
>   That thus so madlie thou did didst answere me?
>
> —2.2.7–12

R.A. Foakes has argued that Shakespeare may have had the neo-Roman staging traditions of Gray's Inn in mind: an arcade with three marked compartments, each representing a house or *domus* ('Phoenix', 'Centaur', 'Porpentine' [the home of the Courtesan]) (1968: xxxv–xxxvi). 'Home' is thus structurally indicated and, although definitive, implicitly interchangeable. Emerging from or entering into one *domus* confers identity in the minds of the other characters, as much as the stage directions denote true identity with homeland attached ('*Enter Dromio Eph*' in the First Folio).

In Edmund Spenser's *Colin Clout's Come Home Again* (1595), the viewpoint swings from Ireland as home to London as home and back again to Ireland. In *Two Gentlemen of Verona* (1590–1), Valentine says to Proteus: 'Cease to perswade, my louing Protheus; / Home-keeping youth, haue euer homely wits' (1.1.1–2).[7] As Catherine Richardson explains: 'Proteus is "home-keeping" in the sense that he will relinquish the enticing delights of Milan to remain in Verona, not in the sense that he will remain within his house' (2006b: 58). In *King John* (1596) the Duke of Austria promises to Arthur, John's nephew and a claimant to the English throne, that he will resist the lure of his own (national) home to battle for Arthur's: until the 'vtmost corner of the West / Salute thee for her Kinghe', he will not 'thinke of home, but follow Armes' (2.1.314–24).[8] Well through the fifteenth century, the battle for home was usually literal. The houses of the great were castles, built for defence. It was not until the sixteenth century in England, after the ravages of plague and war had truly, experientially receded, that 'home' became visible – not so much *couchant* or *rampant* in defence, but, shall we say, comfortably *dormant*.

'BUILDING IS A SWEET IMPOVERISHING'

How did home emerge as 'refuge' in the domestic rather than the defensive sense? It was first refashioned, and then *built*. The idea of 'home' as 'a dwelling place; a person's house or abode; the fixed residence of a family or household; the seat of domestic life and interests' (*OED* 2a), technically goes back beyond the medieval period,[9] presumably all the way back to Peel's imaginings of caves, hides and favourite pots. But, as Witold Rybczynski rather broadly puts it: 'in the Middle Ages people didn't so much live in their houses as camp in them' (2001: 26).[10] The nobility travelled from one castle to another with their retinues of servants and furniture; the poor lived in two-room longhouses, with a chamber for the family and a byre for the livestock. During the 'Great Rebuilding' of the sixteenth century, as W. G. Hoskins termed it, both the castles of the rich and the longhouses of the poor changed from dwellings of basic defence (against enemies, on the one hand, and nature, on the other) to dwellings to *dwell* in (1953: 44–59).[11] The castle became, architecturally, a house; the house became, figuratively, a castle. By 1763, the prime minister, William Pitt the Elder, ringingly extended the power of the image to the 'poorest man' who 'may in his cottage bid defiance to all the forces of the Crown. It may be frail – its roof may shake – the wind may blow through it – the storm may enter – the rain may enter – but the King of England cannot enter! – all his force dares not cross the threshold of the ruined tenement!' ([1763] 1839: 1.41–2).

The architectural, temporal and regional contours of the Great Rebuilding will be discussed in other chapters; in its simplest model, in the wake of the Black Death (1348–9) and the Wars of the Roses (1455–85), 'for the first time men were free to build as they pleased, unfettered by considerations of defence or feudal obligation' (Airs 1975: vi). '[E]uerie man almost is a builder,' said William Harrison in 1577, 'and he that hath bought any small parcell of ground, be it neuer so little, will not be quiet till he haue pulled downe the old house (if anie were there standing), and set vp a new after his owne deuise' ([1577] 1877: 341).

Be it neuer so little and *after his owne deuise*: these two phrases suggest *pleasure* and *originality*. 'Building is a sweet impoverishing,' as the proverb went (Herbert 1640: fol. C; Ray [1670] 1678: 3). Historians will say more about the impoverishing; the building of *home*, however, is concerned with the *sweet*. Henry Wotton describes the situating of a house ('the *seating* of our selues') as 'a kinde of *Marriage* to a *Place*' (1624: 6); the decision is intimate and profound. Both exteriors and interiors reflected what Lena Cowen Orlin calls the 'exuberance' of the new architecture, with its 'projecting and receding bays, great spiraling chimneys, densely textured surfaces, and contrasting color' (Orlin 2007: 93). Buildings could demonstrate 'wit and intelligence' (Airs 1975: 3). Even cottages were both regionally and individually colourful. As Peel exuberantly puts it, the cottages of the Renaissance countryside 'stand in their own right, as various and handsome as the manors and the castles and the farms. A travelled man can use them as maps': 'the red sandstone cottages of Westmorland', 'the Chiltern cottages of Buckinghamshire, built of local brick and flint', 'the cob cottages of Devon', 'the rubric cottages of Sussex', 'the Cheshire magpie', 'the stone cottages of Exmoor', and 'the incomparable Cotswold cottages' (1972: 40–1).

The interiors of the houses, great and small, exhibited similar exuberant individuality (Figure 1.1). When not alabaster-smooth (Harrison [1577] 1877: 235), the walls could bristle with colour, texture, *narrative*: 'hanged with tapisterie, arras worke, or painted cloths, wherin either diuerse histories, or hearbes, beasts, knots, and such like are stained' (ibid.). Indeed, as George Herbert said of the good parsonage: 'Even the walls are not idle, but something is written, or painted there, which may excite the reader to a thought of piety' (Herbert [1652] 1671: 35). In 1662, Thomas Fuller compared England to 'a house not very great, but convenient' and the shires its rooms; his own plan, in the wake of chorographers William Camden and John Speed, is 'to describe the furniture of those rooms' (Fuller [1662] 1987:1). Harrison marvels at the literal

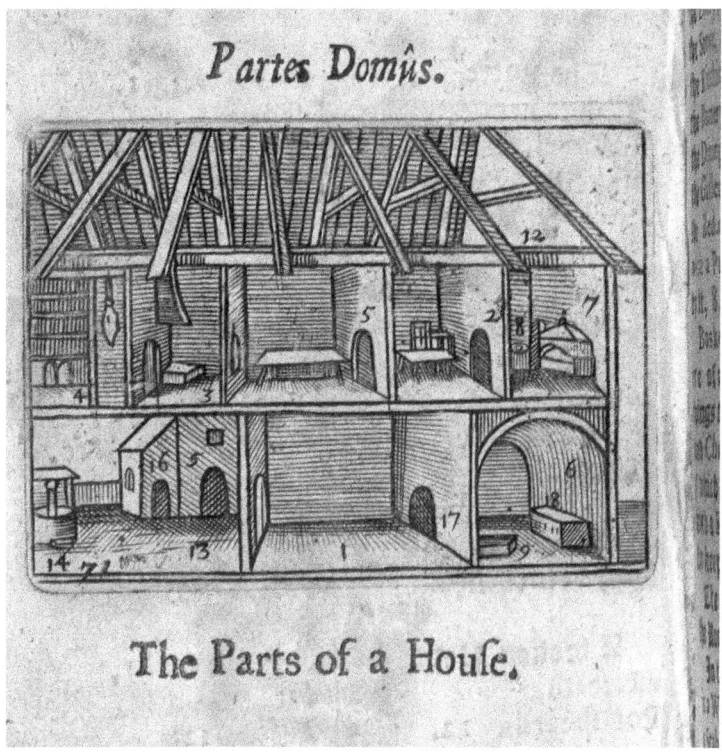

FIGURE 1.1: 'The Parts of a House', Johannes Amos Comenius, *Orbis Sensualium Pictus*, [1658] 1672. © The British Library.

furniture of England's rooms, its 'passing delicacie', and not that 'of the nobilite and gentrie onelie', but even 'the inferiour artificers and manie farmers – haue learned also to garnish their cupbords with plate, their [ioined] beds with tapistrie and silke hangings, and their tables with [carpets &] fine naperie' ([1577] 1877: 238–9). Even the beds of farmers are covered with tapestry (Hentzner [1612] 1797: 64). Harrison is careful to say that he does not speak of all this rebuilding and new luxury 'in reproch of anie man', but rather to 'rejoise . . . to see how God hath blessed vs with his good gifts' ([1577] 1877: 239). Although there was some uneasiness about all this (its impoverishing possibilities, the corruption of luxury, the opening spaces of social mobility), the promise of sweetness lured more compellingly than '*Patch* and long sit, build and soon flit' (Ray [1670] 1678: 21).

Orlin describes the 'house pride' of various Elizabethan Londoners, as that of Eleanor Peerson, for example, 'who was so deeply invested in her home in Aldersgate Street that she rejected a suitor in 1566 because he asked her to move to his place' (2007: 73; and Figure 1.2). John Stow recorded in 1598 that at the west end of Tower Street, there was a faire house, sometime builded by *Angell Dunne*, Grocer, Alderman of *London*; since possessed by Sir *Iohn Champneies*, Alderman and Maior of *London*. He builded in this house an high Tower of Bricke, the first that ever I heard of in any private mans house, to overlooke his neighboures in this Citie. But this delight of his eye was punished with blindnesse some yeeres before his death.

—[1598] 1633: 137

Still, he had built and enjoyed the 'delight of his eye'. During the Dissolution of the Monasteries, Thomas Cromwell took for himself St Pancras Priory at Lewes, 'the finest in all Sussex', and pulled everything down, except for the prior's house, which he renovated for his son, Gregory. 'On going there for his honeymoon the young man writes: "It doth much please me and my wife, & is unto her so commodious that she thinketh herself to be here right well settled"' (Sussex Archaeological Society 1900: 56). In 1629, Robert Herrick was granted the living of Dean Prior, on the edge of Dartmoor, from Charles I; although he initially expressed the Londoner's contempt for country life ('the loathed West'), he came to love his home. His epithalamion on his brother's marriage

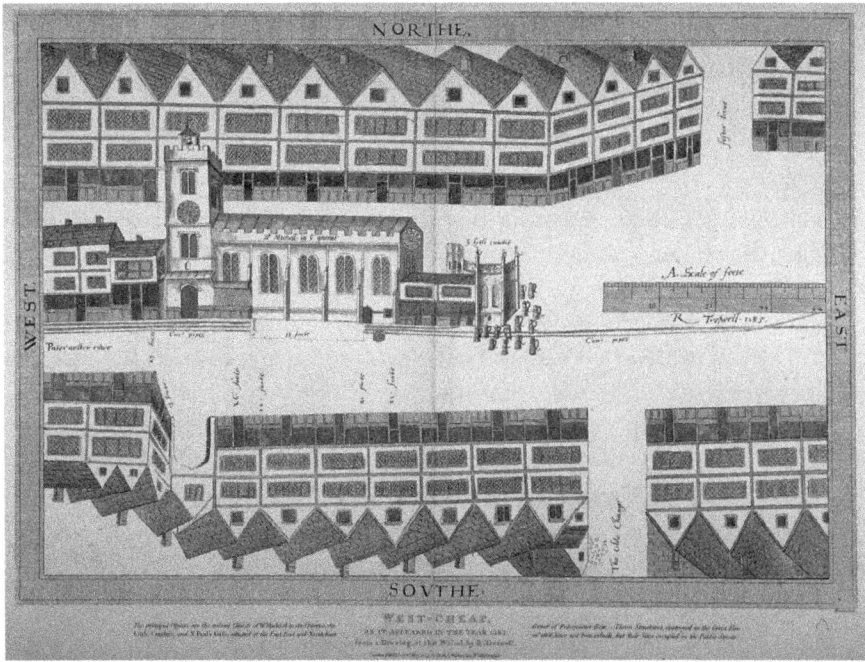

FIGURE 1.2: Cheapside, City of London, 1585 (1814). Artist: Bartholomew Howlett. Plan of Cheapside or Westcheap, as it appeared in 1585; showing houses, St Michael le Querne and the Little Conduit. © Guildhall Library & Art Gallery/Heritage Images/Getty Images.

evokes the pleasures of country quiet and intimacy: unlike the merchant or the sailor, 'thou at home, [are] blest with securest ease'; the daily sounds, scents and visions of meadows, streams, springs, groves, roses, birds and lambs 'make sleep not so sound, as sweet'; within the house, 'thy humble roofe [can] maintain a Quire / Of singing Crickits by thy fire', and thus a 'little well-kept stock doth prove, / *Wealth cannot make a life, but Love.*' The 'Rurall Sanctuary' can be '*Elizium* to thy wife and thee' (Herrick 1648: 35–9).

A garden was part of the sweetness of home.[12] Bacon called it 'the Purest of Humane pleasures' and 'the Greatest Refreshment to the Spirits of Man' ([1625] 1985: 139). In *The Profitable Arte of Gardening*, Thomas Hill notes that besides the 'profit' of a garden (from its herbs and flowers) is 'pleasure, very delectable through the delight of walking in the same ... by the commodities of taking the freshe ayer and sweete smell of flowers in the same' (1568: fol. 1v). From enclosed green spaces for bowls or tennis to kitchen gardens to elaborate knot gardens, the Romantics had nothing on the early moderns by way of pastoral pleasure. John Aubrey regularly notes other peoples' love of gardens: George Herbert had 'a good garden and walkes' ([17th c.] 1949: 40); John Milton 'always had a garden where he lived' where he would 'walke three or four houres at a time' (ibid.: 71); and Sir John Denham, although he had 'better seates' than the parsonage house at Egham, 'did take most delight' in it:

> In this parish is a place called Cammomill-hill, from the cammomill that growes there naturally; as also west of it is Prune-well-hill (formerly part of Sir John's possessions), where was a fine tuft of trees, a clear spring, and a pleasant prospect to the east, over the levell of Middlesex and Surrey. Sir John tooke great delight in this place, and was wont to say (before the troubles) that he would build there a retiring-place to entertaine his muses. ... He delighted much in bowles, and did bowle very well.
>
> —Ibid.: 82–3

Even one of the proverbs that seems sceptical of the sweetness of home is glossed by the proverb-collector for its peculiarly comforting English adaptation:

> Where ever a man dwells, he shall be sure to have a *thorn-bush* at his door. No place no condition is exempt from all trouble. *Nihil est ab omni parte beatum. In medio Tybride Sardinia est.* I think it is true of the thorn-bush litteral sense, [sic] Few places in *England* where a man can live but he shall have one near him.
>
> —Ray [1670] 1678: 209

At least one of the thorn bushes native to the UK is *Prunus spinosa*, or blackthorn, material for cudgels and canes, with creamy white flowers and the dark fruit 'sloe' – of 'sloe-eyed' compliments and sloe gin fizzes. If an Englishman *shall* have a thornbush near him, might that be 'shall' as in 'voluntary action' rather than 'compelled to' (*OED* 3a, 8b(b))?

REPRESENTING SPACES

To what extent is 'home' the *representation* of home? How do textual representations of home align with real homes in the Renaissance? In one sense, they do not. However richly infilled actual interiors might have been with 'tapistrie, Turkie worke, pewter, brasse, fine linen, and thereto costlie cupbords of plate' (Harrison [1577] 1877: 238), with colour and texture and pattern and fabric and light, with tiles and wainscottings and carvings and shining alabaster, with featherbeds and curtains and books and pets and all 'the paraphernalia of everyday life' (Fleming 2014: 5), the stage directions and literary descriptions of Renaissance interiors are notoriously spare. The domestic scenery of printed plays and early prose fiction is drawn by word and gesture, as in *The Merry Wives of Windsor* (*c.* 1597):

> *Enter Mistris Quickly, Simple, Iohn Rugby, Doctor, Caius, Fenton.*
> Qu. What, *Iohn Rugby*, I pray thee goe to the Casement, and see if you can see my Master, Master Docter *Caius* comming: if he doe (i' faith) and finde any body in the house; here will be an old abusing of Gods patience, and the Kings English.
>
> —1.4.1–4[13]

By Mistress Quickly's words we know we are in an interior, in which the casement window becomes spatial direction. 'Space is in fact produced as actors describe it,' says Catherine Richardson, and 'setting is constructed primarily through the language that the characters speak and the gestures that they make' (2006b: 54). It parallels what I have called 'implied space' in late-seventeenth- and early-eighteenth-century prose fiction, where ordinary interior space is rarely visually detailed; rather, we are given a sort of floor plan, a blank space called the 'Chamber' or the 'Parlour', where the characters' *actions* call up the bed, the chair, the doorway, the whip, as they are beckoned by the plot (Wall 2006: 124–5). In both drama and fiction, the *text* is sparsely furnished.[14] The dramatic text, like the prose fiction, assumes the infill. It is not until the second half of the late eighteenth century that texts begin to furnish their own spaces.

The stage itself, however, was not as empty as once thought. Neil Carson has argued that Philip Henslowe's theatrical inventory, with its 'two mossy banks, no less than three trees, as many tombs, and one Hellmouth . . . suggests a state more cluttered than is sometimes imagined' (1988: 52–3). Orlin has argued for even more clutter; analysing the often ephemeral inventories beyond the probate, she argues, suggests the 'vastness of the world of lost records and the eccentricities of documentary preservation' (2002: 106). Orlin makes visible the 'things with little social life' – the 'fittings' – that fill up the visuals of the stage as well as the house. Museum directors now work towards representational infill: '[Atmosphere] is something that is tremendously difficult to create in period rooms, particularly if it is to be done without sacrificing historical accuracy,' says Hannah Fleming of the Geffrye Museum (Fleming 2014: 5), because, as Jeremy Aynsley and Charlotte Grant observe, 'real rooms rarely represent a single historical moment, being accretions over time' (2006: 13). But a sense of reality emerges with 'the inclusion in the displays of smaller, more ephemeral objects – the paraphernalia of everyday life' (Fleming 2014: 5).

Even so, the 'cluttered' stage of the Renaissance remains spare compared to the novelistically described sets of Ibsen. Even two mossy banks and three trees do not add up to the play-specific arrangements in the late-eighteenth-century stage directions of Matthew Lewis:

> *A gloomy subterraneous Dungeon, wide and lofty: The upper part of it has in several places fallen in, and left large chasms. On one side are various passages leading to other Caverns: On the other is an Iron Door with steps leading to it, and a Wicket in the middle.* Reginald, *pale and emaciated, in coarse garments, his hair hanging wildly about his face, and a chain bound round his body, lies sleeping upon a bed of straw. A lamp, a small basket, and a pitcher, are placed near him. After a few moments he awakes, and extends his arms.*
>
> —1798: 88 [5.3]

Why does the 'paraphernalia' of everyday life appear so rarely in the textual spaces of the Renaissance home? I have argued that the novels, poetry and eventually drama of the eighteenth century were infiltrated by the emerging empiricist, religious and commercial habits of description in the seventeenth century (along with the rise of country-house tourism, auctions and mass-produced furniture and objects). For the sixteenth- and early-seventeenth-century reader, on the other hand, word or gesture was enough to evoke the full visual immediacy of the implied. Richardson argues that for the familiar space of home, 'the metonymic representation which the stage space offers, of a part of a house against which the whole is measured, makes the whole domestic interior present without the need for scenery' (2006b: 63). On the other hand, 'mansions of men like Capulet or the palaces of Cyprus or Elsinor, with their halls, closets, great chambers and balconies in their minds, involved recourse to the imagination, rather than the memory' (ibid.: 61). Both cases –

the 'homeliness' of home and the exoticness of the palace – even on the 'cluttered' spaces of the stage, are visually evoked or implied more than presented or represented. The extent of the visual lies in the reciprocally imaginative act of the viewer or reader. The *textual* texture of 'home' is different in the Renaissance; it lies less in the telling than the implying.

MANAGING HOME

Perhaps it is because the routines of home, the 'expectation[s] of synchrony' and order (Douglas 1993: 274) in both country house and cottage, were more *routinized*, more parallel, more uniform, than they can possibly be today, that their details needed less telling. Mary Douglas treats the dark side of homemaking, its 'tyranny' of 'censorship' and 'surveillance', its 'control over mind and body' (ibid.: 277). Twentieth-century feminism generally aspersed home and domesticity as a culturally forged prison. The Renaissance itself recognized that home is not always where the heart is: the subgenre of 'domestic tragedy' emerged to explore the home as locus of household darkness, of adultery (the wrong hearts) and murder (cutting out hearts). The proverbs recognize – by scolding – women who are not domestically inclined. Are you young and pretty (or think you are), and pleased with it? 'The more women looke in their glase, the lesse they looke to their house' (Herbert 1640: fol. B2 [Ray [1670] 1678: 60]). Those who prefer 'silkes and satins' will 'put out the fire in the kitchin' (impoverish the house) (Herbert 1640: fol. 912, D8 [Ray [1670] 1678: 24]), or at best, prove only that 'fine *dressing* is a foul house swept before windows' (Ray [1670] 1678: 8). For those who don't like to cook, 'All ... dishes are chafing dishes' (ibid.: 7). 'A woman's work is never at an end,' says the proverb; '*Some adds*, And washing of dishes' (ibid.: 60). Point taken. 'Home is homely, yea, and to [too] homely some tyme.'

And yet, the proverbs that spring to mind when asked what 'home' means are never the nasty ones. Susan Fraiman (2017) has recently argued eloquently for the pleasures of 'extreme domesticity' – the sort of homebuilding fashioned even on the edges of society. A number of Renaissance scholars have reconsidered the empowering possibilities of housekeeping, from mistress to maid. A variety of textual evidence suggests that, then as now, those who enjoy the creating and maintaining home find pleasure in order and comfort. Thomas Tusser argued (well, versed) for the mutual pleasures of husbandry and huswifery:

> Be house or the furniture never so rude,
> Of husband and husbandry,—thus I conclude,
> That huswife and huswifery, if it be good,
> Must pleasure together, as cousins in blood.
>
> —Tusser, [1573] 2013

For those making a home, 'House-keeping . . . as a refuge is set' (ibid.).

'The wife is the key of the house,' says the proverb (Herbert 1640: fol. D7v [Ray [1670] 1678: 29]). Richardson comments on 'the prominence of the keys which symbolize the most important quality of domestic space, its capacity to be controlled and contained' (2006b: 58). While that control and containment may result in Douglas's unpleasant tyranny – and such nasty households are a favourite of literature – happy domesticity may be like Tolstoy's happy families: there is less of a story to tell. But, in addition to the 'sweetness' of building a house, there are the pleasures of control and containment as imaginative interior *creation*. Assuming that *having* 'tapistrie, Turkie worke, pewter, brasse, fine linen, and thereto costlie cupbords of plate' is merely for the sake of *displaying* them misses the point that it is perfectly possible to arrange those things in a way that instills a quiet, private satisfaction ('a little house well fill'd' (Ray [1670] 1678: 63)). There is pleasure in economy, in efficiency, in small beauties – in the determination of *spaces*, the arrangement of *things* and the managing of *persons*. 'All things are soon prepar'd in a well-ordered *house*' (ibid.: 14).

The physical spaces of home can shape the behaviour of its occupants. Alice T. Friedman has examined the lives and letters of the Willoughby family of Wollaton Hall in the second half of the sixteenth century to show how a gentleman could alter his architectural space to transform his domestic relations. 'Sir Francis Willoughby was never free from discord, intrigue, and dishonesty' (Friedman 1989: 53–4), and so he constructed a house designed to 'alleviate tension and to facilitate new ways of living'. Separate spaces were allotted to different members and activities of the household, and 'more extensive and varied spaces were devoted to entertainment and private leisure' – innovations that signalled an important architectural departure from the 'socially enmeshed world of the manor house' (ibid.: 68–70).

Inside the home, things often require a certain micromanaging. Margaret Paston, for example, displays her eye for detail and her skill at negotiating the physics of domestic space in a letter to her husband, describing some new arrangements:

> Letter 224. Margaret Paston to John Paston.   1453   JAN. 30.
> I have taken the mesure in the draute chamer, ther as ye wold your cofors and cowntewery [writing desk or board] shuld be sette for the whyle; and ther is no space besyde the bedd, thow the bedd wer remevyd to the dore, for to sette both your bord and your kofors ther, and to have space to go and sitte be syde. Wherfor I have purveyd that ye shall have the same drawte chamer that ye had befor ther, as ye shall ly to your self; and whan your gerr is remevod owte of your lytil hous, the dore shall be lokkyd, and your baggs leyd in on of the grete doforis, so that they shall be sauff, I trost.
> —Paston family [15th c.] 1983: 2.281

She ends with tenderness, underlining that this has not been an irksome task: 'I pray yow that ye be not strange of wryting of letters to me be twix this and that ye come hom. If I myght I wold have every day on from yow' (ibid.: 2.282).

Master Allwit is delighted with his household arrangements in *A Chaste Maid in Cheapside* (1630): as long as Sir Walter Whorehound is keeping Mrs Allwit, he's in clover: 'I am like a man / Finding a Table furnish't to his hand' (Middleton [1630] 1969: 1.2.1–2). He finds it 'the happiest state that euer Man was born to', where he can walk out before breakfast and find all in good order and good supply at another's expense (ibid.: 1.2.21–9). By the end of the play, with Sir Walter successfully prevented from marriage, the Allwits find themselves so 'richly furnish't . . . [with] Houshold-stuffe' that they decide to 'let out Lodgings . . . and 'take a House in the Strand' (ibid.: 5.1.167–9):

> We are simply stock't, with Cloath of Tissue Cussions,
> To furnish out bay-windows: Push, what not that's quaint
> And costly, from the top to the bottome:
> Life, for furniture, we may lodge a Countesse:
> There's a Cloase-stoole of tawny Veluet too,
> Now I thinke on't Wife.
>
> —Ibid.: 5.1.171–6

Paradoxically, the plenty of *things* they have frees them; their furnishings can make a home for a countess, while they prefer to be more nomadic in lodgings, as they had preferred maintenance to ownership. Sometimes, 'home' is simply the 'sweet *discourse*' of accord that comes with a marriage of 'like blood, like good, and like age' (Ray [1670] 1678: 7, 56): 'In troth a match Wench,' says her husband happily (Middleton [1630] 1969: 5.1.170).

Somewhere in between the arrangement of things and the management of persons is that necessary condition for many homes now and most then: a dog or a cat. Paintings of Renaissance interiors regularly reveal houses plentifully stocked with this other tier of inhabitants (Figure 1.3). Johann Comenius sets out for the child the hierarchy of domestic animals:

> The Dog   1. with the Whelp   2. is the Keeper of the House.   The Cat   3. riddeth the House of Mice;   4. which also a Mouse-trap, 5. doth.   The Squirrel,   6. The Ape,   7. and the Monkey,   8. are kept at home for delight. The Dormouse,   9. and other greater Mice, 10. as the Weesel, The Martin, and the Ferret, trouble the House.
>
> —Comenius 1672: 54–5]

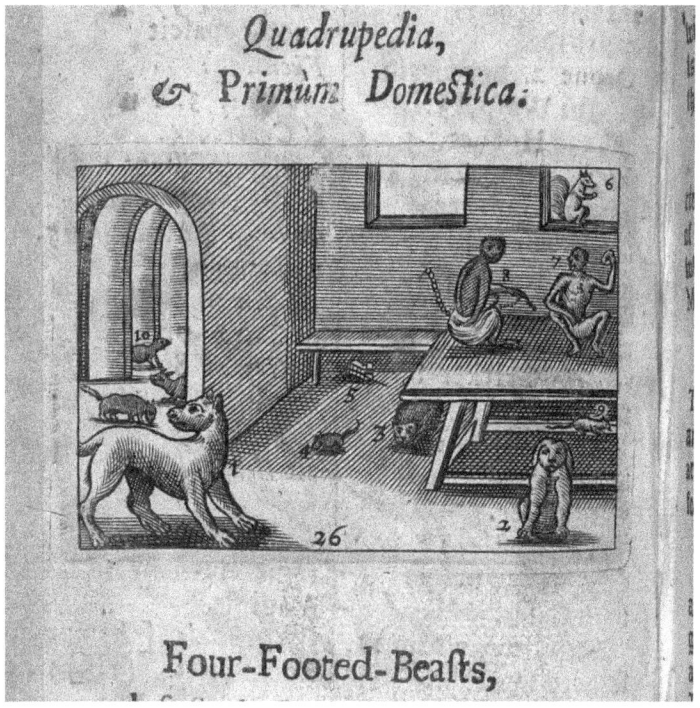

FIGURE 1.3: 'Four-Footed-Beasts', Johannes Amos Comenius, *Orbis Sensualium Pictus*, 1672. © Courtesy of The British Library.

Apart from the squirrel, ape and monkey, the animals seem to exist either for utility or as nuisance. But clearly the dogs and cats could be beloved pets as well (Figure 1.4). William Harrison approvingly chronicles the hunting dogs and watch dogs and fight dogs ('there is no country that may (as I take it) compare with ours in number, excellency, and diversity of dogs' [Harrison [1577] 1968, 1994: 339]), but he manages to include the 'gentle kind' of dog, such as 'the spaniel gentle, or comforter'. Paul Hentzner agreed: 'The dogs here are particularly good' (Hentzner [1612] 1797: 63). More tellingly, *The Young Children's Book* (*c.* 1500) instructs: 'Make thou nother cate ne hond / Thi felow at thou tabull round' (Furnivall 1868: 25).[15] The implicit reason behind this is, of course, *because you really want to*. Poor hapless Mavillia in Nicholas Breton's *The Miseries of Mavillia* would be 'at play, either with the Catte, or a little Dogge, or making of a Babie, of an olde ragged cloute' until her foster-mother the laundress would come in bringing a 'rodde' to end *that* bit of fun (Breton [1580] 1929: 2.115). Robert Herrick clearly watched with interest as 'The brisk Mouse may feast her selfe with crums, / Till that the green-ey'd Kitling comes' (Herrick 1648: 39). A 'green-ey'd Kitling' is distinctly more fetching than your basic household mouser. And the homely details of William Baldwin's allegorical

Beware the Cat ([1533, 1570] 1988) perhaps betray a tighter connection to this world than originally intended. Here, Mouse-slayer 'telleth on her story':

> While I was with this woman I was alway much cherished and made of, for on nights while she was a-praying, I would be playing with her beads and alway catch them as she let them fall, and would sometime put my head in the compass of them and run away with them about my neck, whereat many times she took great pleasure, yea and so did Our Lady too. For my dame would say sometimes to Her, 'Yea, Blessed Lady, I know thou hearest me by thy smiling at my cat.'
>
> —Ibid.: 41

The marginal note nods: '*Old women love / their cats well.*' But that does not fool any catperson, Mr. William 'Cat Lover' Baldwin. The next marginalium confirms the old woman's perception that even the Virgin Mary is delighted:

*The image
laughed to see the cat play with
her dame's beads.*

One of the pleasures of having as well as being 'the key of the house' (Ray [1670] 1678: 29) is managing the rhythms of its days and the patterns of its people.

FIGURE 1.4: Portrait of Henry Wriothesley, 3rd Earl of Southampton, with cat, attributed to John de Critz (1551–1642), *c.* 1603. Wikimedia Commons, public domain.

In Deloney's *Jack of Newbury*, the lively widow first individually invites her three suitors to a dinner at her house, where she promises a clear answer. Dressing her house and herself 'fine and brave', she greets the hopeful priest, tanner and tailor, who '[look] strangely one at another'. She carefully seats them all, flattering each with his place at table ('Women think *Place* a sweet fish' [Ray [1670] 1678: 59], but so, it seems, do men), offering cushions that do not cushion the blow: she will have none of them. She explains why she has done it this way: 'for I ever doubting that a concluding answer would breed a farce in the end among you every one, I thought it better to be done at one instant, and in mine owne house, than at sundry times and in common tavernes' (Deloney [1597] 1859: 22–6). She is every bit as adroit in managing her domestic space to her advantage in a will of wits with men as Defoe's Moll and Roxana or Haywood's Fantomina. Home, where one has the keys, can be a place of power, both spatial and social.

And sexual. The widow then plans her next move, to get strapping young Jack the apprentice as a husband. In a cold, cold Christmastime, she 'mad a great fire, and sent for her man John: having also prepared a chaire and a cushion, she made him sit downe therein, and sending for a pinte of good sacke, they both went to supper'. Then, frisky lady, she in 'a merriment [plucked] off his hose and shooes, and caused him to be laide in his masters best bed, standing in the best chamber, hung round about with very faire curtaines'. After a decent interval, 'the widow being cold on her feet, crept into her mans bed to warm them', and 'John, being a kinde young man, would not say her nay, and so they spent the rest of the night both together in one bed' (ibid.: 27–8). Perhaps needless to say, her cunning plan worked, and Jack proved himself to be one of the 'Good Husbands that loveth good houses to keep' (Tusser [1573] 2013: xxiii).

FROM THE MARGINS

'Home' may be 'a person's house or abode; the fixed residence of a family or household' (*OED* 2a), but, as we all know from proverbs, if not from experience, a house is not always a home. Lytton Strachey described his feelings as a small child in his family's large Victorian house (which was 'size gone wrong, size pathological'): 'When one entered that vast chamber [the drawing room], when, peering through its foggy distances, ill-lit by gas-jets, or casting one's eyes wildly towards the infinitely distant ceiling overhead, one struggled to traverse its dreadful length, to reach a tiny chair or a far-distant fireplace' (Strachey [1922] 1971: 18, 20). Strachey quite possibly experienced the same existential crises of Austen's young Fanny Price in her first encounters with the spaces of Mansfield Park: its grand, over-large rooms, the distant little white attic where she is stashed away, the staircase where she is found sobbing by Edmund (Austen [1814] 2003: 12–13). What about the people in the corners of the Renaissance home – the children and the servants?

In some ways, in early modern England, children *were* servants, regularly ejected from the centres of their own homes to work in others'. Andrea Trevisano was shocked:

> The want of affection in the English is strongly manifested towards their children; for after having kept them at home till they arrive at the age of 7 or 9 years at the utmost, they put them out, both males and females, to hard service in the houses of other people, binding them generally for another 7 or 9 years. . . . And on inquiring their reason for this severity, they answered that they did it in order that their children might learn better manners. But I, for my part, believe that they do it because they like to enjoy all their comforts themselves, and that they are better served by strangers than they would be by their own children.
>
> —[1500] 1847: 24–5

His nineteenth-century editor glosses: 'The severity of parents at this time was so great, that the children perfectly loathed the sight of them; nor did their discipline relax as they grew older, "for daughters, grown women, and sons, gentlemen of thirty and forty years old, might not sit in their presence without leave, but stood like mutes bare-headed before them"' (ibid.: 75 n. 38).

This sounds a bit grim, I must say. But it is true that outsourcing children to others' homes to learn manners or a trade was a well-recognized practice. *The Babees Book* (*c.* 1475), addressed to 'yee Babees [children] in housholde that done duelle', is all about how they 'Shuld haue [behave]' when occupying the houses of the great (Furnivall 1868: 2). There are instructions for entering a room ('Stert not Rudely; komme Inn an esy pace; / Hold vp youre heede, and knele but on ooe kne / To youre sovereyene or lorde' [ibid.: 3]); for standing at attention ('Youre heede, youre hande, your feet, hold yee in reste ;. . . Lene to no poste whils that ye stande present / Byfore your lorde' [ibid.: 4]); and for behaving at table ('Youre nose, your teethe, your naylles, [keep from pykynge' [ibid.: 6]). *The Young Children's Book* (*c.* 1500) sums it all up: 'Dame curtasy fore-bydes it the' (ibid.: 23). All of this seems part of Mary Douglas's sense of the 'tyranny' of home, its expectations of synchronicity, its rhythms of rank, servitude and subservience – the contributing parameters of why children might 'perfectly loathe' their parents or desperately want to leave 'home' and never 'reproduce it when they set up house' (Douglas 1993: 277).

But individual situations were, of course, more finely grained. Richard Mulcaster, headmaster of Merchant Taylors' and St Paul's schools in the late sixteenth century, debates the question about 'whether it be better for the childe to boord abroad with his maister, or some where else or to come from home daily to schoole' (Mulcaster 1581: 226). The case may be made for either decision, but it is clear to him that, all things being equal, 'certainely the parentes house is much better', because if 'the parent himselfe be carefull and wise withall', he can be 'as good a furtherer in the training, as he is a father to the being of his owne child' (ibid.: 226).

And children are adaptable. As Strachey puts it, 'Submerged by the drawing-room, I inevitably believed that the drawing-room was the world. Or rather, I neither believed nor disbelieved; it *was* the world, so far as I was concerned' ([1922] 1971: 27). It is a sort of Heideggerian 'thrownness' (*Geworfenheit*), of finding yourself occupying a certain intersection of space and time, a 'corner of the world', and coming to terms with it. Even those on the margins can learn to feel at home. Strachey tells of dreams in which he was back at 69 Lancaster Gate, and 'a feeling of intimate satisfaction' would come over him (ibid.: 17). After Fanny Price returns to her 'real' (parental) home in Portsmouth and finds herself assaulted by its noise, dirt and disorganization (not to mention careless, indifferent parents), she finally realizes that 'Mansfield was home' (Austen [1814] 2003: 338). We can grow into the spaces in which we find ourselves.

Servants *qua* servants were, by definition, clustered around the edges, keeping things clean and shiny and running for others. It could be demanding and unending. In *The Miseries of Mavillia* (1580), Mavillia's '*Third time of Miseries with the Shepheards wife*' involves the very young gentlewoman being defrauded of her gold crowns and put to work as a 'double servant, and halfe a Mistresse':

> I must serve thee olde Woman, I must learne to spinne, to reele, to carde, to knit, to wash buckes, and by hande, brew, bake, make Mault, reape, binde sheaves, weede in the Garden, milke, serve Hogges, make cleane theyr houses, within doores, make beddes, sweepe filthy houses, rubbe dirtie ragges, beate out the olde Coverlets, drawe up old holes: Then to the Kitchin, turne the Spitte . . . then scoure Pottes, wash Dishes, fetch in Wood, make a fire, scalde milke Pannes, wash the Cherne and butter dishes, wring up a Cheese clout, set every thing in good order.
>
> —Breton [1580] 1929: 2:135

Breton's 'prolix, prolific, euphuistic, alliterative, didactic' prose is achingly 'pad[ded] with mundane details' of Mavillia's daily life, as Catherine Loomis puts it (2016: 21). Things did not change much for the servant over the next few hundred years. In 1739, the working-class poet Mary Collier catalogued the exhausting repetitions of *The Woman's Labour* within the closed, cyclic spaces of the heroic couplet, thinking surely that 'Our first Extraction from a Mass refin'd, / Could never be for Slavery design'd'?

But there is a more empowering side to it. The eighteenth-century landscape gardener Humphry Repton confessed that the 'most interesting subject' he had ever known was the 'View from [his] humble Cottage' (1816: 235). In several places, he describes what he calls the concept of 'appropriation', which in its technical sense means 'the views from a house' of scenes which 'evidently belong to the place . . . not so much for the purposes of gain as of pleasure and convenience' (ibid. 1805: 110–11). But, over the course of his writings, 'appropriation' evolves to imply a more rudimentary kind of ownership and pleasure therein. Even the most enchanting scenery 'will not long engage our interest, without some appropriation; something we can call our own; and if not our own property, at least it may be endeared to us by calling it *our own Home*' (ibid. 1816: 235). 'Appropriation' becomes less a matter of ownership or display and more a sort of psychological alignment with one's own pleasure, the *feeling* of ownership simply through a conscious relish of the visible – open to anyone. *Calling* it home can make it so.

Even a servant is capable of appropriating the spaces she inhabits, wielding a sort of ownership of knowledge and intimacy with the things and people she maintains and serves. As Amanda Flather has argued, 'The early modern house was an arena that resonated with power and symbolism for servants throughout the early modern period even in more modest middling-sort homes' (2011: 184). David Fairer has elegantly argued that Mira, the narrator of Mary Leapor's poem *Crumble-Hall* (1748), treats her inhabited servant's space in the old fifteenth-century manor house not as that of the 'alien within' or of the oppressed worker, but as one who knows the house intimately, is a sustainer of its rhythms, a mistress of its secret spaces and the warm busy underworld of the kitchen (2006: 223–36).

The rhetoric of service can display a grammar of ownership, as in the instructions for tending 'The Buttery' in *John Russell's Book of Nurture* (c. 1460):

> Son, when thy souereignes table is drest in thus array,
> kouer all other bordes with Saltes; trenchers & cuppes theron ye lay;
> than emperialle thy Cuppeborde with Siluer & gild fulle gay,
> thy Ewry borde with basons & lauour, watur hoot & cold, eche
>   other to alay.
> loke that ye haue napkyns, spones, & cuppis euer y-nowe,
> to your soueraynes table, youre honest for to allow,
> also that pottes for wyne & ale be as clene as they mowe;
> be euermore ware of flies & motes, y tell the, for thy prowe.
>
> —Furnivall 1868: 131–2

Although it may be his lordship's table, it is *your* cupboard, *your* ewery board, *your* honour and credit ('honeste'), and *your own sake* ('prowe', advantage, profit, weal). The possessives declare the power of responsibility in arrangement, the possibility of pleasure in 'gay silver', the satisfaction in 'enough'.

On top of that, as Andrea Trevisano marvelled, apprentices could make their way in the world through hard work and marrying the master's widow:

Nevertheless, the apprentices for the most part make good fortunes, ... above all, those who happen to be in the good graces of the mistress of the house in which they are domiciliated at the time of the death of the master; because ... [the widow] usually bestows herself in marriage upon the one of those apprentices living in the house who is most pleasing to her[.]

—[1500] 1847: 26

After all, Jack of Newbury married his master's widow, and 'they lived long together, in most goodly, loving and kind sort, till in the end she dyed, leaving her husband wondrous wealthie' (Deloney [1597] 1859: 35).

'HOME' AS VERB

Like (and unlike) Sir Francis Willoughby of Wollaton Hall, Lytton Strachey was fascinated by the ways in which a house can shape its occupant:

Those curious contraptions of stones or bricks, with all their peculiar adjuncts, trimmings, and furniture, their specific immutable shapes, their intense and inspissated atmosphere, in which our lives are entangled as completely as our souls in our bodies—what powers do they not wield over us, what subtle and pervasive effects upon the whole substance of our existence may not be theirs?

—Strachey [1922] 1971: 16

That is the house acting on us: that is Mansfield Park enlarging Fanny's conceptions of space, shaping her sense of order and propriety, betraying her and comforting her. That is Penshurst bestowing itself, metaphorically speaking, on household, tenants, neighbours, guests. That is Wollaton Hall sorting out the family disputes. That is the house calming, soothing, refreshing: 'Seek home for rest, / For home is best' (Tusser [1573] 2013).

Strachey gives us a quintessentially modernist take on house as agent of change: 'We find satisfaction in curves and colours, and windows fascinate us, we are agitated by staircases, inspired by doors, disgusted by cornices, depressed by chairs, made wanton by ceilings, entranced by passages, and exacerbated by a rug' ([1922] 1971: 16). Yet, we see even in this reactive representation that its active centre is really the historically and psychologically specific example of 'us' – since not *everyone* finds inspiration in doors or disgust in cornices. (Although possibly everyone has been exacerbated by a rug.) We might say that a house becomes a home to the extent we respond *happily* to it in the process of creating and dwelling in it, and to the extent we *consider* it 'ours'.

Certainly many of the most self-satisfied proverbs about 'home' concern the appropriation of and the functioning within its fundamental economic rhythms:

'Everything is of use to a housekeeper' (Herbert 1640: fol. A4); 'In a good house all is quickly ready' (ibid. [Ray [1670] 1678: 14]). The pleasures of home are not dependent on class or wealth: 'My house, my house, though thou art small, thou art to me the Escuriall [Spanish palace]' (Herbert 1640: B8); '*Love* lives in cottages as well as in Courts' (Ray [1670] 1678: 16). A proverbial wedding blessing outlines: 'A little house well fill'd, a little land well till'd, and a little wife well will'd' (ibid.: 63). In fact, if it's *yours*, it bests *anyone's*: 'Dry bread at home is better then rost meate abroad' (Herbert 1640: C8v [Ray [1670] 1678: 13]). It is 'the *Comfortablest part*' of one's 'owne *Life*' (Wotton 1624: 82). The eighteenth-century tourist John Byng, Viscount Torrington, loved to criticize other people's homes and properly rearrange them on his own terms (imaginatively speaking, of course). A sort of Miniver Cheevy, he especially disliked modern improvements, preferring Raby Castle in its Elizabethan rather than eighteenth-century decor (Byng 1934: 3.156–7). Yet, devoted traveller that he was, he, too, declared that 'home is the happiest place' (ibid.: 1.53). 'A mans *house* is his castle' (Ray [1670] 1678: 158), no matter how 'homely', because he *feels that way about it*. It is more than a legal refuge: it is a phenomenological one.

'*Houses* are built to Live in, and not to Looke on,' as Bacon said ([1625] 1985: 135). 'The *seating* of our selues,' said Wotton, is 'a kinde of *Marriage* to a *Place*,' an act of commitment, intimacy, permanence, identification. An *act*: the way 'we inhabit our vital space', said Bachelard, 'how we take root, day after day, in a "corner of the world"'. *Dwelling*: the word is both noun and verb, 'a dwelling-place, habitation, house' (*OED* 3) and the present participle of 'to have one's abode; to reside, "live". (Now mostly superseded by live in spoken use; but still common in literature)' (*OED* 7). The dual functions of 'dwelling' as *abode* and as *living in that abode* are not replicated by 'house' and 'housing' or 'home' and 'homing'. The dictionary does not seem to capture the variant richness of 'dwelling' as *more than* residing in, living in. Perhaps that is why the word dwells more 'commonly in literature'. Another definition brings us closer to Strachey's lively relationship with wanton ceilings, depressing chairs and entrancing passages: 'To spend time upon or linger over (a thing) in action or thought; to remain with the attention fixed on' (*OED* 5). This connotation gives us 'dwelling' simultaneously as noun and verb, expressing the phenomenological relationship between house as noun and home as verb, and thus 'home' as the act of inhabiting as well as the ('vital') space of habitation.

> Now, PENSHVRST, they that will proportion thee
>   With other edifices, when they see
> Those proud, ambitious heaps, and nothing else,
>   May say their lords haue built, but thy lord dwells.
>   —Ben Jonson, 'To Penshurst' ([1616] 1947: ll. 99–102)

CHAPTER TWO

Family and Household

JOANNE BEGIATO

INTRODUCTION

In 1523, Reynold Peckham left instructions in his will that he be buried beside the grave of his uncle, William Peckham, Esquire, in the Church of St George, Wrotham, Kent. Esquire to the body of Henry VIII, Reynold was a wealthy landed gentleman with substantial lands. In his will, he mentioned among other relatives, his brother and his nephew, and he made arrangements for the custody and marriage of his ward, another nephew. He also directed his executors to provide a monumental brass depicting a man, a woman and children, with a Latin inscription, to be set upon his grave within six weeks of his death.

Historians have variously recorded Peckham's status as 'lifelong bachelor' and 'childless widower' (Fleming 2004: 79; Thomas 2009; Tucker [1974] 2006: 233). For them, the brass indicates the increasing social value attributed to children, demonstrates people's concerns to determine their posthumous image by communicating to the future an ideal status, or illustrates that children were so fundamental to the status of patriarchal manhood that wife and children needed to be imagined if they did not exist. In fact, Reynold had been married, although his wife, Joyce Culpepper, predeceased him in 1523. Ralph Griffin's record of sepulchral memorial brasses in Wrotham, described the brass that was placed upon Reynold's grave following his death in 1525 (Griffin 1915: 11; Weever 1631: 326). It included Reynold in armour on the left and his wife Joyce on the right. Although Reynold requested 'children' to be depicted on his 'fair stone', he did not mention any offspring in his will, hence historians' assumption that Reynold was childless. Certainly, the brass depictions have not survived. Griffin referred to Thomas Fisher's drawing of the brass, made around

1800, and noted that all the shields Fisher recorded as accompanying the brass were now lost. So, too, were the additional representations of two children; already lost when J.G. Waller visited the church in 1840 and made another record of stones and brasses.[1]

So, what should the historian of family and household make of all this? Speculating on Reynold's paternal status can, indeed, tell us something, although we can now reject the discredited thesis of a chronological improvement in the status of childhood and children during this period. These recorded moments in Reynold's life reveal the significance of parental, religious, reputational and dynastic feelings which extended beyond one individual's lifespan. Being a parent mattered, but historians need to be mindful of the precarious nature of family life before assuming anyone's childless status. With the high rates of infant and child mortality, it is possible that Reynold and Joyce bore children, but that they predeceased him and were not therefore mentioned in his will. Nonetheless, as a pious man, he had still wanted them to be memorialized as part of his family. Indeed, Reynold's concerns at the time of writing demonstrate a diachronic understanding of family, whose bonds did not disappear when a family member died, something which historical demographers' accounts of the composition of families and households often miss. Reynold's arrangements for his death also illustrate the expansiveness of his family and household. This was no simple nuclear family, a category which earlier historians of the family saw as the defining set of relationships to be investigated, since the key members of his nuclear family were absent due to mortality. Reynold's will and his place of burial also speak to family members' close attention to wider kin and to parental-style responsibilities beyond biological children. In sum, it shows that Reynold experienced numerous different kinds of 'family' during his lifetime thanks to its precarious nature, the mutability of family relationships and the inclusivity of assorted individuals within any one household. Despite the focus on wider rather than closer kin, these aspects of his family and household relationships could be the source of powerful emotions.

This chapter will argue that the history of emotions offers the most effective conceptual framework to understand family and household in the two centuries spanning 1450 to 1650. Both were constituted through the nexus of feelings and attachments that bound together individuals of various kinds, whether related through marriage or blood, co-resident or absent. It is also an approach which moves on from the rather stagnant state of the history of the family that had emerged by the last decade of the twentieth century. Until recently, a student had two approaches to choose from when studying households and families: 'structural' or 'affective'. On the one hand were structural accounts of increasing nuance and complexity, which identified broad regional patterns of marriage and inheritance, and family and household size and composition (Hajnal 1965; Laslett 1965; Laslett and Wall 1972). On the other were social history analyses of families, typically relatives related by blood and marriage and their servants, which focused on the extent to which family relationships were founded on love over time and social rank (Stone 1977). These two approaches could at times seem incompatible. Over the last decade, however, emotions history has flourished, which can be defined as a conceptual approach to understanding the changing nature of emotions in different times and places, and the ways in which this shaped human experience. Innovative historians have begun to apply it to provide insights into family and household structures and composition, as well as illuminate lived experiences of gendered inequalities in interpersonal relationships and subjectivities. This chapter first briefly outlines this shift in scholarly interests. It then applies a history of emotions framework, moving beyond more conventional organization around relationships or life-phase, instead to examine the family and household through the themes of connections and constituencies, which captures their mutability, dynamism and various permutations far more effectively.

FAMILY AND HOUSEHOLD: STRUCTURES AND FORMS

Scholars have long debated the terms family and household, attempting either to impose overarching categories in order to measure their composition and form over time, or to understand their contemporary meanings and complexities across Renaissance Europe. Initially, scholars distinguished family from household and kin by applying a measure of relatedness and co-residence; at the risk of crude generalization, a family was whoever lived in the household, although for demographic purposes non-related individuals were removed from the category, focusing on what might be called 'ties of reproduction' (Fleming 2004: 2–3). Historical demographers, for example, attempted to chart the broad patterns of household composition.

For them, two types of families could be identified. The North-West European nuclear form, consisting of parents and children, with unrelated servants, and the Mediterranean extended form (sometimes referred to as 'stem'), with variations in composition but usually consisting of more than one married couple, perhaps including generational couples (parents plus one married offspring and their family) or two married siblings and their families (for a critical overview, see Goldberg 2010: 22–8; Cavallo 2010: 11–12). These family forms were correlated with other regional patterns that demographers detected. Delayed age at marriage and a significant minority of never-married people were correlated with areas where nuclear families predominated and 'universal' marriage prevailed with very young women marrying older men with regions where extended families were present (Fleming 2004: 19–23).

When demographic analysis was combined with studies of property transmission, kin density could also be assessed. It was argued that areas that showed least worker mobility demonstrated high kin-density. If this did not strictly conform to the category of extended families where two generations co-resided, then it demonstrated 'functional' extended families where local aid from kin was accessible to nuclear families. Areas experiencing most geographical mobility showed reduced kin density and a higher prevalence of nuclear households. Historians saw these conditions as driven by mortality and economic opportunity in medieval England, with weaker kin-density more likely to prevail by the early modern era (Razi 1981). If household composition here represented family, then scholars also extrapolated that these different household types shaped power hierarchies. Marriages between similar-aged couples were seen as more equitable than skewed-age unions; multigenerational households were expected to provide more patriarchal authority for one man, but also lead to challenges given competition between adult men for resources.

Twenty-first-century scholarship has, however, shown these patterns to be simplistic, requiring some degree of special pleading to keep distinct such categories as nuclear, extended and functional-extended. It also exposes the difficulties of mapping them onto life-courses, time periods and geographical regions in any satisfying way. Sandra Cavallo sums up the revision of these outdated approaches by observing that 'geographical homogeneity' is an illusion and, even more worrying, that the interpretations of these family forms were driven by 'ethno-centric assumptions' (2010: 12). What has emerged in the last decade instead is a picture of household complexity, with very local economic conditions determining which family members formed a household. It is now clear that in the Renaissance, people experienced many different kinds of family members co-residing because families were disrupted by death and remarriage, seasonal working practices and types of employment and religious conventions. Trying to plot the size of the average household thus becomes ever more reductive, given its changeable nature over its own life-course and variation according to local conditions such as proximity to epidemics, economic opportunities or levels of wealth (Fleming 2004: 66–7). Equally, what records of household membership cannot fully capture is that a family consisted of any of the following configurations: a variety of kin and step-kin, such as spouses, widowers, parents, children, siblings, uncles, aunts, grandparents; non-kin, including servants, apprentices, employees, nursemaids, sick-nurses, wet-nurses, unrelated fostered children; and, depending on denomination, spiritual kin.

Indeed, contemporaries tended not to distinguish between family and household as separate entities; for instance, they typically described servants who shared their dwelling as part of both family and household, as Figure 2.1 shows (Gordon 2008: 86). Recent scholarship has tried to capture this experience by coining the term 'household-family' (Tadmor 2001). An historical demographic approach also risks being too functionalist because it sees families as primarily reproductive forms. Accounts which prioritize marriage, for

FIGURE 2.1: *A Family Saying Grace Before the Meal* by Claeissins or Claeissens, Anthuenis (Antoon) (1536–1613), 1585. © Private Collection/Bridgeman Images.

instance, neglect households not structured around marriage, such as those shared for economic security, by single women or men, or formed following the cessation of marriage through death. Similarly, as Reynold Packham's monument suggests, a family does not stop being a family when some of its members die. Furthermore, one of the striking features of family life that emerges from studies of late medieval and early modern households from all levels of wealth is the degree of movement of people into different households. Infants were sent to wet-nurses or wet-nurses came to live with their charges, older children went to train as servants or apprentices or were fostered and adopted in other households. The sick and poor were cared for and nursed by paid and unpaid carers, and lodgers or boarders shared family homes (Broomhall 2008: 18).

THE IMPACT OF EMOTIONS ON CATEGORIES, GENDER AND POWER

What do we do with this more fragmented picture of family formation and life? The risk of such a position is that all families look different from one another, which is true but unhelpful for historians of family life, whose job it is to contextualize and historicize family life. Family and household were, in practice and ideology, the building blocks of society and their role and meaning, as well as people's experience of them, was subject to historical forces. Yet, this is far easier to do at the microlevel, as Cavallo (2010) recommends, where the influence of society, economy, religion and politics and the complexity of their interactions can be identified in detail. It is a far less tenable task when surveying family and household across two centuries and a wide geographical area. This is where an emotions framework is helpful. In the first place, it resolves some of the issues of who to include in a study. As Susan Broomhall explains, it shifts the focus to the 'connections forged by members of household communities', and the emotions that shaped interactions between these people drawn together by shared economic, social and biological needs, rather than relations forged only from marriage or blood (2008: 1). This chapter follows her advice, since it means that we can focus on relationships, as people did at the time, and accept they may be temporary or longer term, shaped by events and activities, rather than by inflexible categories.

Second, using the history of emotions as an overarching conceptual framework tackles some of the shortcomings of the 'affective' model of investigation. This had the limitation of attending only to love, with scholars generally measuring its depth, and consequently categorizing relationships in one of two oppositional ways: affective or instrumental. It also placed constraints on who could be included in such a study: generally only spouses, parents and children were, because it was assumed that only 'close' marital or blood links forged such affection. Moreover, it restricted the social groups included, since such historians tended to assume that only life-writings could give information about family feelings (love) because, until the nineteenth century, most ego-documents were written by an educated, elite minority (Fleming 2004: 53–4). By reconceptualizing what investigating emotions in the past aims to achieve, however, it is possible to resolve this supposed problem. The historian of emotions is concerned with the full range of feelings, recognizing that emotional relationships include anger, anxiety, grief, fear, apprehension, pain and suspicion, as well as love (in its diverse forms) and desire. This also means that most of the records used to capture family life can be used, such as court records, literary works and conduct books.

Third, scrutinizing the emotions that circulated within the household facilitates a more expansive account of the family that is neither structural nor affective; it is inclusive since it does not depend on rigid characteristics of relatedness, is less synchronic in nature and not dependent upon co-residence. With emotions as our conceptual category, it becomes clear that people included household members unrelated by blood or marriage in their understanding of family. Attention to emotions also reveals that families were reconfigured in temporary forms around emotional cultures, such as those following bereavement or during pregnancy and childbirth. Moreover, it enables us to extend our understanding of family to encompass family members who were rarely co-resident. As Broomhall observes, ideas about emotional relationships transcended physical boundaries and were played out by people at a distance (2008: 16).

Fourth, emotions history nuances family life by revealing that feelings interacted with power to act upon and disrupt age and gender hierarchies, birth, rank and occupational order. Studies recognize that while emotions in the household create and reproduce subordination, they can also unravel it (ibid.: 5, 14–16). As this chapter will show, this breaks down a tendency to apply binaries when analysing the family. It helps us to move away from placing ideal and reality in opposition or at a distance from each other (previously explained through ignorance or rejection of conventions). It prevents us defining hierarchical relationships only through the categories of dominance and subordination (and thus seeing them as based on obedience or subversion or mediated by reciprocity and negotiation). It shows instead that gender ideals were not simply inculcated to favour men, but could be trained in both sexes as simultaneously an instrumental tool and an intrinsic value. As Broomhall explains, the household 'offered a set of rules to order the emotional content of individuals, whether strangers or blood relatives' which are thus, of course, historicizable (ibid.: 4).

This chapter thus insists that the dwelling group is too limiting a category by which to measure family, and that temporal and spatial fluidity should not militate against recognizing an enormous variety of family relationships (Cavallo 2010: 8–9, 27–8). Again, it is important to emphasize that these relationships involved emotions and did not require co-residence. Studying the Lisle Letters of the 1530s, exchanged between Lord Lisle and his servant Husee, Catherine Mann argues that they indicate that 'household ties were predicated on good feeling, affection, and understanding, rather, perhaps, than duty or proximity' (2008: 127). It also deliberately shakes off the shackles of structural and affective models, together with their organizational formulations and suggests that we think of family and household in terms of connections and constituencies. Connections rather than co-residence are the key factor for inclusion in this examination of family and household. This recognizes the constellation of emotional ties between those who resided, for more than a brief visit, in the household or who were bound by ties but at times did not co-reside and, admittedly, largely in the case of the elite, therefore relied upon correspondence as the means by which the familial relationship was maintained. As Jacqueline Van Gent and Broomhall's analysis of the Nassau family indicates, siblings were not just part of family and household as children when they co-resided, but continued to be so, even as they moved between each other's dwellings (2009: 152).

A constituencies approach aims to capture the sense of family as a group of individuals (perhaps an 'emotional community', Rosenwein 2006: 4) who had shared interests, which extended beyond the walls of a dwelling, consanguinity or affinity, and which included people who formed family-households based around other kinds of activities, such as single women sharing a home for economic advantage or to avoid local authorities' harsh regulations, and individuals living together with shared occupations and professional interests. As Broomhall's collection demonstrates to magnificent effect, the social unit of the household structured its residents' identities and interactions with other communities (2008: 2). With these framing formulations in mind, the rest of the chapter is divided into sections around the powerful and motivating feelings of love and hate, sex and suspicion and the ties of responsibility and reciprocity. It also explores the impact of emotions in constructing and mitigating various temporary and more longstanding bonds and hierarchies.

LOVE AND HATE

The family and household were the location of physical and emotional reproduction: loci in which loving relationships were forged but also broke down. Hence, historians have tended to investigate only these two: love and hate, oppositional yet intertwined emotions through marital relationships. Historians of family and household in the Renaissance period have been caught up for some time in speculating about the extent to which marriage was based on mutual love. Early scholars, such as Lawrence Stone (1977), saw an increase in the making of marriage for love from the late medieval period, when he deemed it did not serve as a basis for a union, to the seventeenth century, when at least Protestants were increasingly attuned to the necessity for companionate marriage. Others have rejected such a crude periodization, pointing to numerous examples of love and affection in the fifteenth and sixteenth centuries, such as that expressed between Margery Paston and the family's bailiff, Richard Calle, in the late 1460s (McCarthy 2004: 93). Nonetheless, historians have struggled to accommodate their idea of love with noble families arranging marriages between children for social and political advancement. Scottish Highland chiefs of clans in the sixteenth century, for example, used marriage as either a way to reinforce internal clan cohesion or to form and maintain external alliances. The union in 1571 of Helen, daughter of John Grant, fourth of Freuchy, and Donald, son of Angus MacDonald of Glengarry, cemented a bond between the two clans. It bound MacDonald to his promise to assist Grant in his activities, defend his lands from attack and help recover stolen goods in the event of an attack (Cathcart 2008: 130–2). Pragmatic unions are observed in other social groups. Middling-sort unions wed according to economic wherewithal, and in times of need poor and widowed individuals married to secure a basic level of economic provision for themselves or their young children.

Of course, it is easier to reconcile such a variety of unions with love, if we define love according to understandings applied at the time (Reddy 2012).

Marital love was understood to develop over time, and thus be consistent with a union constructed for instrumental reasons out of which romantic love could grow. Interestingly, the supposed absence of love in marriage is generally constructed by historians as damaging for women, not men. Thus, courtly love is cast as largely theoretical and favouring noblemen, not their objects of desire: symptomatic of families' sacrificing women's happiness to dynastic interests. Any notion of love in the patriarchal context of marriage is viewed as primarily serving men's benefits. Men held the most power in the family over their dependents; yet, contemporaries saw love as offsetting or limiting their desire to exert their will. The instrumentality of this is clear, seemingly constructed merely to facilitate women's acceptance of their husbands' authority and thus enabling them to proffer obedience (Fleming 2004: 54–5).

Scholarship attuned to gender has nuanced much of this account. Wives had more authority in certain household circumstances, such as when their husbands were absent or because they held property in their own right (Sandvik 2005: 112–13). The sixteenth-century Nuremberg couple, Magdalena and Balthasar Paumgartner's correspondence reveals her considerable agency which resulted from his extensive travels in Europe as a merchant (Ozment 1989). Furthermore, married women garnered degrees of autonomy and power through the emotions engendered in situations such as childbirth, childrearing and care of the sick, although we need not see this as wrested from husbands. Hannah Newton's account of parental care of sick children in sixteenth-century England reveals that fathers nursed their ill offspring as much as mothers did, with both feeling the same levels of emotional distress (Newton 2012: 4–5). Accounts of early modern marriage now stress the space it offered for spouses to negotiate their relative positions of authority along gendered lines, but enabling a flexibility that cut across these gender restrictions that placed wives in a subordinate role, as Figure 2.2 vividly shows (Barclay 2011). It is also acknowledged that noble women were trained in feminine virtues for instrumental reasons, aiding their capacity to exercise female forms of authority within the family, rather than simply to ingrain obedience (Pollock 1989). Tracy Adams' work on fosterage in early modern French noble families reveals that efforts were aimed at cultivating them into gentle, amiable young women. This helped manage the conditions of this collective style of living, which did not centre on biological relationships. However, the virtues of piety, chastity and amiableness were not inculcated simply in order to make women submissive. Appreciated in themselves, the values were also intended to enable a woman 'to better exercise influence': a form of diplomacy to be exercised by women in a system that forged political contracts and created chains of influence between families. The values, supposedly modelled by the noble women in whose families they were fostered, were intended to 'help them to enter successfully into the system of exchange through which one gained power' (Adams 2008: 111).

FIGURE 2.2: *The Four Conditions of Society: Work* by Jean Bourdichon (1457–1521). © Bibliothèque de l'École des Beaux-Arts, Paris, France/Bridgeman Images.

Work on masculinities reveals that patriarchal manhood was itself precarious, undermined by wives' sexual and moral reputation, and by their economic contribution to the domestic economy (Shepard 2006). Less often acknowledged is that lack of love and affection was as detrimental to men's wellbeing as to women's. Perhaps our questions of these sources need to be reconfigured to ask what love meant for both spouses when separation and divorce remained either unavailable or damaging. As such, it is more useful to acknowledge that successful marriage was always understood to be constructed on several pillars: love, sex, economic stability and compatibility of various kinds, which were as essential for husbands as to wives. Those with additional means sought to secure dynastic, financial and political advancement through it, although this was not necessarily in opposition to these concerns.

The counterpoint to studies that seek convincing evidence of marital affection are those which expose marital violence. Julie Hardwick (2006), for instance, explores individuals', communities' and courts' negotiations of the parameters of the prerogative of husbands to use force to discipline their wives in seventeenth-century France. The patriarchal structure of society and family governance in this era provided men with the right to correct insubordinate dependents, although it should always be remembered that violence was not considered acceptable by secular or canon law or in popular culture. Men were not supposed to let themselves be bested by their women, in the endless battle of the sexes for dominance, but, for all that examples of men's horrific abuse of their wives can be found all too often, the protection of women from abuse was carried out at several levels from family to Church and state (Bailey and Giese 2013). Moreover, boys were typically trained to channel anger into appropriate forms and not display uncontrolled rage (Foyster 1999a). Since marital abuse stems from a man's desire to control his wife, and its incidence remains shockingly high in societies deemed relatively egalitarian, we should be very cautious about condemning late medieval and early modern marriages for being structured to accommodate and condone the blows of husbands against wives.

SEX AND SUSPICION

The household was the site of both legitimate and illegitimate sexual acts; the former in the marital bed, the latter in a variety of liminal spaces within the dwelling and its environs. These acts and the meaning surrounding them also shaped notions of family relationships. Marriage was a union that conferred mutual care and companionship and was expected to be founded on mutually satisfying sexual relations. St Paul's statement upon the 'marital debt' in 1 Corinthians 7 was unequivocal about the centrality of sex in marriage:

> to avoid fornication, let every man have his own wife, and let every woman have her own husband. Let the husband render unto the wife due benevolence: and likewise also the wife unto the husband. The wife hath not power of her own body, but the husband: and likewise also the husband hath not power of his own body, but the wife.

Moreover, one model of sexual reproduction saw mutual orgasm as a necessity for conception, which presumably encouraged satisfying sex for women as well as men (Kingsley Kent 2012: 14–15). It is perhaps not surprising then, that marital sex was understood not simply to serve reproductive ends, but also to sustain a married couple in their union and to strengthen the relationship.

Yet, the family and household consisted of family members who directly threatened this legitimate sexuality. Spouses were regularly reminded of infidelity's risks for household and gender reputation. Throughout the period, bawdy tales and, in the later part of the period, conduct advice, and popular customs such as charivari, rough music and Skimington rides mocked and reprimanded men whose wives cuckolded them (Burke 2009: 279–80). Being seen by one's community as weak and unable to satisfy or control a wife's sexual appetite not only undermined a man's personal identity, it also threatened his standing in his community as governor of his household. Furthermore, husbands' adultery was often very close to home; in imagination and practice, men engaged in sexual relationships with their household maids. These were often exploitative relationships, although there could be some degree of female volition. In 1627, in Venice, one maid brought a defloration case against her master Bortholomio Agazi, a spice merchant. She apparently agreed to exchange her virginity for a dowry, but sued him when he failed to provide it (McGough 2010: 41–2). As such, while servants were understood to have potentially affectionate relationships within their family of employment, the more sinister side of this was their perceived role in causing conflict and tensions. The potentiality and reality of master–maid sexual relationships meant that mistress–maid relationships could be fraught and constructed around mutual mistrust. As such, court records from cases of illegitimacy inevitably reveal the fear, anger and hatred as well as, occasionally, care and pity emanating from these relationships. Often, wives were obliged by their own lower position in the household hierarchy to support their unfaithful husband, even when he had clearly exploited a dependent, the maid. Marko Lamberg (2008: 172) thus identifies suspicion as the main feeling characterizing mistress–maid relationships in Stockholm, 1450–1650.

RESPONSIBILITIES AND RECIPROCITIES

At various points in the family life-course, most households were filled with children. Although family sizes varied and not all households were formed around fertile married couples, nevertheless children, whether biologically or socially related, were usually present. Procreation was considered the purpose of marriage and, unless infertile, couples had children, although their numbers varied according to rates of infant mortality and, perhaps, the practice of family limitation. Moreover, older children entered households as employees, kin and through fosterage (Gager 1996). Despite previous scholarly debates about the degree to which late medieval and early modern society conceptualized and valued childhood, and parents emotionally invested in their offspring, the consensus is that parents were expected to love their children and do their best to establish them for adult life, which often meant securing training for them in other people's households. Love could ameliorate power hierarchies. It is perhaps as fathers that this is most evident. When sons behaved badly, or sought to follow an occupational route other than that planned, their fathers might be more likely to accommodate their position due to their love (Cavallo 2010: 22).

As noted earlier, love has had different definitions in the past, but there are continuities where parenting is concerned, revolving around responsibilities and reciprocities. Mothers and fathers were to give their offspring care, compassion and religious and educational or employment training, all of which necessitated considerable emotional and financial investment, and the exercise of authority. In return, children offered affection, respect, duty and care. These parenting bonds extended across generations. For example, grandparents would take on the duty of care for their grandchildren when their children died, as Lucy Laumonier's study of late medieval Languedoc reveals. For instance, a reciprocal arrangement was forged between Guillimeta and her deceased daughter's husband that he and her orphaned grandson would provide and care for her, and offer her reverence like a good son would his mother. In return, the widower secured a home and place to work for his son as well as, perhaps, a carer for the child (Laumonier 2016: 110).

Societies set, monitored and judged parental performance of their responsibilities for children, typically through scriptural tenets, custom and law. In post-Reformation Scotland, for instance, parents' duties to their children were publicly declared through the baptismal ceremony. The ministers' sermon made it clear that parents were admonished, 'that ye nourish and bring up the children of God's favour and mercy ... So ought it make you diligent and careful to nurture and instruct them in the true knowledge and fear of God' (Hollander 2008: 67). Melissa Hollander shows that the Kirk placed particular emphasis on fathers being educated and well equipped for their role as moral, spiritual and social head of house (ibid.: 68). In England, by contrast, god-parents took this role, selected from the family's extended relatives or social network. In fact, parents were still intended to secure their offspring's spiritual education, with the choice of god-parents establishing links between generations and families (ibid.: 70–2). Moreover, maternity and paternity carried reputational benefits and those who failed in their roles lost their standing (Krausman Ben-Amos 1997: 13–14).

Parental roles were often performed in relation to other people's children. Fosterage was a widespread practice, with families fostering children in order to train the child in the necessary gendered social and/or occupational skills required for adulthood. It was also part of a patronage system, wherein children were sent into a household of a higher social rank. In any of these situations, an emotional relationship between the child or adolescent and the family in which they were fostered could develop. In 1584, Duncan Campbell of Duntraein and his wife Agnes Nikolleane agreed to foster the son of Duncan Campbell of Glenorchy. Their formal bond stated the motivation for the fosterage: to ensure 'luife and favour suld be and contenew betwex the housis of Glnurquhay and Duntrone'. Still, this did not preclude the obligation of care for the child. Agnes was bound as foster-mother to 'do hir dewtie to him in all thingis according to the custome and condition of ane favorabill fostermother' (Cathcart 2008: 137). Even at the more general level, emotions shaped expectations and behaviour in this relationship. Tracy Adams' analysis of guides for fostering girls in early modern noble French families reveals that they advocated strategies to create pleasant atmospheres for the girls as well as training them to be agreeable. This was intended to cultivate an atmosphere of mutual affection, in order to transmit skills to the women and facilitate the success of this form of extended family (Adams 2008).

Poorer households boarded a range of children, too. In the later sixteenth century, John Harrys of Essex boarded his daughter Elizabeth with Philip Baker, in London, 'for a certain time, to th'end his said daughter might learn some breeding' by being in London. The Bakers kept Elizabeth for ten years until she married, perhaps an indication of each party's satisfaction with the arrangement (McIntosh 2005: 63). Some took in illegitimate and orphaned children. Joel Harrington (2008) demonstrates that parentless children of all ages, citizen and non-citizen, were circulated in early modern Nuremberg, a minority organized by the state, but most following horizontal relationships among neighbours and friends. Again, this had a financial aspect. The Collectors of the Poor accounts from 1579 to 1596 of Hadleigh, Suffolk, show that the town paid elderly married couples, themselves in receipt of poor relief, to board young children. As McIntosh observes, the town fathers believed both parties would 'benefit from the economic, physical, and emotional stability of such arrangements' (2005: 71–2). In 1580, John Rede, a London vintner, arranged that his sister Elizabeth and her husband take in an illegitimate child, presumably so that the mother, Agnes, could work or find a spouse. The contract was for several months, and Agnes signed a bond promising to pay for her child's boarding. When she later married, her husband continued to pay the couple for several years. When the mother and her new husband then requested the return of the child, the foster parents refused and sued Agnes for the higher boarding amount originally agreed in the bond she had signed. It would seem that they had been happy to be paid the lower amount and keep the child, only demanding the higher sum with the prospect of giving it up. This surely resulted from the development of family-feelings for the child, and was not solely driven by the regular sum paid, otherwise the couple would have sued earlier (ibid.: 66).

BONDS, RIVALRIES AND TENSIONS

Siblings lived together for at least part of their childhood, periodically separated by wet-nursing practices, training, education and fosterage. During this time, they learned their place in the hierarchical family and social order, shaped by birth order, sex and, more broadly, by their family's status, wealth and religion. Although differentiated in this way, most brothers and sisters will have known

FIGURE 2.3: *Two Sisters and a Brother of the Artist* (also called *Three Children with Dog*) by Sofonisba Anguissola (*c.* 1532–1625), *c.* 1570–90. © Corsham Court, Wiltshire/Bridgeman Images.

that brothers took precedence over sisters, as Figure 2.3 suggests, and that boys and girls were reared for different purposes, with marriage the aim for girls unless they were intended for religious seclusion, while a wide variety of employment was open to their brothers. They encountered these gendered rules through their clothing, activities and religious instruction. Van Gent and Broomhall's study of an aristocratic Nassau family between 1570 and 1650, for instance, notes that gifts were often gendered, with boys receiving toys or educational gifts, while girls were given gifts that emphasized their appearance (2009: 143–65, 150).

In many cases, siblings dispersed in adulthood; but their relationships continued to be a significant feature of family life. Detailed accounts of children's lives as siblings are scarce for this period, but studies that attend to the emotional exchanges between adult siblings in correspondence exchanged during long-distance separation reveals considerable interaction. Van Gent and Broomhall's study of the twelve legitimate children of William the Silent in the later sixteenth and seventeenth centuries, for example, reveals numerous 'exchange acts', from visiting one another and gift exchange, to fostering children (ibid.). Unsurprisingly, given gendered property ownership, sisters circulated service to siblings, while brothers sent material aid. Van Gent and Broomhall also reveal how emotions shaped the siblings' relationships as adults in ways that contributed to, and reshaped, familial power norms and hierarchies. Child-bearing could reshape family order, with women gaining more power and influence regardless of their own birth order by having children first, particularly sons. As Van Gent and Broomhall observe, the 'ability to have children as well as their sex caused envy and competition to emerge' among siblings (ibid.: 157).

The vocabulary of emotions they used to some extent confirmed gender constructions and age conventions. The Nassau sisters were more likely than brothers to articulate feelings in letters; the corollary was that when brothers did express emotions, these feelings were deemed more authentic and powerful. Younger siblings were more likely to be effusively grateful and proffer services, although this was instrumental and anticipated elders' care in return (ibid.: 147–9). Other emotional vocabularies were strategical, demonstrating or renewing preferred familial connections, such as a mother naming her newborn after another family member, or a sibling flagging up favourites among brothers and sisters to give one individual leverage over another (ibid.: 152). This meant that adult siblings would align with other siblings in order to undermine other family members, perhaps an older brother or the family patriarch. In the Dutch Nassau family, elder siblings expressed negative emotions to younger siblings about still older siblings (ibid.: 155).

In noble families, dynastic political authority was the subject of dispute between siblings, with brothers jostling for power. Disputes frequently occurred when a father died and transferred property and power to one male successor. This led to horizontal disputes between brothers, largely operating as peers since they were equal before the law. Erica Bastress-Dukehart's work on early modern German noble families reveals that gender was also a key factor in such dynastic jostling and negotiation for power. She focuses on brother–sister conflict, wherein despite their unequal legal position, women attempted to achieve their own ambitions. Such conflict reveals that noble women often expected to support themselves, rather than be dependent upon a brother's financial protection, because these women inherited movable goods of value, which included rents and mortgages from family-owned properties, and their high birth meant they were trained for the task of managing this property. It also demonstrates that the making of marriage and transmission of property were both integral to noble dynastic strategies. As such, sisters' actions were just as significant in altering a family's political fortunes as their brothers' (Bastress-Dukehart 2008).

This does not mean that women were entirely passive objects, despite the extreme lengths to which brothers went to regain control. Bastress-Dukehart examines three early modern German cases from the early fifteenth to mid-sixteenth centuries in which noblemen placed their sisters under house arrest, denying them access to the wider world and repudiating the efforts of state and Church to intervene on the women's behalf. Bastress-Dukehart argues that the meaning of a sibling's defiance affected the brother whom they resisted differently, according to their sex. A brother's challenge tested his male sibling's right to rule, while a sister's defiance questioned her brother's capacity to rule, since his inability to control his sister intimated his inability to manage his other responsibilities. As such, men might act with especial severity in controlling defiant sisters who resisted their authority, typically when a sister wished to marry a man of lower social rank, or refused to renounce rights to natal property. Indeed, in some cases, a man who defied higher authority's demands and intervention in his family's affairs could improve his family's social and political reputation (ibid.).

Other types of relationships had the potential to construct emotional bonds, as we saw above between surrogate parents and children, but also between masters, mistresses and their servants (Broomhall 2008: 19). Servants in this period were taken on in smaller households as well as constituting the vast entourage of noble families; in the former they included women, in the latter for much of this period they were male. Employed from adolescence (defined by historians as life-cycle service), generally single and learning employment- and life-skills until their own marriage or maturity, they were drawn from their masters' kin, neighbourhood or trade. Servants' sex and intended training shaped their roles within their household-family, and perhaps their treatment. There is evidence of good and bad relationships. Some degree of emotional intimacy or dependence is perhaps evident in masters' and mistress's bequests of property and cash to their servants. In 1611, Marjorie Clutton died, with a huge estate worth £1,468. 1s. 4d. She made bequests to her daughter and cousin, but also left £5 each to her 'old servant' William Reeve, to 'her man Goodyer', to her maid, and to the poor, with 2s. 6d. to another maid. Although Karen O'Brien interprets this as evidence of family feeling, it is perhaps significant that the Nantwich widows and single women who left cash for servants also left similar sums to the poor. It may well be that leaving money to servants and the poor was a charitable and virtuous act as much as a sign of familial affection; of course, the two were by no means incompatible (O'Brien 2016: 137). Indications of greater and lesser affection survive. When Ann Wright died in 1634, she differentiated between her servants, giving her favourite servant £10 and the rest 40s. (ibid.: 138).

As with all intimate relationships, there is also evidence of tensions; the failure of trust and suspicion which some mistresses and maids encountered from each other is discussed above (Fleming 2004: 72–6). Masters could have a very instrumental and exploitative attitude towards their servants, particularly maid servants who were vulnerable to sexual abuse in the patriarchal household. Indeed, late medieval bawdy and humorous literary tales often featured maids who were objects to be used by both masters and mistresses for their own ends. In one mid-fifteenth-century Burgundian collection of tales, masters pronounced that their maids' bodies were their masters' to possess. In other stories, mistresses exploited maids to serve their own ends, whether to sexually satisfy an undesired husband or facilitate an affair (Bibring 2008). Yet, it would be a mistake to see servants as universally passive and oppressed or without emotional depth. There is no doubt that the domestic servant was considered socially inferior to the master of the household, subjected to another through contract or bloodline, as well emotionally (Gordon 2008). Yet, emotional connections and vocabularies were another way to resist other family members' power. Broomhall observes that early modern representations of servants, suggested that moral householders should fear servants because they impacted upon the household's honour. Thus, masters and mistresses' perception of the threat of their servants' potential or actual disobedience and its repercussions for household reputation gave servants some emotional power (Broomhall 2008: 22, 30). The embeddedness of servants in kin and community in this era could be interpreted as providing some degree of protection for the servants, either because their employers were related by blood or marriage, or because their families were near enough to be called on for support. Similarly, this may have afforded some servants a position of negotiation, which at least alleviated their inferior status within the household or gave them some leverage in negotiating an amenable situation.

ANXIETY AND GRIEF

Family relationships were reconfigured time and again in response to life-stage events, such as birth and death. Each of these instances was prefigured by a period of time in which families and households were changed by the corporeal demands of pregnancy and sickness, and in each case the constituency of the household reformed to meet these events' challenges. Pregnancy placed demands upon families, whether due to the mother's physical needs and capacity to work, expectations upon a father to provide materially and psychologically for his wife's state, or in wealthy households where anticipation of childbirth might also include extensive ceremonial arrangements. In many different social ranks, family members moved around or communicated with each other in order to monitor, facilitate and participate in the pregnancy and its culmination. Where written evidence exists, it is clear that pregnancy elicited a number of emotions for the parents and their household-families, primarily anxiety, apprehension, fear and pain, hope, joy and gratitude. As I have argued elsewhere, this emotional vocabulary, expressed in conversation, presumably, as well as letters, helped families navigate the stresses of this condition. It forged further bonds between spouses, but also between them and family members, for example when mothers sought guidance and support from their own mothers or mothers-in-law (Begiato 2017).

As noted earlier in this chapter, emotional events and vocabularies enabled people to subvert traditional hierarchies. Thus, mothers used the various emotions associated with pregnancy and birth to construct female authority and make demands or challenge patriarchal authority (Begiato 2016). For example, Broomhall argues that Catherine de' Medici used her correspondence with the Spanish Court about her daughter Elisabeth de Valois, Queen of Spain between 1559 and 1568, to legitimize her authority to direct her daughter's care during childbearing. This authority was established through her knowledge of the intertwined health and emotional well-being of pregnancy and childbirth (2002). Furthermore, the ability to share feelings of anxiety helped bridge the difficult transitions from one phase of life to another, and helping neutralize the fear of the arrival of the child, an unseen 'stranger' (Begiato 2017). Unfortunately, pregnancy also had a sinister side, in that it was a time of increased incidence of violence in some marriages, perhaps related to its potential to undermine traditional patriarchal hierarchies. Court cases of marital violence reveal that a husband's abuse of his wife frequently occurred during her pregnancy. Indeed, husbands were warned not to strike wives during this time. St Bernardino (1380–1444), for instance, included this admonition in his recommendations that husbands rely on correcting wives through words rather than blows (Fleming 2004: 57).

Childbirth also led to the circulation of family members and carers between households and temporary instantiations of emotional constituencies. Renaissance women drew upon their husbands for support and various services as childbirth came closer. Nonetheless, the event itself was predominantly a female occasion, with men waiting for the delivery of the child, while women took the key roles: a group drawn from the mother's family (especially the child's future maternal grandmother) and friends, as well as the professional services of the midwife. The rituals of childbirth materialized collective female action, with the birth chamber physically and symbolically enclosed by blocking out daylight. The lying-in period following birth (ideally a month), in which a mother was given time to physically recover, also meant that family members stayed for some time in the household to assist with domestic duties and childcare (Wilson 2013: chapter 4). Richer parents would employ a nurse (Wilson 2013: 178–9). Historians have debated whether these customs, and the churching ceremony that followed, indicated a rite of passage, signified society's belief in women's inferiority and impurity, or enabled a transitory reversal of gender order by placing women on top (ibid.: 191–8). For our purposes, it is the emotional connotations that illuminate how the relationships within households were malleable both physically and conceptually. When a woman of reasonable means gave birth, her family reconfigured to accommodate those with whom she already had familial feelings. It also temporarily reshaped her relationship with her husband since she was removed from his immediate authority, and their sexual relationship, as well as some of her household labours.

It should be noted that the same circumstances could forge negative emotions that challenged familial relationships. These provisional familial configurations could also be a period of conflict rather than female conviviality (Pollock 1990). Laura Gowing observes that childbirth could lead to tensions between women. The women involved might engage in questioning the mother's behaviour or morality, gossiping and slandering her and arguing with rather than supporting family members. As she points out, when poor women gave birth, and particularly when unmarried women did, the 'Honest matrons who attended did so primarily to uphold parish interest as well as assist the travailing mother' (Gowing 2003: 159, 163). Indeed, Gowing argues that childbirth might be another area 'for the exercise of authority and deference', since the women attending births were by no means social equals. Gentlewomen sometimes attended the lying-in of villagers, and 'poor old women' assisted with cleaning and nursing mothers in labour, as part of the conditional requirements imposed by receiving poor relief (ibid.: 155). The gathering of women during a lying-in period was also potentially disruptive and argumentative; male satirists certainly feared it was (ibid.: 174).

Sickness and death in the family also created a temporary emotional constituency. This was practical, since it led to more people entering and staying in the dwelling when a family member was ill and known to be dying, including medical professionals, paid carers and attendants, clergy and kin (Brady 2008: 194). Following death, there were a number of religious and customary rituals surrounding funeral rites and bereavement and grieving, which forged links between the community and family. As Andrea Brady argues, both sickness and death created new emotional bonds. This had the potential to cut across social hierarchies, temporarily creating equity between family members, and embodying affection, since not only did paid carers minister to sick family members, servants who were ill could be cared for by their employers (ibid.: 192). In the early seventeenth century, Jane Stephens, a maid in Alice and William Payne's household in Canterbury became ill and died a couple of weeks later. She slept in the same chamber as her master and mistress and during the night she sickened, she called out that she was dying. At that, William leapt up and lit a candle and Alice got her warm broth. In the next two weeks, Alice provided solace, support and food and William applied himself to helping Jane sort out her property and will. In the end, Jane died in the Paynes' home, surrounded by female friends and neighbours, all presumably facilitated by her employers (Hallam 1996: 69–71).

TRUST, SERVICE AND SUPPORT

Restricting the study of families and households to those with parents, children and servants at their centre ignores household-families composed of different members who were, nonetheless, bound by feelings such as trust, service and support, which shaped both their living arrangements and their emotional lives. Figure 2.4, for example, depicts the wealthy German merchant Jakob Fugger at work with his clerk in his office. An excellent example is Marcantonio Sabellico's household based around the profession of teaching. In the late fifteenth-century, this Venetian family was composed of Sabellico and his son, along with a number

FIGURE 2.4: Jakob Fugger in his office, 1518, German School, sixteenth century. © Private Collection/Bridgeman Images.

of male amanuenses, tutors, foster carers, students and servants; women being largely absent. By his teenage years, Sabellico's son was hosted by other households in Ferrara and Padua, and Sabellico took in his brother's son to educate him, as well as boarding adolescent residential students in his household. Neither proximity nor co-residency was critical in shaping this household-family. Ruth Chavasse points out that his authority as pater-familias extended over his own residence and those where he sent his son to board. Although composed predominantly of unrelated or distantly related individuals, the correspondence between members of his household reveals strong bonds. This was not without instrumental cause since the members were financially dependent upon Sabellico, but it was founded on feelings of trust and care (Chavasse 2008).

Another household in which the main familial relationships were forged between its male members was in the scholarly Godfrey household in France, in the mid-seventeenth century, whose members were employed in pedagogy. Caroline Sherman notes that while the patriarch, Theodore Godfrey, paid his clerks and copyists a good salary in exchange for fidelity and effort, he also entered affective relationships with them. Travelling in his advanced years, two of his amanuenses accompanied him to carry out their work and physically care for him, as well as keeping his son up to date with his father's health and activities. The amanuenses were afforded the permanent status of younger son or brother. As with younger brothers, they were only allowed to express themselves in more childlike emotions such as wonder, fear, gratitude and anxiety. Like some of the siblings discussed above, whose acceptable modes of communication were determined by their relative birth order, an amanuensis was the individual to whom a 'superior' expressed displeasure. They therefore could construct affective alliances which offset patriarchal relationships, such as a clerk allying with a son against a domineering father (Sherman 2008: 155, 158).

In noble families, it is possible to examine the ways in which service constructed affective relationships through the correspondence between its unrelated household members. An example is the relationship between Lord Lisle and his high-ranking servant and agent in London, Husee, laid bare in his communications with his master and mistress in the 1530s, when they resided in Calais. Mann shows that Husee deployed a language of obligation and feeling engendered by duty. This secured his position and offered him a safe platform from which to defend his actions and offer criticism of his employers. Husee frequently explained his actions in his letters to his employer, Lord Lisle, through a vocabulary of loyalty and duty. What is particularly interesting is that he deployed a gendered mode of contact in his letters to Lord and Lady Lisle. Not only did he draw on ideals of 'good lordship' and 'good ladyship' to negotiate his position with both, but he also corresponded with Lady Lisle in such a way that potentially subverted the power relationship between him and his master. As well as requesting her intervention in his letters, Mann argues that he constructed his duty towards her as devotional, establishing a certain gendered intimacy that was not replicated in his letters to his master (2008: 126–7).

There is less detailed evidence surviving of such households at lower social levels, although court cases and records of governance offer some clues to alternative forms of household-families forged around support. There are examples across Europe of several single women living together. Local authorities frequently viewed single women as sources of social disorder, masterless women who were not under the authority of father or husband. Many forbade unmarried women from living and working independently, although, in fact, women's pay was usually too low to make this viable anyway. For authorities, controlling single women thereby prevented the moral disease of prostitution, and limiting their capacity to find employment prevented them from undermining married men's ability to earn enough to keep their dependents. A Coventry Ordinance of 1492, for instance, forbade single women from keeping a house or chamber by themselves or with another, and required them to go into service or leave the city, all strategies which brought them under a master's authority (Froide 2005: 19–25; Peters 2003: 24–6). Still, some single women did form households together, although usually related, such as sisters, and of some means (Froide 2005: 22–3, 54–5, 71–3). While possibly composed of both non-kin and kin, some of these relationships may have stimulated or depended upon feelings such as affection, obligation or trust.

Another way to achieve a household-family that was more economically viable was for women to take on unrelated children, part of the plethora of makeshift economies. Thus, urban women boarded children who attended local schools. In the sixteenth and seventeenth century, Christ's Hospital, London, sent out illegitimate and orphaned children to be wet-nursed in the suburbs, and cities paid 'foster mothers' to take parentless children into their homes. Lone women with children might also board with male householders, presumably as a way to secure a more respectable living and avoid concerns over their masterless state. Most of the evidence of modest households doing such work comes from institutional or court records, and thus does not always record details of everyday lives and feelings, yet it is clear that, at the least, these relationships would result in reciprocal obligations (McIntosh 2005: 61–2). In the 1560s and 1570s, for instance, Elizabeth Watson, came from London to board with Thomas Freman of Leominster. She stayed for about four months and then left, returning the next year with her two-year-old child, boarding again for nearly four months, and leaving again. She also paid Thomas to board a second child. During this time, Thomas loaned her cash and paid some debts, while Elizabeth claimed she had loaned him a larger sum (ibid.: 2). Such temporary constituencies may well have forged trust and support, and, as this case shows, when trust failed, had the capacity to engender a number of far more negative feelings.

CONCLUSION

This chapter shows the value of attending to emotions as the framework for exploring family and household in Renaissance Europe. Attention to the full range of emotions that was created by family life and household connections reveals the extensive web of relationships that constituted family and household, their variety, their mutability, their temporality (both short and long), and the ways in which these changed over time and location. This overview of emotional ties also points to the significance of emotions themselves in shaping family life and the people whose relationships constituted family and household. Feelings determined behaviours, shaped gender and age hierarchies for good or bad, and influenced the interactions between individuals, households, communities and states.

CHAPTER THREE

The House

DANAE TANKARD

In February 1617, an argument was brewing between two clerics' wives, Elizabeth Mead and Thomasine Blaxton, both living in the Cathedral close of the small provincial city of Chichester in Sussex. Elizabeth and three other women were visiting Ann Newman at her house in the 'Little Cloisters', when Thomasine turned up at the front door accompanied by her son, 'much enraged and incensed' and shouting, 'Where is this impudent baggage?!' At the time of her arrival, Mead, Ann's sister, was in 'some upper room or chamber' whilst the other women were in the kitchen. Ann opened the door and called for her sister, who came downstairs and then, in 'the entry between the . . . stairs and the kitchen', the two women traded insults 'both being . . . violent and furious in their communication [and] ready to fly in one and others face' (WSRO/EP/III/5/1: 48–53). What had caused Elizabeth and Thomasine to fall out is unknown and is of no particular relevance here, but the spatial dynamics of their argument are of interest since they offer an insight into the domestic environment in which these women and their neighbours lived. We know rather more about Ann's house than the sketchy details provided by this case because it is recorded in a parliamentary survey of Cathedral-owned properties carried out in 1649 and 1650 (discussed in more detail below). It was on the east side of the Little Cloisters and consisted of an 'entry' and four 'low', or ground-floor, rooms, including a 'fairly wainscoted' parlour. There was a cellar beneath one of these rooms and five chambers above them, that above the parlour being 'well wainscoted'. This was, then, a good house in a central location, suitable for a man like John Newman, who is described in contemporary records as a 'gentleman'. The house had one major disadvantage, however: one of its upper chambers was located over the 'common houses of office' or privies shared by all the houses that made up the Little Cloisters; the smell from this must have permeated its rooms, particularly during periods of hot weather (WSRO/Cap I/30/2: 87–90).

This chapter is about urban and rural housing in England during the period *c.* 1450 to 1650. It adopts a case study approach, examining houses in some detail within a relatively small geographical area rather than attempting a broader overview of the country as a whole. It is divided into two parts: the first part is concerned with rural housing in parts of southern England, especially Sussex; the second part focuses on urban housing in London and Chichester. The focus of the chapter is on 'ordinary' housing, the type of housing lived in by the majority of men and women in these areas, rather than the elite housing of the few. The layout and uses of space within houses are examined and the way that these varied according to location, size of property and time period. Houses are also contextualized by considering their relation to ancillary buildings, structures and services such as detached kitchens, privies and wells.

RURAL HOUSING

With a reduced population in the fifteenth and early sixteenth centuries, land was plentifully available and rural wages levels were relatively high. Basic living standards rose and the number of landless, or near landless, households declined. The prosperity of the peasantry stimulated new house-building, which reached a peak between *c.* 1440 and 1520. The quality of these buildings is reflected in the large number that survive today (Dyer 2003: 356–7). There were, nevertheless, considerable variations in wealth. By the late fifteenth century, the peasantry was differentiated into three broad socioeconomic groups: yeomen, who typically held between 80 and 100 acres; husbandmen who held between fifteen and thirty acres and labourers who each held a few acres and who undertook waged work to supplement their income (ibid.: 358). Rural trades and craftsmen straddled these three broad bands; the more substantial – tanners, clothiers and millers, for example – lived like yeomen, whilst the status of others was more similar to that of husbandmen and even labourers.

The economic fortunes of many rural inhabitants changed over the course of the sixteenth century. Rapid growth in population after 1520 combined with steep price rises and worsening wage rates to produce an increasingly impoverished rural labouring class. As we shall see, one consequence of this was a lack of affordable housing, leading to a proliferation of illegally erected 'cottages'. In contrast, many yeomen did well out of the changed economic conditions, expanding their agricultural production and profiting from higher market prices. They enjoyed an enhanced standard of living, reflected in an increase in the number and variety of their household possessions (Wrightson 2002: 116, 135–40, 159–60, 182–90). The late sixteenth and early seventeenth centuries is also the period which has been termed the 'Great Rebuilding', when many medieval houses were remodelled and new houses were built to a different domestic plan (Hoskins 1953: 44–59; Machin 1977: 33–56). Also benefiting from the economic conditions were substantial landowners, who used their increased wealth to build themselves what have been termed 'prodigy' houses. One such was Sir Thomas Pelham of Laughton in Sussex, lord of the Rape of Hastings, who, in 1595, built himself a new mansion at Halland in East Hoathly, partly financed by the profits from his ironworks at Waldron (Wrightson 2002: 185; J.E.M. 1981).

The defining feature of the late medieval rural house was its open hall, with a centrally located open hearth. This type of house survives in two principal forms: the so-called 'tripartite' house with additional rooms adjoining the hall at each end and the 'bipartite' house which had rooms at one end only. Of the two types, it is the tripartite house that predominates in the historical record and so it will be considered first.

In the tripartite open-hall house, the house is entered via a door at its 'lower' end. This gave access to a 'cross passage', with an opposing door on the other side of the hall. Going off the hall at its lower end were two ground-floor service rooms and a staircase giving access to a first-floor chamber. Adjoining the hall at its 'upper' end was a ground-floor chamber or parlour, with stairs leading to an upper chamber or bedroom. The rooms at this end of the house effectively formed a self-contained suite, providing the householder and his wife with private accommodation. The spatial significance of the upper end of the hall was created by the use of double-height, unglazed, windows on either side of the house and the 'dais beam', which crossed the upper-end wall horizontally just above head height. This part of the hall was where the 'table and its frame', with its associated form or bench, was located. In some cases, the bench might be fixed to the timber frame with decorative panelling behind it; in other cases, it was movable. A wall cloth – usually painted – was typically affixed to the dais beam (Martin, Whittick and Brisco 2017: 46–8, 66–71).

Whilst tripartite houses followed a standard layout, there was considerable variation in their overall size – some were smaller than others. Surviving buildings that have been surveyed in East Sussex all have an upper storey at each end but, elsewhere, in Hampshire for example, there are extant examples of single-storey houses with three ground-floor rooms (Tankard 2012: 48–50). Externally, these houses were also distinguished by the style of timber framing and by the use of 'jettying', where part of the upper floor extended out over the ground floor. The main advantage of jetties in urban houses on constricted sites was that they increased upper-floor space by as much as 20 percent but, in rural areas, where plot size was not a concern, their use was aesthetic. Since the cost of constructing a house with jetties was higher than the cost of constructing one without them, they were also undoubtedly an expression of status. In open-hall houses, jetties might be restricted to one or both ends. Where jetties projected forwards at the front of the house, they created the recessed-hall wall characteristic of the so-called 'Wealden' house. In the countryside, Wealden houses are (with a few exceptions) only found in Kent, Sussex and the southern part of East Anglia, but as an urban house type they have a national distribution (Martin, Whittick and Brisco 2017: 27–35, 39–44).

These houses would have been located within a farmstead, with a barn, probably a stable and perhaps a cattle shelter, pigsty and poultry house surrounding or adjoining to a yard (Martin 2006: 27–32). Many of them are also likely to have had a detached kitchen. After houses and barns, detached kitchens were the most common type of building in South-East England in the fifteenth and sixteenth centuries. Very few have survived, and those that have are typically large, multi-room, two-storey buildings. These might more accurately be described as 'service blocks', with downstairs rooms used for baking and brewing and upstairs rooms providing storage and additional sleeping accommodation, perhaps for male servants. Many kitchens are likely to have been little more than a single-room, single-storey outhouse. Detached kitchens were usually located at the back of the house near the lower end, and were accessed through the rear doorway of the cross passage. In some instances, they were connected to the house by a covered passage (Martin, Whittick and Brisco 2017: 99–102).

We can examine the form and function of a tripartite open-hall house in more detail by looking at an example re-erected at the Weald and Downland Living Museum in West Sussex (Figure 3.1). 'Bayleaf' is a Wealden open-hall house, originally from Chiddingstone in Kent, constructed in two phases. Its earliest part, which has been tree-ring dated to *c.* 1405–30, consisted of the open hall and service end. This was probably attached to an earlier high end, which was replaced around 1510. At this date, the house was occupied by a yeoman called Thomas Wells, who farmed about 100 acres of land. The house follows the conventional late medieval plan of a communal open hall, with service rooms at the lower end and a private chamber at the upper end. The upper chamber above the service rooms is accessed via a staircase at the rear of the hall. The upper chamber at the upper end of the hall is accessed via a staircase in the ground-floor room; there is evidence that a hatch over the stairwell originally allowed this room to be closed off. This room also includes an integral privy, projecting out over the end wall which may originally have had a chute directing the waste downwards to an external pit. Whilst not unknown in rural houses, integral privies like this one were relatively rare; most rural houses are likely to have had external privies in a backyard (Tankard 2012: 55–60, 63–4, 74–6).

Bayleaf is entered via opposing doors at the low end of the hall opening into a cross-passage, which is divided from the hall by short screens. The floor of the upper chamber at this end projects out over the cross passage, creating what is

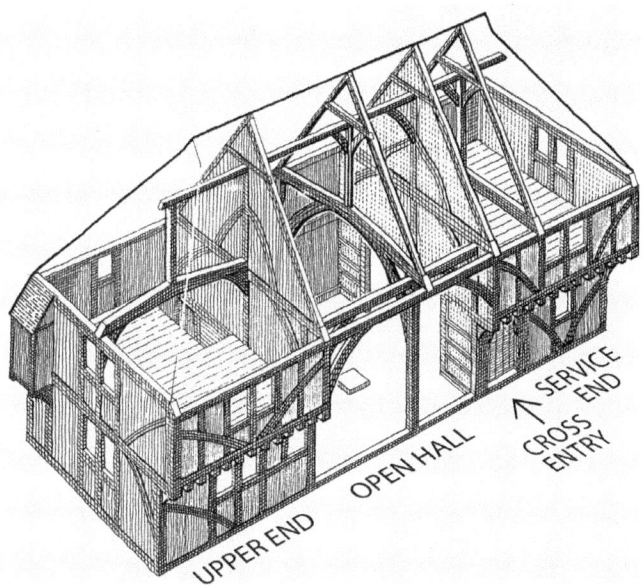

FIGURE 3.1: Cutaway plan of Bayleaf, 1978. © Richard Harris/Weald and Downland Living Museum.

termed an 'overshot cross passage'. The lower end of the hall has no windows; in contrast, the upper end has double-height windows, emphasizing the spatial significance of this part of the house (Tankard 2012: 74–6). The earliest probate inventories surviving for Kent are from 1565 and there are none for any of the sixteenth-century occupants of Bayleaf (KHLC/PRC/10/1; Martin, Whittick and Brisco 2017: 105–24, 147–71). However, they are still useful for looking at the most likely names and uses of the house's various rooms. The hall was a general multifunctional living space; probate inventory evidence suggests that even where houses had separate kitchens, day-to-day cooking often took place here, too. The twin service-rooms at the lower end of the house are likely to have been used as a buttery and a pantry, the former to store ale and perhaps cider, the latter to store foodstuffs. The upper chamber at this end of the house is likely to have been used as a bedchamber for the household's children and female servants and possibly also for storage. The ground-floor room at the upper end of the house is likely to have been used as a parlour, a private withdrawing room for the use of the householder, his wife and their guests. The upper chamber, with its integral privy, would have been the principal bedchamber used by the householder and his wife, but possibly also shared with younger children or a female servant (Tankard 2012: 74–6).

Whilst there are considerably fewer surviving examples of the bipartite open-hall house, they are likely to have been relatively common, probably outnumbering their larger tripartite neighbours. In these smaller houses, it was typically the high-end rooms that were excluded, instead they had a service room at the lower end with a chamber above it. Two examples of these smaller, bipartite, houses are Ruth Cottage in Beckley (pulled down in 1972) and Silverden in Northiam, both in East Sussex and both built in *c.* 1450. Each house had an open hall with an overshot cross passage at the lower end, a single ground-floor service room with a chamber above it. Ruth Cottage had a width of just 4.65 metres and a ground-floor area of 36 square metres (Martin, Whittick and Brisco 2017: 40, 48, 121, 133, 134). There is little evidence for one-roomed houses during this period; none can be identified amongst surviving buildings and few appear to be recorded in sixteenth-century probate inventories (ibid.: 45, 51). However, since one-roomed houses or cottages are known to have existed in the seventeenth century, their absence from the historic record at an earlier period is probably misleading; poorer householders are less likely to have made probate inventories and the smallest houses are less likely to have survived.

The late fifteenth and sixteenth centuries were a period of transition in rural housing. New open-hall houses continued to be built and many older open-hall houses retained their medieval form but they coexisted with new houses that were built with a first floor throughout and heated by an internal chimney stack, and some former open-hall houses had chimney stacks inserted and their halls floored over. In most cases, these changes did not significantly alter the external appearance of the house or the internal configuration of space. Chimney stacks were usually located against the back wall of the hall or at its lower end, either against the service-room wall or freestanding, backing onto the cross passage. This arrangement allowed the house to retain its traditional upper and lower ends. The flooring-over of the hall provided an additional first-floor chamber, which formed part of the private suite of rooms accessed via a staircase in the parlour. This room usually had its own fireplace. However, in some instances, the insertion of a chimney stack led to a reorientation of domestic space with service rooms moving to the former upper end and the parlour moving to the lower end. By the late sixteenth century, some houses had glazed windows, but these were typically only in the principal rooms such as the parlour and parlour chamber; less important rooms and those at the back of the house continued to be unglazed (ibid.: 75–98; Martin 2000: 26–31). It was during this period that detached kitchens began to go out of use; instead, kitchens came to be integrated within the main range of the house, frequently as an additional room beyond the service end. Other services previously associated with the detached kitchen, such as brewing and baking, were relocated to lean-tos or outshuts, attached to the exterior of the house (Martin, Whittick and Brisco 2017: 99–102).

By the last quarter of the sixteenth century, a new house form had emerged which broke significantly from the domestic plan of its medieval predecessors

(Figure 3.2). In this new form, entry to the house was via a small, centrally placed lobby which faced onto the end of an axial chimney stack. This type of house is called a 'lobby-entry house' and typically had two or three lineally arranged ground-floor rooms. Although there were other possible arrangements for fully storeyed houses, the lobby-entry plan was widely adopted. Room terminology in these houses varied but in the three-room plan one of the rooms was a kitchen (sometimes referred to as a hall), the central room was usually the main living room (variously described as a hall or a parlour) and the end room was a service room. These houses also had at least one additional service room in an external outshut. In some cases, outshuts could be accessed via an internal doorway from the house; in others, access was via a separate, external doorway (Johnson 1993b: 89–105).

An example of one of these new-style houses is 'Pendean', originally from the parish of Woolavington in West Sussex and now re-erected at the Weald and Downland Living Museum (Figure 3.3). The house was built in c. 1610, replacing an older building, during the tenancy of Richard Clare, a yeoman farming about 40 acres. Although there is no surviving probate inventory for Richard Clare, there is an inventory for a later occupant, Nicholas Austen, who died in 1697 (WSRO/EP/I/29/215/35). In this house, the room on the east side with the largest fireplace was the kitchen; there is structural evidence that this room originally contained an oven but, by the late seventeenth century, this had been moved to a newly constructed outshut, which became the house's bakehouse. The central room, with a slightly smaller fireplace, was the hall and the unheated room at the house's west end was the milkhouse or dairy. When first built Pendean had one rear outshut which may originally have been used as a brewhouse. A staircase in the kitchen led up to the kitchen chamber, which gave access to two further chambers, a heated 'hall chamber' and a 'little chamber' at the house's west end. Its original windows were unglazed but it is likely that they would have been glazed by the time Nicolas Austen lived there in the late seventeenth century (Tankard 2012: 79–80, 85–6, 96–7).

Many of Richard Clare's poorer neighbours would have been living in considerably smaller houses or cottages with little or no land. Seventeenth-century cottages varied in size and layout: the smallest cottages consisted of a single ground-floor room with an end smoke-bay or chimney stack; the largest were of four rooms, two on the ground floor and two on the first floor. These small cottages usually also had outshuts, providing an external service room. Many new cottages were built as encroachments on manorial 'waste' or commons. An act of 1550 specifically protected the occupants of these 'wasteland' cottages, provided their enclosures were of less than 3 acres. However, rapid growth in population and worsening levels of poverty meant that, by the late sixteenth century, unregulated cottage building had become a matter of public concern and there were calls for statutory controls. In 1589, a

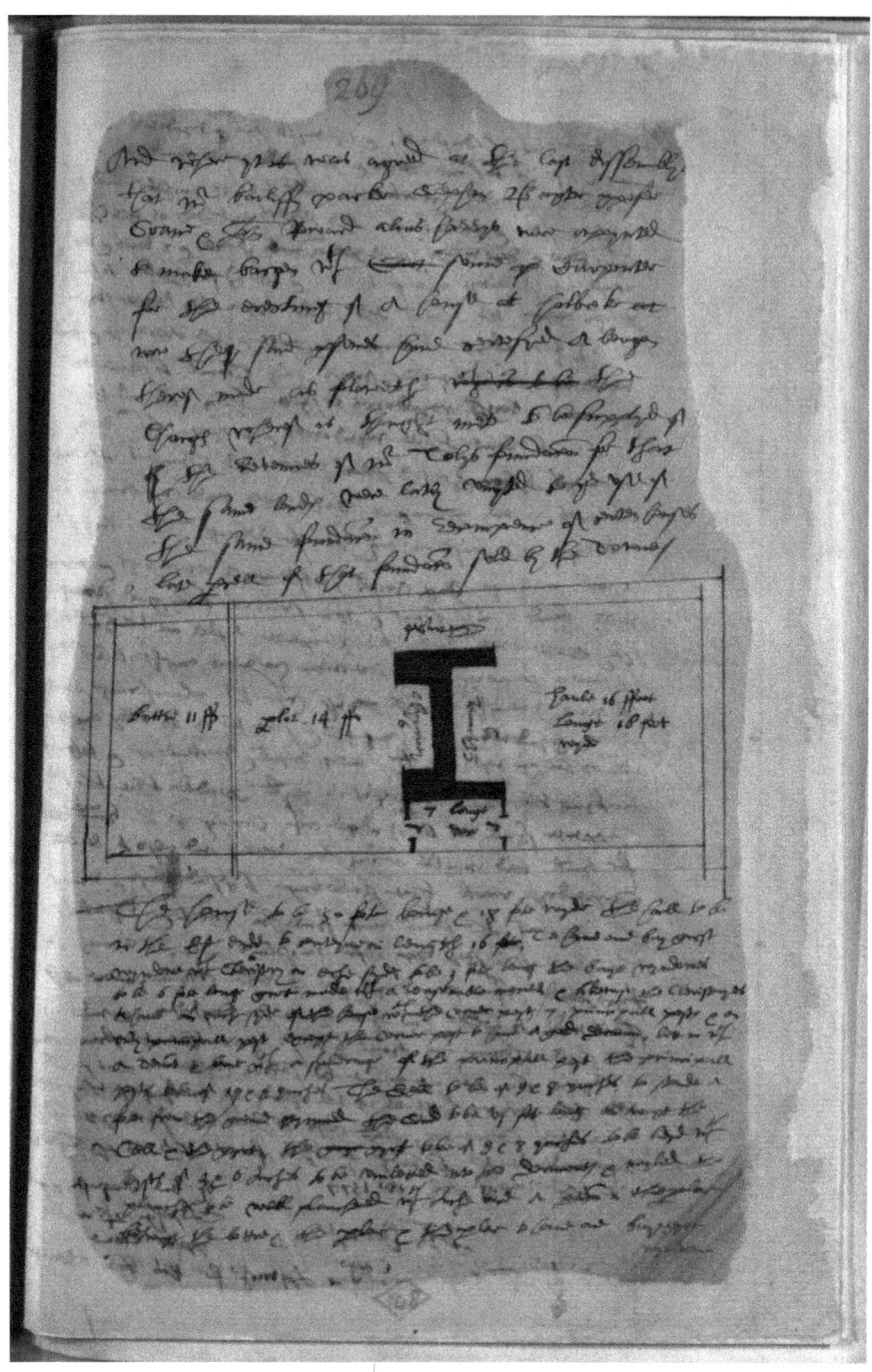

FIGURE 3.2: Plan for a new lobby-entry house at Holbrook, Suffolk, 1577, showing three ground-floor rooms, a 'buttery', a 'parlour' and a 'hall'. Ipswich Record Office, C/4/3/1/1: 269. © Suffolk Record Office, Ipswich Branch.

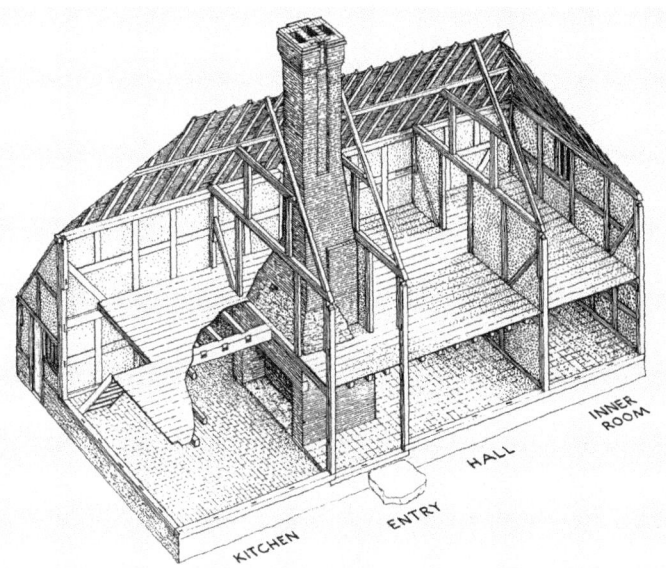

FIGURE 3.3: Cutaway plan of Pendean, 1977. © Richard Harris/Weald and Downland Living Museum

statute was passed entitled 'An act against erecting and maintaining cottages', which made it illegal to build a cottage without 4 acres of land, to convert a building into a cottage without 4 acres of land, or to 'willingly uphold, maintain and continue' a cottage without 4 acres of land. There were various exemptions in the Act: cottages in towns or cities, for example, and those inhabited by any 'poor, lame, sick, aged or impotent person' (31 Eliz. C. 7 (1589), cl. 1–5). Prosecution was vested in any of three authorities: the manorial lord at his court leet, the justices of assize and the justices of the peace. The justices of assize and the justices of the peace were permitted to make decrees allowing the continued habitation of cottages built without 4 acres of land for a set period of time 'upon complaint' made to them – petitions made to them either by the cottager or on his or her behalf (Tankard 2011: 18–20).

Whilst the legislation did not explain the rationale for the four-acre requirement it was evidently based on a view that this was the minimum amount of land that a household needed to remain self-sufficient. The legislators' underlying concern was that cottage inhabitants should not become a financial burden on their communities and, for this reason, the 1589 Act should be seen as part of the developing poor law legislation of the late sixteenth century (Tankard 2011: 26–30). The economic significance of the cottage is reflected in the wording of many of the petitions that came before the Sussex courts. For example, in 1641 some of the inhabitants of the parish of Thakeham petitioned the court of quarter sessions sitting at Chichester to allow a poor parishioner, John Stowell, to 'continue' his cottage. They told the court that Stowell had:

> lived in the said parish about some sixteen years and maintained himself, his wife and child in an honest and industrious way by his labour and industry and has of late been visited with sickness and lameness of limbs in so much that if [he] should now be deprived of his dwelling house being an aged man himself, his wife and child is likely to be a weekly charge to the parish.
>
> —WSRO/QR/W43: 44/7

There is enough evidence in records surviving from the Sussex courts of quarter sessions and elsewhere to show that these small cottages were properly constructed, usually with a timber frame, occasionally from stone. For example, in a petition presented to the court of quarter sessions in Chichester in 1627, Robert Pearlie, a poor husbandman with a wife and eleven children, informed the court that he had been given a frame for a new cottage by the manorial lord of Madehurst but, despite this, and having obtained permission from a justice of the peace, his neighbours would 'not suffer him to set up the same frame' (WSRO/QR/W21: 23/59). An undated letter of c. 1600 to Sir Thomas Pelham, lord of the Rape of Hastings, informed him that William Garrom had 'bought a house ready framed to set up' and requested Pelham's licence so that he could 'go about it' (BL/Add MS 33058: 33). And a letter of c 1610 to Pelham from his cousin, Elizabeth, informed him that a shingler, Thomas Blatcher, had 'a frame set up for a little house' but that he was being prevented from doing so by Pelham's steward (BL/Add MS 33084: 34). Fuller descriptions of two cottages are included in the parliamentary survey of the manor of Pevensey made in 1649. The first cottage, occupied by Widow Knight, with an adjoining stable and garden plot, was located at the west end of Pevensey Castle. The surveyors recorded that: 'the said cottage and stable is built shed-wise against the castle wall of timber and mud walls and covered with thatch'. The second cottage, built on waste near the castle wall, was occupied by 'one Purchin'. This cottage was described as: 'new built with stone walls and well covered with tiles'. Both of these cottages had two ground-floor and two first-floor rooms (Tankard 2011: 32; Daniel-Tyssen 1871: 280–1).

In four-roomed cottages such as these, typically the heated ground-floor room was the hall or the kitchen and the unheated room was the buttery, the latter often doubling up as a workshop of some kind. For example, the buttery of Robert Pullengen, a shoemaker living in Stoughton in West Sussex, was used for brewing and dairying but it was also where he made his shoes: his probate inventory of 1622 records that this room contained his 'lesses' (that is, his lasts) and 'all working tools'. Upstairs, Pullengen's 'hall chamber' was used for sleeping, whilst his 'buttery chamber' was used for storage: this room contained

'22 pairs of shoes and leather' as well as hemp, hops, sixteen cheeses and a spinning wheel (WSRO/EP/I/29/189/4).

There were also 'cottages' that were constructed using more rudimentary methods. In 1605, the rector and thirteen of the inhabitants of the Sussex parish of Ripe informed Sir Thomas Pelham that John Pegden's 'small cote' had been 'pitched in the ground and placed in the king's highway', suggesting a structure built with earth-fast poles rather than being properly timber framed (Tankard 2011: 33–4; BL/Add MS 33058: 51). Poor men and women might also take up temporary residence in agricultural buildings: Thomas Blatcher, his wife and four children had been forced to live in 'an end of a barn' for more than a month and were unable to have a fire because of the 'hay and straw that lies there' (BL Add MS 33058: 54). In the Wealden area of Sussex, many of those unable to find accommodation elsewhere bedded down in the furnace houses attached to ironworks, of the kind owned by Pelham in Waldron (WSRO/QR/W19: 14/80; WSRO/QR/W53: 54/37).

URBAN HOUSING

In contrast to the relative economic prosperity of the countryside, the late fifteenth and early sixteenth centuries were a period of economic contraction for many of England's towns and cities. Demographic decline meant that there was less demand for goods. During this period, cloth production on which the economies of many towns had been based shifted to the countryside and many port towns lost part of their overseas trade to London (Wrightson 2002: 105–7). The socioeconomic structure of towns and cities was considerably more complex than that of the countryside: affluent merchants and professionals rubbed shoulders with lesser trade and craftsmen; larger cities also had a sizeable rump of urban poor – some settled, others highly transient. The population of most towns did not begin to grow again until later in the sixteenth century but it then grew rapidly, keeping pace, or in some cases exceeding, national population trends (ibid.: 125, 164).

LONDON

London was always a case apart. Its population grew exponentially throughout this period from about 40,000–50,000 in 1500 to about 400,000 in 1650. It also became increasingly dominant in the nation's economy (Harris Sacks 2000: 22; Wrightson 2002: 108). Since London's death rate consistently exceeded its birth rate, this increase was wholly the result of inward migration – it has been estimated that the city needed an average of 6,000 migrants a year to replace its losses and continue to grow. Inward migration appears to have peaked in the 1570s, a result of deepening rural poverty forcing poor men and women off the land and an influx of religious refugees from the continent (Wrightson 2002: 165; Schofield 1984: 142). This rapid growth in population put a significant strain on housing stock. A royal proclamation of 1580 had prohibited the erection of new houses on new plots within three miles of the city but small cottages and tenements continued to be built on areas of open ground and new housing was also created through the subdivision of larger buildings, including former inns, and the conversion of sheds, barns and other outbuildings into dwellings (Baer 2000: 13–39). Some of this was within or immediately adjoining the city's walls but new areas of housing also developed in London's suburbs, particularly to the east in areas such as Radcliffe, Whitechapel, Limehouse and Shoreditch (Schofield 1994: 144–5; Baer 2000: 13–39, and 2008: 61–88). John Stow noted the rapid encroachment of new housing on formerly open space in his *Survey of London* of 1598. In Whitechapel, for example, he observed that a common field, which should have been 'open and free for all men', was now covered with 'filthy cottages' and other 'purprestures [illegal encroachments], enclosures and laystalls [dung heaps]' (Stow [1598] 1994: 384). The Dissolution of the Monasteries provided a considerable stimulus for new housing. Some former monastic houses were converted into grand houses for the nobility; other former monastic sites were redeveloped into new housing estates, such as that developed on the former site of St Bartholomew's Priory, discussed below (Schofield 1984: 140–2).

Much of the following discussion is based on the early-seventeenth century house plans drawn by painter-stainer and surveyor, Ralph Treswell (*c.* 1545–1616), which have been extensively analysed by John Schofield. Treswell's main commissions in London were for Christ's Hospital between 1607 and 1611 and the Clothworkers' Company in 1612 (Schofield 1987: 1–2). His surveys show ground-floor plans and include outbuildings, yards and gardens; they also show the position of doorways, chimneys and stairs, but not usually windows. Most walls in Treswell's plans are coloured grey and shown as less than a foot thick, presumably indicating timber framing; some thicker walls were evidently of stone. Red is used to show brick-built chimneys, wells, garden walls and some exterior walls. Brick-built back-to-back chimneys were common in London houses by 1500 and Treswell's plans show that even one-room plan houses had at least two heated rooms which were serviced by a single chimney stack (ibid.: 17).

Upper floors are not shown in plan but are described with room measurements given in accompanying text. Many of the houses shown in these plans would already have had quite long histories. Of those that can be securely dated, the earliest are a row of five two-room plan houses facing onto Abchurch Lane constructed around 1390. Whilst the original form of these houses may have undergone some alteration over the ensuing period of occupation, the surveys, nevertheless, give a good idea of the type of housing that was available in London between 1450 and 1650 (ibid.: 11, 28).

Treswell's surveys show that brick houses were still rare in pre-Fire London; it remained, in John Evelyn's words, 'a wooden city'. In *A Character of England*, Evelyn described the city as a 'very ugly town', consisting of 'a wooden, northern, and inartificial congestion of houses, some of the principal streets so narrow as there is nothing more deformed, and unlike, than the prospect of it at a distance' (1659: 10). The narrowness of the streets and congestion of houses were exacerbated by the use of jettying, with upper stories projecting out into the street. New jettied houses were built in the sixteenth century but, by 1600, jetties appear to have gone out of fashion, possibly in response to civic legislation which sought to restrict their use because they caused a public nuisance, for example by blocking out light to neighbouring properties (Schofield 1987: 28).

Using Treswell's surveys, Schofield has divided London's houses into four types. Type 1 houses only had one ground-floor room but could be up to six storeys high. Examples of these can be seen on Treswell's survey of houses in West Smithfield and Cow Lane (Figure 3.4). Entry to these one-room plan properties, created out of a former inn called the Maidenhead, was off Cow Lane via a narrow passage into Pheasant Court, running between the properties of Thomas Anderson and John Showell. To look at one of these, the house of William Haslom facing onto the eastern side of Pheasant Court had a shop on the ground floor with stairs giving access to a second-floor chamber and a third-floor garret, both rooms containing fireplaces. Haslom, like those inhabiting the other one-room plan houses around Pheasant Court, had no private outside space. He and his neighbours shared three common privies located against the east wall of the Court (ibid.: 11–15, 132–4).

Some one-room plan houses would have been built as 'rows', a term used to describe a range of houses constructed as a single structural unit. A significant new development of one-room plan row houses was built in the fairground of the former priory of St Bartholomew between 1597 and 1616 by the site's new landlord, the third Baron Rich. Approximately 175 small houses were built, mostly to a uniform plan, with a cellar, a ground-floor shop, single chambers on the first and second floors and a garret. Evidence of tenants' occupations recorded in a survey of 1616 shows that the majority were artisans, with tailors predominating. They would have used their small shops as workshops. The earliest houses in this development were timber-framed but houses built from the second decade of the seventeenth century used brick for their external walls (Leech 1996: 201–13, 225–30).

The more numerous Type 2 houses were of a two-room plan over three or more floors. An example of this type is the house of Christopher Askwith in West Smithfield, which faced onto the Smithfield Pens and backed onto Pheasant Court (Figure 3.4). Entry to the house was through the shop; stairs within the shop gave access to the upper floors. Behind the shop was a kitchen with a

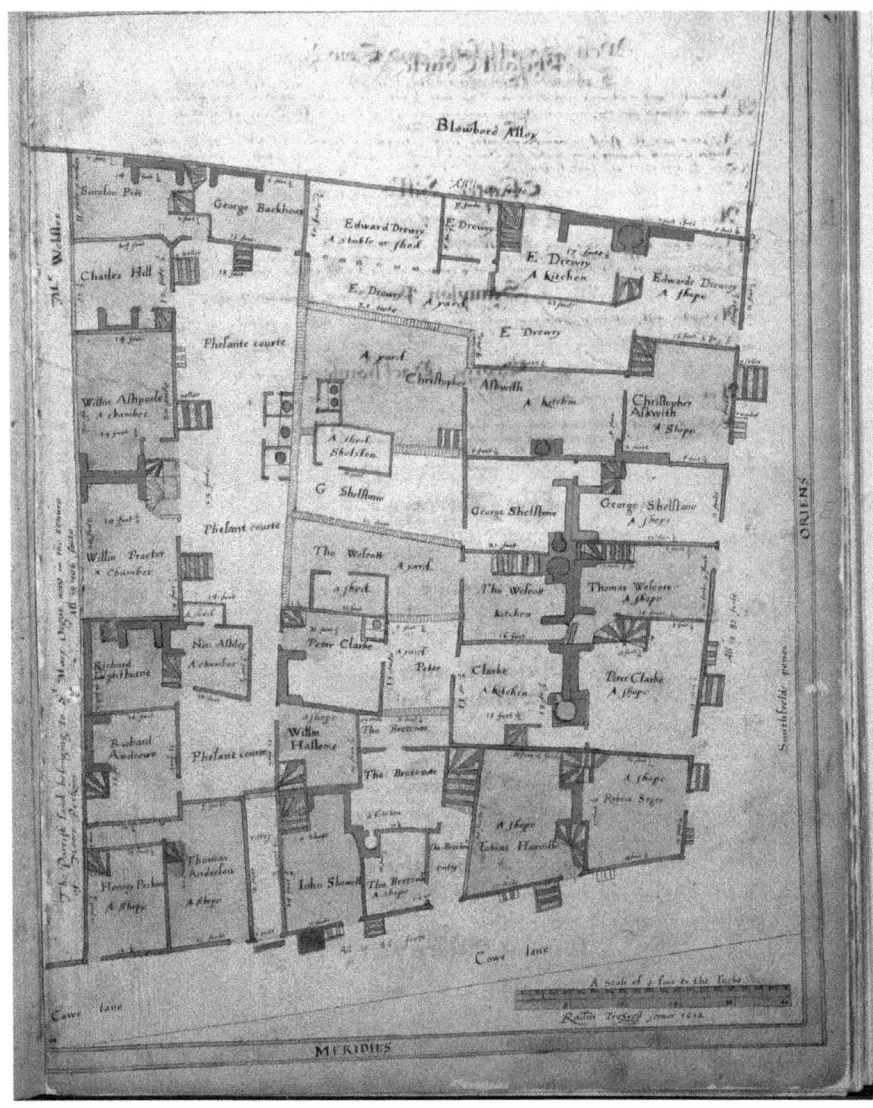

FIGURE 3.4: West Smithfield and Cow Lane surveyed by Ralph Treswell, 1612. CL/G/7/1: 31r. © The Clothworkers' Company.

fireplace and oven; to the rear was a yard with an enclosed privy. Going upstairs, on his first floor, Askwith had a room which Treswell described as a 'chamber' (presumably used as a hall or a parlour) facing out onto the street and a rear chamber over the kitchen; on his third floor were two further chambers; there were two garrets in the roof. Stairs at the front and rear of the house gave access to cellars beneath the shop and kitchen. We know that Askwith's house was jettied because Treswell describes his first-floor chamber as 'jettied out toward the Pens' (Schofield 1987: 15, 132–4).

Type 3 were medium-sized houses, with three to six ground-floor rooms in the main range. An example of this type is the house of Jacques de Bees and which was entered through a passage or 'entry' off Fenchurch Street between properties in the tenure of James Dyer and James Sutton. On his ground floor, de Bees had a hall and a kitchen, both with fireplaces, and a wash house (the latter presumably containing a water pump). On the western side of the house was a substantial garden with a well; along the back of the plot was a shed containing an enclosed privy. Access to the upper floors was via a staircase in the entry in front of the hall. These stairs probably also led down to the two cellars since no other staircase is shown. De Bees' upstairs accommodation extended over Dyer's ground-floor shop and kitchen and his own entry (ibid.: 15, 72–3).

Type 4 is a miscellaneous group of larger properties which include courtyard houses and inns (the latter not discussed here). These largely retained their medieval layout and form. Larger houses were often located behind smaller, but taller, street-facing houses, which meant that they might be entirely hidden from public view. For example, Sir Edward Darcy's two-storey house, which

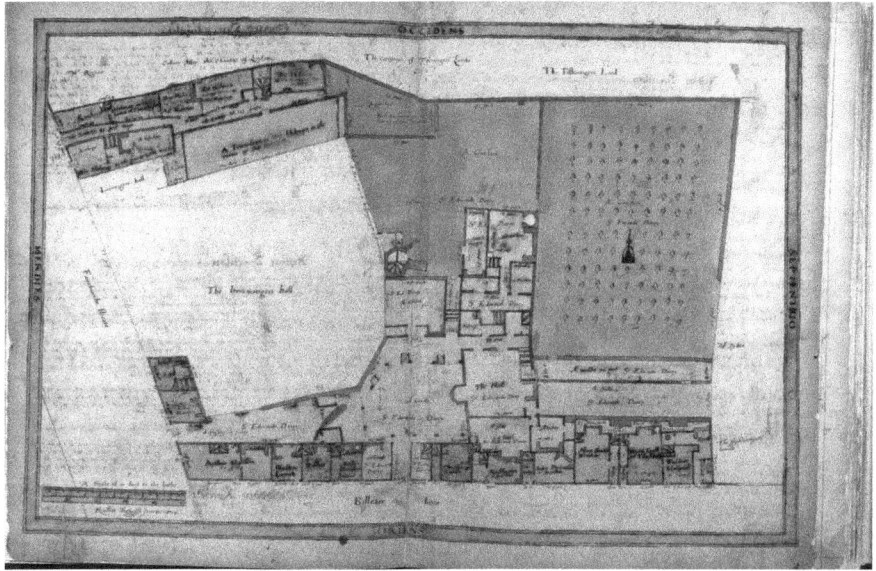

FIGURE 3.5: Fenchurch and Billiter Streets, surveyed by Ralph Treswell, 1612. CL/G/7/1: 15v–16r. © Clothworkers' Company.

had briefly served as the Fullers' Company hall in the early sixteenth century, was entered via a passage from Fenchurch Street on the south, which ran through a smaller property tenanted by Arthur Harrison (Figure 3.5). At the end of the entry, a gatehouse gave access to the courtyard at the front of the house; from here, the house could be entered either via a substantial hall on its eastern side or via service rooms to the west. Its eastern perimeter was bordered by a row of eight one-room plan houses of two-and-a-half or three-and-a-half storeys, with entries onto Billiter Lane; between two of these small houses a further gateway provided a second point of access to Darcy's courtyard. On the western and north-western side of the house were his extensive walled gardens; his southern garden included a brick tower (Schofield 1987: 15, 74–5, and 1984: 160–2).

The majority of small and medium-sized houses surveyed by Treswell which faced onto the street had a shop as the ground-floor front room, sometimes with a warehouse behind it. In slightly larger houses, separate warehouses were located across small yards or, in the largest houses, around a courtyard (Schofield 1987: 22). The 1625 probate inventory of wealthy haberdasher, Richard Wilcox, who lived in the parish of St Magnus the Martyr, recorded that at the time of his death his shop and warehouse contained cloth and stockings to the value of some £1,050 (approximately £100,000 today), including 'northern' and 'Devon' kerseys, 'Manchester' and 'Welsh' cottons, says, perpetuanas, bays, fustians, satins and 440 pairs of men's 'hose'. Wilcox's house also contained a 'counting house', where he would have made up his accounts and written his business letters. Counting houses were usually small rooms located on the ground floor at the back of the shop or warehouse (TNA/PROB 2/825; Schofield 1987: 22).

Some larger London houses had a hall on the ground floor, which was comparatively lofty and open to the roof. Sir Edward Darcy's hall, which had a semi-octagonal bay window facing onto the courtyard, would have been fully open when first constructed but by the time it was surveyed in 1612, it must have been partly ceiled since Treswell records an upper chamber 'once part of the hall with a fair passage into it'. It contained a large brick fireplace against its northern wall (Schofield 1987: 74–7). Darcy's hall is likely to have functioned as a grand entry rather than a living space, with limited furniture and walls decorated with weaponry, hunting trophies and possibly the royal, or the family's own, coat of arms (Leech 2000: 1–10). In smaller houses, where the more limited ground-floor space was used for shops and warehouses, halls were usually located on the first floor. First-floor halls were a feature of London housing by 1400, and in Treswell's surveys were especially common in houses of one- and two-room plan. In the two-room plan, the hall always occupied the front room over the street. Some houses also had a parlour, which could be located on the ground floor or on the first floor. Parlours are first mentioned in better houses in the mid-fourteenth century and had become widespread by 1600 (Schofield 1987: 17–19). They were intended to be private and relatively intimate spaces. Sir Edward Darcy's ground-floor parlour adjoined his hall on its eastern side and was approximately half its size (ibid.: 74, 76–7). The different functions of the hall and the parlour are already evident in fifteenth-century probate inventories. For example, at the time of his death in 1468, the hall of wealthy London draper, Thomas Salle, was furnished with tapestry hangings, bankers and cushions, stools, tables, trestles and an array of weaponry. In contrast, his parlour was more richly furnished with hangings, bankers and cushions, a carpet, stools, turned chairs, a bird cage and the chronicles of London in two volumes (TNA PROB 2/5; Leech 2000: 3).

From the early fourteenth century, service rooms, including kitchens, might be on the first floor but, in a large number of cases in the Treswell surveys, the kitchen remained on the ground floor. In two-room plan houses, like that occupied by Christopher Askwith, the kitchen was located immediately behind the shop. However, ground-floor kitchens could also be located in a separate building at the back of the yard; John Dorrell's house in Pudding Lane had a substantial detached kitchen behind his yard, with a 'chamber or garret' over it. Many houses also had a service room called a 'buttery', which could be located on the ground or first-floor; Darcy's house had two ground-floor butteries, forming part of a suite of service rooms with a kitchen and 'water house' at the western end of his hall (Schofield 1987: 19–20, 74–7, 110–11, 132–4).

Darcy's water house indicates that his house had an internal water supply but most Londoners had to make do with an outside well in a backyard which might be shared between properties. Households living in houses without private wells took their water from London's street pumps and public conduits. Where properties contained some open space, privies were located in the garden or the yard, sometimes within or adjacent to the kitchen building. In some cases, they formed part of the structure of the external kitchen, but were entered through a separate door; in other cases, they were entered through the kitchen. Their location allowed them to be used for the disposal of food waste. Privies could also be incorporated into the structure of the house; Darcy's house had a 'little house of office' on his first floor, in addition to two external privies in his garden. Privies connected to stone-lined cesspits, either directly if on the ground floor or via a chute if on an upper floor (ibid.: 21, 22–4, 27, 74–7). Properties sometimes shared a common cesspit and disputes over who should bear the cost of repairing and cleaning these frequently came before the city's Viewers – men appointed by the city to adjudicate property disputes (Orlin 2007: 160–3).

Smaller dwellings were created by subdividing houses, either through internal partitioning or by leasing out individual rooms. Ralph Treswell's plan of properties surrounding Pheasant Court in Smithfield records that a cellar measuring 6.9 metres by 4 metres beneath the houses of Samson Pott and

Charles Hill was home to Edward Lee (Schofield 1987: 133–4). Subletting to 'inmates' or lodgers was also common (Baer 2008: 76–9). The combination of dividing houses and taking in inmates led to extremely crowded living conditions. In 1637, a house in St Martin Ironmonger Lane in the city was home to smith, John Holmes, and his family, William Drywood, his wife, maid and lodger, three 'ancient' widows and an elderly 'milk woman', Magdalen Hall (ibid.: 79). At the bottom end of the housing market were the converted barns, stables, coal houses, privies and sheds that were used to house London's poorer inhabitants; these would more accurately be described as 'dwellings'. Between 1635 and 1638, some 1,846 'offending' dwellings were listed in certificates returned to the Privy Council, the majority located in the city's sprawling suburbs rather than its centre (ibid.: 62, 65–6). A certificate for 1636 described three houses in Turnmill Street in Clerkenwell constructed on the foundations of former pig sties from 'such slender' materials that they put the inhabitants at risk; another, for 1637, reported two 'base' sheds in Long Acre near Covent Garden, built over a rubbish heap and inhabited by a blacksmith (TNA/SP 16/345/92; TNA/SP 16/370/80; Baer 2008: 64). These micro-dwellings or 'mouse halls' could be as little as 3.6 metres square and were typically of one storey (TNA/SP 16/305/87; Baer 2008: 65). Into one such shed in 1637 crowded carpenter, Henry Hill, his wife and their five children; into another, cobbler, Simon Reddish, his wife and four children (Baer 2008: 69).

CHICHESTER

From the nation's capital we move to the small provincial capital of Sussex. Chichester, on the western edge of Sussex and close to the south coast, was a small walled city with a population in 1625 of about 2,500 (Figure 3.6). Within the walls, the city was divided into four quadrants by its principal streets, which radiated out from a central market cross and there were two suburbs beyond its west and east gates, St Bartholomew and St Pancras. As the seat of the bishop, it was the ecclesiastical centre of Sussex, as well as being an important administrative and trading centre for the western part of the county, with goods exported through its harbour at Dell Quay, approximately three miles away (Fletcher 1975: 8–9). Prior to the Dissolution of the Monasteries, approximately 60 percent of property within the city was in religious ownership; some of this was subsequently acquired by the city corporation but the Cathedral retained ownership of many city-centre properties (Morgan 1992: 2–6).

The most detailed information about houses in Chichester during this period is from a survey of Cathedral-owned property undertaken on behalf of the Interregnum Parliament in 1649 and 1650 (WSRO/Cap I/30/1, 2). This can be supplemented by the Cathedral's own records, including accounts of expenditure on its properties covering two periods, 1513 to 1514 and 1533 to 1538, and by

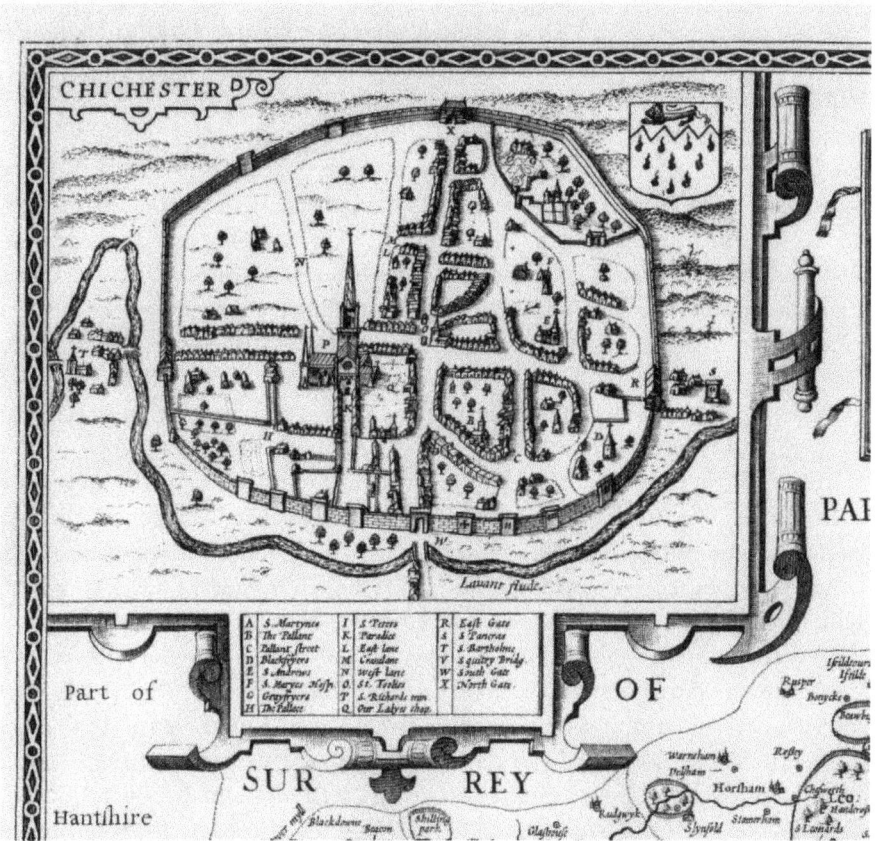

FIGURE 3.6: John Speed's map of Chichester, 1610. © West Sussex Record Office.

probate inventories which survive from 1580 onwards (WSRO/Cap I/23/1: 69–107, 129–38; WSRO/EP/I/29).

Most of the houses described in the parliamentary survey were relatively small and of only two storeys; many also had a garret in the roof and a cellar. Although the survey gives no indication of construction methods or appearance, other sources, and extant houses, indicate that they were timber-framed with tiled roofs; some were jettied at the first floor (WSRO/Cap I/23/1: 69–107; Haines 1879: 222). When first constructed, many of these houses are likely to have had an open hall set parallel to the street, either with a single ground-floor chamber at one end and an upper chamber above it, or with ground-floor and first-floor chambers at either end of the hall in the classic tripartite medieval-house style. Prior to 1500, many of these houses would have had open hearths but, by the early sixteenth century, chimneys are likely to have become increasingly common, either constructed of wood or brick (WSRO/Cap I/23/1: 73v, 93r, 98r, 132v, 133r). Despite the obvious fire hazards, wooden chimneys persisted in urban houses into the late sixteenth century: in Rye at the eastern end of Sussex, the town corporation was making strenuous efforts to force their removal as late as the 1580s (Martin, Clubb and Draper 2009: 160–2). In the early sixteenth century, kitchens appear to have already been integral to the house but some properties had external bakehouses. For example, in 1532 or 1533, the Cathedral paid a thatcher and his 'man' 20d. for two days' work to thatch Thomas Barber's bakehouse in East Street (WSRO/Cap I/23/1: 75v). External bakehouses had gone by the seventeenth century; they are neither recorded in probate inventories nor in the survey. Most houses are likely to have unglazed windows until at least the mid-sixteenth century, when window glass became more widely available. Glazing may at first have been reserved for the principal rooms, such as the parlour and parlour chamber.

Although there is no evidence of when Chichester's open-hall houses were floored over, the process is likely to have been complete by the late sixteenth century. Some houses were fully floored from their construction, an example being the double row of vicars' choral houses in the Cathedral's 'Little Cloister', built around 1400. When first built, each of the twenty-four houses had a front door leading into a ground-floor chamber or hall with a staircase opposite the door leading up to a first-floor chamber. These houses were built of stone, with internal timber partitions, and each had a rear stone chimney stack. In the late sixteenth century, the twelve original houses on the west side of the Cloister were rearranged into four larger houses with more substantial gardens (Tatton-Brown 1994: 237–9). Those on the east side must also have been rearranged into larger houses at some point because the parliamentary survey records them as having multiple rooms. That leased by Richard Roberts, for example, had a ground-floor hall, kitchen and two other 'small' rooms, with three first-floor chambers and, as we saw at the start of this chapter, John Newman's house had four ground-floor rooms and five first-floor rooms, one of which was located over the 'common houses of office' shared by all the houses in the Little Cloisters (WSRO/Cap I/30/2: 87–92). The eleven tenements 'adjoining together under one frame' on the south side of West Street, known as 'Bishop's Row', are also likely to have been fully floored from their construction. These were timber framed and had brick chimney stacks, probably at the back. In the early sixteenth century, Peter Joiner's house at number 1, Bishop's Row had a ground-floor shop, hall and kitchen; in 1537, John Sury at number 8 was provided with boards to erect a 'pentice booth' over his entry and hall 'to keep the storm away from the walls and doors' and 200 bricks to mend his chimney (WSRO/Cap I/23/1: 98r, 109r, 134r, 136r).

Evidence from the parliamentary survey and from probate inventories suggest that halls were always on the ground floor and that some houses also had a ground-floor parlour. Some also included a street-facing shop; sixteen of the eighteen houses owned by the Cathedral on the west side of South Street contained shops (WSRO/Cap I/30/2: 122–66). The smallest houses listed in the survey had only two ground-floor rooms, typically a shop and a kitchen, and between one and three first-floor rooms. However, the majority were larger, with at least four ground floor rooms – perhaps a shop, a hall, kitchen and buttery, at least four first-floor rooms, a second-floor garret and a cellar. Cellars were entered from the street; there are numerous complaints in the city's court leet about occupants' cellar doors lying 'open to the street' or being 'very dangerous', causing a potential hazard to passers-by (WSRO/ChiCity/K/3: 1; WSRO/ChiCity/K/6: 2).

References to parlours being wainscoted suggest that they were intended to serve as the best room. Jane Squire's house in West Street, for example, had a hall, wainscoted parlour, kitchen, wash house and buttery on its ground floor, five first-floor chambers and a cellar (WSRO/Cap I/30/2: 224–8). Evidence of furnishings from probate inventories confirm that, by the late sixteenth century, the parlour had precedence over the hall as the house's most important social space. The house of wealthy ironmonger, William Moore, in St Pancras, for example, recorded in an inventory of 1582, included a hall and a parlour, both with fireplaces. The former contained relatively functional furniture, including a 'short plank table with two posts in the ground', one 'short joined form', 'two planks for benches' and some cooking equipment, the latter contained (amongst other things) 'a turned chair', 'a little chair', 'a looking glass', 'buckram' [a coarse linen] window curtains, six 'thrum' [tufted] cushions, a tester bed with red and green fringed curtains and a truckle bed. The reference to window rods and curtains in the parlour indicates that its window was glazed (WSRO/EP/I/29/042/2).

Outside space was usually limited to a small yard, sometimes including a well or a pump which might be shared with a neighbouring property or properties (WSRO Cap I/30/2: 181-89). For houses without a private water supply there was a common well or pump in West Street and a public conduit in East Street (WSRO/Cap I/30/2: 195; WSRO/ChiCity/K/3: 2). References in the Cathedral's accounts to repairs to 'privy houses' suggest that these were located in the backyard as, presumably, were the 'noisome' pig sties that were presented from time to time at the city's court leet (WSRO/Cap I/23/1: 73v, 79v, WSRO/ChiCity/K/6: 2). Some houses also had small gardens. A few of the properties described in the survey had more substantial outside space, with 'fair' gardens and stables. William Baldwin's property on North Street, for example, had a large gated courtyard, with a stable and 'hay room' in it and a 'large fair garden', fenced on one side and with a new brick wall on the other (WSRO/Cap I/30/1: 129–33). The problems of disposing of human and animal waste are well documented in the records of the city's court leet: in 1574, John Osbourne was threatened with a fine of 3s. 4d. if he continued to throw the contents of his chamber pots out into East Street and there are innumerable references to malodorous heaps of animal dung in front of stables, houses and in public places (WSRO/ChiCity/K/2: 2, WSRO/ChiCity/K/6: 2).

Although Chichester was a smaller and less congested city than London, its poorer inhabitants still found it difficult to secure affordable housing and there is evidence that at the lower end of the housing market, multiple occupancy and the subdivision of houses were relatively common. For example, at the court leet in 1574, William Woods was presented for harbouring 'diverse persons', including 'Underwood and his wife,' Philip the 'Hyllyear' and his wife and 'one sick', whose name the ward constable had been unable to ascertain, and, in 1649, 'diverse poor people' were living in a former vicar's house within the Cathedral precinct, apparently placed there as an act of charity by William Aldridge, one of the vicars choral (WSRO/ChiCity/K/2: 6; WSRO/Cap I/30/2: 75–6). Evidence taken from witnesses in a tithe dispute heard in the Peculiar Court of Chichester in 1630–1 and 1632 also reveals that many of the houses in the area of the city called 'The Pallant' had been subdivided into smaller units, housing two or three families (WSRO/EP/III/5/2: 54–82, 90–134). In most cases, the occupants were living as 'distinct families', with their own cooking facilities, access to a yard or a garden and a separate front door. But some of the poorest residents lived communally, renting single rooms and sharing facilities. Widow Aylwin, John Green and John Shewbridge, for example, were described as living together in one house, 'not as distinct families for that they dress their meat and eat their meat altogether in one room and at one table and have the said house in common amongst them' (WSRO/EP/III/5/2: 67v). Others were forced to live in converted outbuildings: Richard Stone, described by a witness as 'a very poor man', and his wife, Mary, lived in a 'skilling' or lean-to attached to the side of Henry Bane's house (WSRO/EP/III/5/2: 94v).

The two extra-mural suburbs at the city's west and east gates, St Bartholomew and St Pancras, had been substantially destroyed during the siege of Chichester of 1642 and during the city's subsequent occupation by a parliamentary garrison. Much of the housing in St Bartholomew remained in ruins in 1649, when the survey was undertaken and the parish church, rectory 'and the greatest number of the houses within the said parish' were described as 'ruined and demolished' (Thomas-Stanford 1910: 53, 57–8, 62; WSRO/Cap I/30/1: 72–7). The parish of St Pancras appears to have been even harder hit: a petition of 1651 to the justices of the peace complained that: 'by reason of the burning and pulling down of their houses the chiefest of the inhabitants are now gone and the poor increased, being twice so many as formerly have been' (Fletcher 1975: 158, WSRO/QR/W71: 8). Many of those whose houses or small cottages were destroyed are likely to have taken up residence in temporary structures of the kind erected by John Pegden in the Sussex parish of Ripe in 1605. Others were probably forced out onto the road, seeking shelter in barns and furnace houses.

CONCLUSION

This chapter has surveyed a range of urban and rural house types that were in existence between 1450 and 1650. There was, as we have seen, a considerable variety in housing during this period, with some marked differences between houses in urban and rural areas. London led the way in the sophistication of much of its permanent housing stock, with many of its houses having brick chimney stacks from *c.* 1500. Limited ground space in a congested city and the need to accommodate business activities on the ground floor dictated the form of London's houses, with multiple storeys and living accommodation on upper floors. Growth in population in the late sixteenth century put increasing pressure on London's housing stock; areas of open land were built over, houses were subdivided and barns, sheds and even privies were pressed into use as dwellings. In contrast, in Chichester, space was at less of a premium; houses were typically of two storeys and halls and parlours were on the ground floor. Nevertheless, within the city's walls, some poorer residents were forced to cohabit or to take up residence in converted outbuildings, and the destruction of housing in its two extra-mural suburbs caused considerable hardship. In the countryside, the open hall, with its centrally placed hearth, continued in use into the sixteenth century but over the course of the century many houses were adapted by having a chimney stack inserted and their halls floored over. By the end of the sixteenth century, a new domestic plan had emerged, typified by lobby-entry houses such as Pendean. Surviving rural buildings, homes to prosperous yeomen and the better-off husbandmen and trade and craftsmen, represent the better end of the housing market. As in London, significant growth in population had put severe pressure on existing housing stock by the late sixteenth century. This is reflected in the proliferation of 'wasteland' cottages, which, after 1589, were regulated by statute and the fate of families like the Blatchers, encountered earlier living in 'an end of a barn', who had great difficulty in securing a permanent home at all.

CHAPTER FOUR

Furniture and Furnishings

CATHERINE RICHARDSON

FURNITURE, FURNISHINGS AND THE HOUSEHOLD

I geve and bequethe unto the said Maude my daughter one greate brasse potte in full recompence and Satisfaccyon of all hyr Childes parte and porcyon of my goodes and Cattells . . . a cowple of pewter platters & a Candelsticke.

—Geater (2016: 176)

With these goods, Edmond Wilson, a goldsmith of Birmingham in England, discharged his responsibilities to the married daughter who was to receive his dwelling house after her mother's death. It was 16 February 1564/5, and he was buried just over a month later. In June, an inventory of his goods was taken by four of his neighbours, recording £17 13s. 2d. worth of property in his hall, best chamber, other chamber, kitchen and buttery, as well as his goldsmithing wares, sheep, pigs and corn. The pot is clearly a symbolic gift, intended to stand for the responsibilities of a father towards his children, and provision had probably already been made for Maude earlier in her life in the form of a dowry, as she was by the time of his death a married woman. Edmond owned two pots, which were kept in the hall where he cooked, and valued, with his pan, kettle and skillet, at 10s. As the key cooking item he owned, a brass pot was symbolic of hearth, home and sustenance; having two meant he could leave his wife with the other one for the duration of her widowhood. The pewter and candlesticks given to Maude were also in the hall, and giving them away left the table and seating, a modest amount more pewter and the rest of the cooking goods. Not very much, in other words.

It is fairly certainly this Edmond the goldsmith who made the set of items from which Thomas Marshall the tanner's bequest to his daughter Elizabeth was made, in his earlier will of 1551: 'to off my syllver spones that Edmond Goldsmythe dyd make' (Geater, 2016: 103).[1] These two wills, linked by the identity of a maker of domestic goods, both give specific instructions for the passing-on of household stuff to women of the next generation. Between them, Edmond and Thomas's bequests raise interesting questions about the relationships between household goods, personal possessions, individuals and their homes in the early modern period. Fairly unremarkable as they are – similar examples could probably be proliferated from probate materials for almost any place in Europe for which last wills and testaments exist – they offer insight into a distinctive way of thinking about and using the connections between things, rooms and people.

These bequests suggest that goods had their own specific places within houses, ones that defined both their own use and the use of the room within which they were kept. But they also indicate that, despite these close associations, things were thought of as belonging to people and not to domestic spaces, moving most often at critical stages in the lifecycle such as marriage and death. It would be possible to suggest, from the descriptive specificity and careful choice that are written into these documents, that the bequeathers were well aware that objects in motion took with them practices and ideals that aided the transfer of social status and familial practice from one household and one generation to the next.

These documents also make it clear that the provenance of things – their manufacturer and materials provided ways of identifying them – was a part of their identity, and that possessions might make connections between houses within the same community and much further afield, too. By recording his purchase from Edmond in his will, Thomas was able to broadcast the association between their domestic material cultures (a relationship of commercial transaction, style and craftsmanship) more broadly. Methods and materials of making and the relative qualities of things articulated domestic space and made it effective on a daily basis; together, as a group, formed the household, both in the memory of its inhabitants and on the paper of the inventories in which its goods were enumerated.

Such conceptual aspects of furniture and furnishings are much easier to see further up the social scale and in communities in which domestic display was more self-consciously articulated. In Italy at the end of the fifteenth century, for example, Giovanni Pontano discussed 'the social virtue of splendour', stating that: '[t]he acquisition of furnishings is the "duty of the splendid man"' (Lindow 2007: 139–40). This essay might have started in the *sala* of Renaissance Venice, then, but it begins in a hall in mid-sixteenth-century Birmingham to make the point that reading carefully shows the wide social and geographical applicability of such patterns of thought and behaviour in early modern Europe. While comparative analysis of these practices across the continent over 200 years is only possible as a series of snapshots that allow us to think about similarities and differences, and to pose questions for future detailed work, it does seem possible, nevertheless, to identify two broad developments across the period considered here: first, people owned many more domestic objects at the end of it than at the start, across a wide swathe of the social scale; second, rooms were used in more specific ways, increasingly for unique purposes and by individuals either on their own or in less mixed social groups – in this period, sleeping in one's own bedroom, for instance, became more likely – and furniture was therefore more segregated, less flexible and movable, and had a closer and more stable association with the room in which it was kept. In some ways, these two ideas are in tension with one another. The fashionable tendencies seen in the ownership of larger numbers of goods led to objects being replaced before they were worn out, and therefore a higher turnover of things, whist their closer association with rooms ensured that, for the duration of their residence in the house, they stayed put.

This essay aims to answer two fundamental questions in relation to such evidence. First, what things were likely to have been found where in houses: which items were conventional and which unusual or uncommon in each room; how did their configuration relate to the use to which the space was put; and how widely applicable were these uses across the social scale and in different countries? Second, how did people navigate and negotiate these spaces: if lists of goods in rooms gives us a temporally 'flat' sense of their significance, homogenous in terms of the interest they may have aroused, how might questions of manufacture, purchase and provenance, of colour, texture and pattern, and of display and concealment suggest those objects which were noticed most and those which faded into the background of the renaissance home?

FURNITURE, FURNISHINGS AND SOCIAL STATUS

The Elite

Imagining how furniture and furnishings might help us to negotiate these houses, we might begin in the hall of Hardwick Hall, Elizabeth Talbot, Countess of Shrewsbury's 'supreme triumph of Elizabethan architecture', built in the 1590s and inventoried in 1601 when newly furnished (Boynton 1971: 1). The room was relatively sparsely appointed, with tapestry hangings 'with personages of forrest worke' on the walls, 15 feet and 6 inches deep and hung above wainscot panelling, three long tables, with six forms and an iron chimney back. The room was lit by two 'great Copper Candlestickes with severall places to set lightes in', hung on ropes and four brass-plate candlesticks on the walls (ibid.:

33–4). It extended through two floors of the building, rising to an impressive height, and occupied the whole central section of the house from front to back, with service and storage rooms on both sides on the ground floor and Lady Shrewsbury's apartments above. The tables and benches suggest large-scale dining, where comfort was not a priority. It was likely to be mainly symbolic of feudal responsibilities, and used on those occasions on which such issues came into play – feasting at Christmas, for instance.

In the minds of the household and its guests, this arrangement of furniture must have connected the room with several other spaces in the house: the Little Dining Chamber and Low Great Chamber on the first floor and the High Great Chamber on the second.

The Low and High Great Chambers were similarly furnished for dining. The former, for instance, was hung with tapestries of the story of David 11 feet deep, so covering most of the wall area, and with portraits of Queen Elizabeth, George, Earl of Shrewsbury, Lord Treasurer Burleigh, Margaret Countess of Lenox and her son Charles, Sir William Cavendish and the elder and younger Mr William Cavendishes, twelve tables of arms and a mirror with the Earl and Lady Shrewsbury's arms on it. The furniture consisted of a long table covered in carpets, two square tables and a cupboard. The numerous chairs, stools and forms with elaborate textile work included 'a Chare of Cloth of golde and silver with a frett of grene velvet and with grene silk frenge' and 'a forme of yellowe damaske with a border of Crimson velvet and golde frenge' (ibid.: 30–1). There was also a stunning array of long cushions, including one 'of Cloth of silver and grene velvet, with a rose imboste in the middest with a golde lace and a golde frenge lyned with washcolored sattin bridges' (ibid.: 31). The overriding impression of this room would have been coloured and patterned textiles: tapestry, turkeywork, fret (strapwork patterns), fringing, striping, tasselling, lacing and spangling, and embroidery (mainly with flowers); the colours gold, silver, green, murray, yellow, red, russet, black, crimson, white, washcolour; the fabrics predominantly cloth of gold and silver, velvet, silk, damask and satin. These were the main rooms for entertaining peers.

Bess also had the option of using a new type of room, however, the Little Dining Chamber off the Low Great Chamber and adjacent to the upper part of the hall below. This room was much smaller and more modestly furnished: wainscoted, it contained a long, carpeted table, turkeywork chair and fourteen joined stools, and was apparently used for Bess's everyday meals in a warmer space (Cooper 1999).

It is the long table, chairs, forms and stools which link these rooms together. The furniture ties individuals to the same surface for eating, whilst distinguishing between them socially and in terms of their authority within the house – Bess must always have sat in the best chair. In the more elegant rooms intended for lavish entertaining, there were larger numbers of tables and the cupboard from which to serve, and a much greater investment in decorative textiles on walls and furniture. The dining room demonstrates the desire to move from large-scale communal meals to more intimate, everyday dinners. It suggests developments in practice in this period, with room specialization, in the context of a profound stability in the use of recognizable forms of furniture.

Moving down the social scale and forward in time, Sir Thomas Puckering of The Priory in Warwick also had a hall with long and square tables, forms and a court cupboard, at his death in 1637. He, too, had a Great Chamber hung with tapestry, but this was a room apparently exclusively for sleeping. The 'great paved Parlor next the garden' contained a long drawing table of walnut and a court cupboard, both with two leather carpets 'belonging' to them, 'nyne highe redd leather chaires quilted, *with* straight elboes foure other lowe chaires of leather suteable foureteene ioyned stooles of Turkeyworke wth greene covers six other ioyned stooles of Orris worke wth greene Covers', and a new parlour with a square table with folding leaves, court cupboard and chairs and stools (Merry and Richardson 2012: 304). Although these rooms were called parlours, rather than chambers as they were at Hardwick, the furniture demonstrates their intended function. We know from Puckering's account book that the house also contained a banqueting house in the garden, which he built in the course of 1620. In this room, he could withdraw chosen guests for a final sweet course – it was a particularly lavish (in the sense of not strictly necessary) addition to the spaces available to him (ibid.: *passim*).[2]

The Middling Sorts

With the exception of the banqueting house, which need not have had such a large table, the configuration of furniture which signals and facilitates eating is recognizably similar in these houses, deployed in equivalent ways across a range of rooms of increasing complexity, and closely related to a dazzling range of textiles in the case of Hardwick Hall in particular, their variety narrowing a little in Warwick as the influence in fashions for matching suites of furnishing impacted on colour diversity. Further examples show the robustness of these comparisons even lower down the social scale: in the large urban property of Robert Rowland als Steyner, a gentleman from a mercantile family who died in Worcester in 1622, a hall offered two table boards with forms, a round table with a foot, 19 joined stools, three cupboards, carpets, cupboard cloths and cushions. There was arras work and fringing here, too, and the main colour was green. Like Puckering's hall, Rowland's housed suits of armour. A parlour also contained a long drawing table board and its frame and carpets, plus another square table, and chairs, stools, forms and a court cupboard. There were arras carpets, fringed and velvet stools, and 'certeyne bushes of fflowers to garnishe the howse' (WAAS, 008.7, fol. 61C). A little parlour provided a similar range:

drawing table, bench, stools and chairs, and another 'square little boord with a lowe foorme' that might have been for children. Rowland's great chamber had a very impressive bed in it, like Puckering's, but also 'crymson vellvett chayres with cases', fringed arras stools and a square table of walnut with its own needlework carpet, a settle and two court cupboards with cloths (ibid.). He could have entertained small numbers in this room, too, so even at the level of the urban gentry, the repetition of dining furniture across various rooms facilitated social divisions.

SMALLER HOUSES

To return to our Birmingham goldsmith, Edmond Wilson's hall contained a table with trestles, a form and a cupboard, and was his only eating space in 1565; this marks the minimum amount of furniture which would enable dining. The room was apparently unembellished with soft furnishings, although this does not preclude the presence of painted wall decoration, of course, to offer colour if not physical comfort. The relative social 'flatness' of this house is striking: its furniture does not facilitate distinctions between individuals dining in different spaces or sitting on different types of furniture, and the lack of soft furnishings means that the experience of sitting, for instance, was not graded into different levels of comfort.[3] This lack of flexibility indicates a smaller and more insular patriarchal unit, and an absence of hospitable leisure time spent with friends and neighbours.

The broad structures are, however, similar, and Bess of Hardwick's Lower Great Chamber essentially only embellishes them in socially meaningful ways; it adds no objects whose purpose Edmond would fail to understand, even though its quality and proliferation of goods would have astounded him. This is not an argument for similarity of quality or visual appearance: Neapolitan court theorist Giovanni Pontano, talking about spendour (in his treatise *De Splendore*, 1498), stated that: 'The base man and the splendid man both use a knife at table. The difference between them is this. The knife of the first is sweaty and has a horn handle; the knife of the other man is polished and has a handle made of some noble material that has been worked with an artist's mastery' (Hohti 2010a: 656). It is an argument for a similarity of function that demonstrates social distinction precisely through shared understanding.

FURNITURE FOR SLEEPING

A similar exercise could be undertaking for the location of and furniture associated with sleeping across the period covered by this volume. It would demonstrate a comparable proliferation of standard pieces of furniture – the bed and its associated furnishings, the latter greatly expanded for those of middling level and above, and chests for storage – and a shift of location to different rooms in the house over the years up to 1650. Wilson has two chambers, a 'best' and an 'other'; the former contains a featherbed with bolster, pillow, covering and tester, and another bed with some bedding. Also in the room are two coffers and a form. The 'other chamber' has a mattress rather than a featherbed, with bolster and covering only, and a trestle table. The presence of the two coffers suggests that Wilson slept in his best chamber, the other perhaps for children or servants, and his covered featherbed indicates a relative level of investment in sleeping. While it is not clear in this particular inventory whether or not the chambers are upstairs, a key distinction between the start and end of our period in England was the 'Great Rebuilding', in which properties were either adapted or newly built with a hall only a single floor high, and chambers could then be inserted on an upper floor. For the middling and lower social groups, gradually from the sixteenth to the eighteenth centuries and at different times across the country, sleeping could for the first time take place in dedicated upstairs spaces (Johnson 1993b; Hamling and Richardson 2017; King 2009).[4]

Rowland had at least twelve chambers for sleeping, so he was able to leave his best bed in his Great Chamber for guests, and slept instead in his Lodging Chamber, with its standing bedstead and wide range of coverings and curtains. The room also contained a further little bedstead, a court cupboard and some stools, but the main space in the document is taken up with descriptions of the contents of several chests (Figure 4.1): one deep one 'under the wyndowe towards the Court', one long one 'next the beddsyde', one 'next the wyndowe towards the church', one great one with £185-worth of plate in it, and one waynscott one 'att the beddes feete' (WAAS, 008.7, fol. 61C). These nested objects – valuable things inside large chests – defined the chamber as a crowded room, whose cluttered spaces provided the comfort of proximity during the night, making theft less likely. Again, the chamber in which the head of the household sleeps must be seen in relation to the others which the house affords, and the beds themselves dictate their own internal hierarchies – Rowland's own is a standing one with a featherbed, mattress and dowl bed (of feathers) on it; the servants' plainer 'bedsteads' with flock beds on them. The contrast between these tall four-poster beds and the lower, uncurtained varieties articulates domestic status.

Lady Shrewsbury's bedchamber at Hardwick Hall was similarly but more elaborately furnished with a bedstead whose posts were: 'Covered with scarlet layd on with silver lace' and whose curtains were embellished with a valence 'imbrodered with golde studes and thissells, stript downe and layde about with golde and silver lace and with golde frenge about' (Boynton 1971: 31). The similarly striped scarlet curtains had red silk buttons and loops so that a servant could close them at night to keep out the cold. Other furniture in the room

FIGURE 4.1: Joined and carved oak chest, 1560–1600. V&A Museum No. 833-1898. © Victoria and Albert Museum.

included a cupboard, folding table, chair and stools, many highly embroidered cushions, her books (with a looking glass, hourglass and brushes), and her various desks, chests, coffers and boxes (25 in total, from 'a boxe paynted and guilded with my Lodres and my Ladies Armes on it, a Yellowe Cotten to Cover it' to 'too trussing Cofers bounde with Iron') (ibid.: 32). Also in the room was 'My Ladie Arbells bedsted,' making the point that higher status made sleeping alone very unlikely – either servants or relatives in one's chamber underlined one's elevated status, complicating our sense of evolving privacy in this period.

In addition to the higher levels of embellishment in richer fabrics and the larger numbers of storage goods which separate Bess's chamber from Rowland's, the room is connected to two further spaces. Amongst storage items in 'a little roome within my Ladies Chamber' are two close stools, one with a silk-fringed cover (ibid.: 32). Rowland's Privy Chamber was apparently in the service rooms behind a central court, and Wilson obviously did not have one. Lady Shrewsbury also had a Withdrawing Chamber with a table, chairs, stools and forms as well as a cupboard, chests and trunks. Such suites of rooms were unique to the highest social groups.

These examples give a sense of the broad similarities and differences between furniture ownership in this period, and they reveal a relatively homogenous pattern of key items such as beds, tables, chairs, stools and chests, as might be expected, with status-inflected increases in the number and quality of objects, in the soft furnishings with which they were embellished and in the number of rooms across which they might be deployed. Such a comparison demonstrates how important it is to see questions of furniture ownership relatively for a given society, and hence why the preceding analysis has concentrated on just one society, England.

Looking across Europe makes it possible to see other forms of organization of furniture and furnishings. It is hard to make direct comparisons because the social configuration of the societies is different and so, therefore, are the broad divisions between the way they arrange furniture across the rooms of their houses. In Renaissance Italy, for instance, in the houses for which most comprehensive research has been undertaken, the long, rectangular *sala* was the main reception room, looking out over the city from a first-floor position, from windows which offered glimpses of furniture and furnishings such as the brightly painted wooden ceilings from the street (Currie 2006: 20).[5] The presence of the *credenza*, a sideboard on which the family's most prestigious tableware could be displayed, marked this room as the main space for dining, especially on significant occasions. At a banquet given in the home of a Florentine in Naples in 1477, 'after eating in the *sala* guests moved to the *camera* . . . to make music', so here, too, there were movements between rooms for different parts of the meal, but rather differently configured (Preyer 2006: 41). At other times, the *sala* became a space for different types of leisure activity, which might take place simultaneously in each of its corners. The main division between the comfort offered by crowded sleeping spaces (in Italy in the *camera*), filled with the owner's most expensive possessions, and more sparsely furnished communal rooms, holds true for both countries (and down the social scale as far as artisans, too) (Cavallo 2006), and the close engagement of mercantile properties with the streets outside their doors and windows is also a feature of other European towns.

The way the distinctions between different spaces distinguished between the middling sorts of these towns and their less prosperous neighbours is also widely apparent. In 1568, in Antwerp, for instance, an inventory was taken of Sebastiaen Cuypers' substantial, nine-roomed house, *De gulden penne*. Sebastiaen was a schoolteacher, and in addition to a schoolroom and sleeping facilities for the pupils, his house also included a 'sumptuously furnished *neercamere* (lower room)' and a 'first kitchen' overlooking the courtyard. In addition to roasting equipment, it contained three cupboards 'stocked with pewter plates, dishes and metal kitchen chattels . . . a mirror, chimney cloths and copper candlesticks' and 'two tables, some tablecloths and a considerable amount of seating furniture' (Baatsen, Blondé and De Groot 2014: 163–4).[6] These well-decorated kitchens, with pictures, cloths, tapestries and rugs, appear to have had a leisure function as they also contained board games (ibid.: 179); they were available to those who had the space to create another kitchen exclusively for the dirtier processes of cooking. In contrast, the sole kitchen in Daniel van Aymeyen's four-room property had fewer goods, but additional furniture – it also contained a bed. Dinner was taken in the *neercamere*, 'where a table and seating furniture were installed' (ibid.: 164).[7] A similar pattern was uncovered by Sandra Cavallo in the *casa* of Genoese artisans where, despite considerable investment in expensive bedding, cooking equipment, tables and seating were often found in the *camera* or *caminata* (Genoese *sala*) as there was apparently no separate kitchen (ibid.: 173). The way sleeping and eating furniture were organized in these properties revealed clear social distinctions between them, as it did for the Birmingham goldsmith with whose furniture this paper began.

Working in this way with probate inventories gives us a strong relative sense of the density and quality of objects within and across houses, but it does offer a temporally static picture that is some way from the lived experience of the household. The rest of this chapter therefore sets out to explore the way the contemporary eye might have fallen upon these rooms – how and why men and women might have had their attention drawn to some objects rather than to others, and what types of relationship the prominence of particular things might have set up between individuals and their furniture and furnishings.

THE PROVENANCE OF GOODS

Death and the Transmission of Household Goods

How did objects enter these houses then, and what was the effect of their provenance on the meaning and function of spaces? After Bess of Hardwick's death, the contents of Hardwick Hall were bequeathed to her son, William Cavendish, and his male heirs 'and entailed to remain at the house' (Boynton 1971: 3). For the elite, in other words, there was a significant connection between carefully chosen furniture and the particular houses for which it had been purchased – often the specific room for which things like hangings had been designed. This indicates one of the key tensions between objects, houses and individuals: things which we might consider personal, such as beds, were often seen as belonging to the house itself, and in England at least there was a category of 'standard': objects without which the house would not be able to operate in a way appropriate to its inhabitants' status.[8] On the other hand, Bess left all the contents of the Pearl Bedchamber (except the hangings) separately to her daughter Mary, Countess of Shrewsbury (ibid.: 3), suggesting the significance of passing on objects of suitable distinction to establish new branches of the family at the same social level.

Lower down the social scale, too, as we saw at the start, objects formed important bequests between the generations, ones that reinforced the significant role which furniture and furnishings played in defining individuals' social positions. In late medieval Douai in Northern France, for instance, the widow Maroie Le Grand 'left her best bed equipped with two pairs of bedclothes, two pillows and a serge coverlet, her good *cotte hardie*, her best *cotte a chambre*, her good *plinchon*, a *banquier* and six of her best cushions to a Jehane De Hainau', following a pattern of the bequest of long lists of personal possessions which had emerged by the early fourteenth century and intensified by the mid-fifteenth (Howell 1996: 6–7). It was a wider phenomenon: 'From Bruges to Lubeck, from Constance to Avignon to Genoa, it seems, people often laboriously named individual objects in wills and distributed them, piecemeal, among friends and relatives' (ibid.: 9). But it was also a reasonably socially diverse one. Such bequests can be found, both in collections of testaments made in advance by 'securely propertied people' such as 'established merchants, *rentiers* or artisan-entrepreneurs', and in wills made by a cleric or clerical notary at the deathbeds of 'simpler people who generally had less property at risk and less sophisticated means of protecting it' (ibid.: 8–9).

In her analysis of these documents, Martha C. Howell insists on the significance of the laws surrounding property ownership for understanding the bequests. She explores the possibilities open to women for keeping the goods which they had brought with them into marriage, past the point where that union was dissolved by death: 'A widow who had been married under contract . . . had a constituted right to the return of the property she had brought to the marriage . . . but she had no straightforward accounting allowing her to separate these assets from an estate likely to be composed of interchangeable and constantly mutating properties' (1996: 35). We might sense the presence of such a legal framework in Edmond's identification of his child's 'parte and porcyon' above. Under these circumstances, 'She would have had every reason to try to mark other goods as her own as well, to label them so unambiguously as hers that, when the marriage ended, she or her heirs would have no trouble identifying and claiming what was hers' (ibid.: 35). This gives us a strong sense of the connections that furniture and furnishings, as a part of a wider bequest strategy, could set up between individuals and household objects throughout the functioning life of the household as a social and familial unit. Seeing a room might mean appreciating the differing patterns of ownership that the objects it contained represented.

And, in Douai, as elsewhere, there were clear gendered elements to these distinctions (ibid.: 36–7). Men and women gave different kinds of objects to distinct groups of beneficiaries, and therefore received different goods, too: in Kent, for instance, young women were more likely to be given pewter and larger numbers of linen goods, and young men received larger numbers of key pieces of furniture (Richardson 2006a: chapter 2). Looking at a room in one's house revealed gender roles and identities through these patterns of ownership. A careful reading of such documents, situated within a clear understanding of the laws and customs dictating ownership and use, can give us a deep insight into how furniture and furnishings shaped daily life – the economic, social and cultural values which were articulated through them – especially in a period in which, for many people, their goods were worth more than their property or their land (ibid.: 33).

Ritual Objects, Courtship and Marriage

The other main point in the lifecycle at which furniture and furnishings entered the household was, of course, marriage. Even relatively humble marriages involved a dowry of goods, and the newly established furnishings of the house therefore included objects from both the bride and groom's families, eventually supplemented by those that were bought when funds allowed. In Renaissance Italy, symbolic gifts were given at all social levels and at all stages in the marriage process, from smaller objects between courting couples to large marriage chests commissioned especially for the bedchamber and decorated with significant iconography such as the coats of arms of the two families involved. These items were intended to have an audience – 'robes in precious material, silver or gilt tableware and embroidered household linens were often carried through the streets' to demonstrate the wealth and importance of the family, sometimes put on show on the night before the wedding, and carefully written into the inventory taken of the dowry (Ajmar-Wollheim and Dennis: 112–13).

As well as demonstrating the status that came with the families' economic and aesthetic power, these objects also fixed the significant ritual moments in the marriage process – they symbolized its events in ways which would last throughout the union and beyond, standing testament to its longevity and productiveness in quasi-legal terms – as contract and sociofinancial bond – but also drawing out the affective memory of those family and friends who were present and marking the passing of the years in their ability to endure whilst bearing marks of use and wear. In Urbino, for example, a *scritta* or written contract was signed by the heads of the bride and groom's family, and surviving maiolica inkwells may have been commissioned to be used at this event (ibid: 107). The food served at banquets held as part of the ostentatious hospitality of the marriage itself may well have been eaten from commemorative tablewares such as maiolica plates, bowls and jugs. Matching borders on surviving pieces suggest they were made to order, and noble and patrician account books show payments for several hundred pieces for particular feasts (ibid.: 114–17). The divergent quality of these products, often embellished with dates and initials as well as signs of love such as hearts, handclasps or rabbits (for fertility), indicate that they were in use down the social scale (ibid.: 114).

Whilst other places in Europe may not be able to compete with the sheer ostentation of Italian practice, there are, nevertheless, examples of courtship gifts, dowry items and commemorative tablewares in countries less given to spectacle around matrimony. In England, for example, Diana O'Hara's analysis of ecclesiastical court cases around the breach of the promise of marriage reveals rich evidence of the giving of tokens of affection throughout the process.

In the case of Elizabeth Williams and William Divers, for instance, a schedule of tokens lists the gifts which he gave her during the course of their relationship, including gloves, purses, a girdle, a pair of knives, petticoat cloth, thimble and points. In addition, she had 'in her keeping' some of his goods, including a candlestick and chamber pot, and he gave to her mother 'in tooken of goodwill to the said Elizabeth' slippers, starch, candles and pots (ibid.: 59–60). Household items only made up a very small percentage of the gifts, but some of the more personal objects such as knives fell into the category of both personal possession and domestically useful good.[9] Used by individuals in the course of their domestic practice, these things marked the formation of a new household.

Partly because of the type of evidence she works on, the gifts O'Hara discovers are lower-status objects, and were less obviously capable of holding ritual significance and surviving to narrate a familial story of commitment, even if the relationships had not broken down. There is, however, other evidence of gift-giving around marriage of a more explicitly thought-through nature. A tin-glazed earthenware mug, painted with geometric decoration and Chinese Wanli-derived 'birds-on-rocks', flowers and insects in blue, is inscribed 'WILLIAM AND ELIZABETH BURGES 24TH AUGUST 1631' and '1632' beneath the handle (Figure 4.2). It was probably made at the Pickleherring Pottery in Southwark,

FIGURE 4.2: Tin-glazed mug, English, 1632, inscribed: 'WILLIAM AND ELIZABETH BURGES 24TH AUGUST 1631'. V&A Museum No. 3839-1901. © Victoria and Albert Museum.

London, a factory run by Christian Wilhelm, erstwhile dealer in cobalt turned potter, hence the blue-and-white colouring. These objects were likely to have been mass-produced, with the inscription added at the point of purchase, and they may have been given as wedding gifts.

FORMS OF PURCHASE

In a rather different example, the Exeter merchant, John Hayne, left a book of accounts which start in 1634, just before his marriage, when he was 26. A second-generation cloth merchant from a family long-resident in the town,[10] some of the first furniture purchases that Hayne lists include a cabinet bought at Rouen for £3, which he sends to Susan, his wife-to-be, as a gift. Other courtship gifts include a pair of women's knives, a box for her ruff and a looking glass, muff and 'head brush' bought in London (Brushfield 1901). Such purchases take planning; they use commercial networks and demand financial outlay, which were beyond the reach of many in early modern England. They remind us of the importance of trade within Europe, and, more broadly, of the increased status of goods that had travelled from a different material community – made with different stuffs and processes to those which could be purchased in local markets.

Hayne's accounts allow us to explore a rather more piecemeal approach to furnishing a home to the wholesale acquisition of dowry objects evident in the Italian examples. He made three different types of purchase in the first few years of his marriage: first, bundles of goods bought second-hand, such as a set of curtains and a valence of blue serge with yellow lace and yellow worsted 'French', with two matching chairs and two stools of the same fabric and 'tricking' (ornament), and a fair blue rug, from a local widow (ibid.).[11] Such purchases represent over 40 percent of his domestic expenditure for 1636. Second, he commissions furniture from a local joiner, including a drawing chest, a chair and a table in the study. These purchases indicate a process of negotiation and discussion, followed by waiting, and the work going on in the house. Finally, Hayne's smaller purchases represent occasional acquisitions to attend to immediate needs, and many of them are metal goods for the kitchen, as he sets it up to his wife's liking so that she is able to run it efficiently with her maid. To this end, he buys parcels of goods, including, from John Tucker a brass chafing dish, tinderbox and mousetrap for 6s. 4d. and a latten dripping pan, iron chafing dish, clothes brush, pottle jug, and latten tunner and breader for 7s. 9d. (DRO/Z19/36/14: 25v). The items are often of the same material or materials as one another, they are apparently bought off the shelf, and the occupation of their vendor is usually noted. The collections of objects he lists indicate ways of thinking about domestic needs in relation to local skills, and this might suggest different attitudes towards the objects as used within the house.

The sets of items bought in bulk, the new objects that Hayne commissions himself and the groups of smaller things, are complemented by his wife's dowry objects – a great brass pan, for instance, transported from his in-laws. This range of types of purchase shows different levels of investment in the processes of commissioning furniture and furnishings, and the groups in which they entered the household, both of which must have affected the way they were regarded in the years to come.

Hayne's purchases are probably fairly typical of the way a man of middling status, living in an affluent port town with good links to foreign and domestic markets, furnished his house in the first half of the seventeenth century in England. His less well-off neighbours would have shopped only locally and much less regularly – it is probable that furniture, bought seldom after marriage, was mainly acquired as bequests by those below him on the social scale.[12] The second-hand market may well have been significant for both groups, but it is harder to see in England, where it was apparently less closely regulated, than in other places in Europe such as Venice and Antwerp. In the latter, the 'oudkleerkopers', or guild of second-hand dealers, were in some cases very wealthy men, trading recycled household goods in the town's more elite Friday Market until their decline towards the end of the seventeenth century (Van Damme 2006).

More affluent customers than Hayne spent more money (and time) engaging with London markets, making the most of the opportunities that London afforded for buying goods unavailable in the provinces, where landed gentry were based for most of the year. The capital was becoming a popular destination for shopping in the early seventeenth century as its status as an entertainment centre grew, and new purchasing opportunities opened up with the 'exchanges' – the first shopping centres.[13] This dominance of one capital city contrasted sharply with the situation in other places in Europe. In Italy, for instance, 'diversity and competition' between the towns of the relatively more urbanized area of the northern and central peninsula meant distinct fashions and therefore rivalry for market share (Welch 2005). London, in contrast, became the centre of trade in various types of luxury goods.

The Le Stranges, an old gentry family from Hunstanton in Norfolk, shopped extensively in the markets surrounding their home, as Hayne did, but they also visited London and made the most of its material opportunities: 'On average, someone from the household visited London twice a year, Norwich four times a year, and King's Lynn six times.' King's Lynn provided for their more pedestrian needs, whereas much of their luxury shopping was undertaken in Norwich, where they went to socialize. It 'offered many things that were also purchased in London, such as books, hawking equipment, fine fabrics, clothing accessories, glassware, watches and clocks', and these kinds of elite manufactures marked off a particular type of provincial shopping centre capable of catering to the wealthy (Whittle and Griffiths: 63). Nevertheless, 'money spent in London accounted for around 20 per cent of domestic consumption expenditure, and 10 per cent of overall expenditure', and at no point during the period 1614–28 did they not buy London goods for use in Norfolk (ibid.: 64, 59). In the course of the most extensive trip detailed in the account book, in 1628, they made their most expensive purchase of a crimson damask bed for £84 14s. 4d. They had bought a new black bed for over £50 on a visit eight years earlier, as part of around 120 purchases, including, '£5 worth of books, and gloves, hats, stockings, lace, boots, spurs, cloth, earthenware, brass and ironware, silverware and a new upholstered couch' (ibid.: 58, 61). This gives us a sense of the occasional and irregular nature of even elite purchases of substantial and impressive pieces of furniture.

The markets in which furniture and furnishings were purchased to a certain extent defined the household's social status through their cultural and economic engagement, then. Looking around an early modern room meant appreciating the relative age of the goods – how often they had been replaced – and their provenance – whether they were locally made and bought or whether they had come from further afield. Familiarity with these objects – whether or not one had a similar type of object in one's own home, whether one recognized its material, style and manufacture – was key to the feelings of social parity or distinction, inclusion or exclusion, which furniture and furnishings could create. Linda Levy Peck argues that not only retailers but also consumers 'played an active role in creating their own desires for new goods based in part on seeing, reading, and travel' (Peck: 151). Standing in one place and looking outwards, we can appreciate the growing pull of the exotic as we go up the social scale – goods from a larger town, from a capital city or other centre of fashion, from another part of Europe or even beyond.

GLOBAL TRADE

For some sectors of society, the period covered by this volume was one of profound change in the provenance of furniture and furnishings: it was the start of global trade, and goods such as East Asian ceramics, Japanese furniture and Persian carpets became highly sought after partly because they were exotic in their colours, patterns, textures and forms, and partly because many of the processes by which they were produced were (initially at least) impossible to reproduce in the West. After the capture of Constantinople by the Ottomans in 1453, Europeans began to open up Eastern markets to direct trade, without Arab intermediaries, the Portuguese reaching India in 1498 and China in 1513 (Jackson and Jaffer: 55, 224). Eventually, the Portuguese lost out in these Eastern markets to other European interests and, with several countries represented as trading nations, a period of bulk export began (ibid.: 225). The East India Company was founded in England in 1600, but initially at least it was a poor cousin to its Dutch counterpart, which monopolized trade with Japan because of its access to a much larger market: 'Amsterdam had the whole of northern Europe as its trading hinterland' (ibid.: 144).

Such rivalries affected the goods available in different European countries. Chinese porcelain began to arrive in Britain in the 1560s, but it was mainly obtained by plunder from Portuguese and Spanish ships, rather than by more direct forms of trade (ibid.: 50). At different moments within the long timespan considered in this volume, then, as well as at different points on the social scale, Eastern furniture and furnishings were more prominent within European homes. In the course of the 200 years in which the Dutch East India Company was trading (1602–1795), it has been estimated that 'approximately one million people sailed on a total of 4,789 ships bound for the Indies' (ibid.: 136). This gives us one measure of the significance of the trade. On the other hand, even at the peak of the trade in the eighteenth century, other estimates suggest that 'no more than 1–2 per cent of everything that was consumed in Europe came from outside its borders' (Emmer 2003: 38). Thinking about this sequentially, at the level of the individual household, we might consider that every single traded commodity, brought into a home up until that point full of local wares, became a unique object in its style if not its function – marked off visually from the things which surround it by differences from indigenous domestic cultures.

We can also see such objects as part of a dialogue, one which explicitly drew attention to the relationships between near and far. The furniture produced for Europe was in time so influenced by its eventual market in very different homes to the ones lived in by its craftsmen, that it 'was exotic both in the eyes of the Asian artisans who made it and of the Europeans who used it' (Jackson and Jaffer 2004: 261). And these processes of knowledge exchange around aesthetics and function involved the development of a keen comparative eye. John Albert de Mandelslo wrote in the early seventeenth century that the painted furniture of Gujarat was of 'such a lustre, as none yet could ever imitate in Europe'; the desire to emulate necessitated careful attention to effect, both at the scale of individual pieces and in their relationship to one another – the impact of such impressive effects on a Western room as a whole. But it must also have drawn a wider set of comparisons in the minds of those involved in the production, trade and consumption of exotic domestic objects, between here and there, 'our' ways and 'theirs'. Full contact with Eastern lifestyles, such as that gained by the factors of the various companies trading abroad, showed striking differences: 'When Europeans first landed in Asia they found that there existed neither western-style elevated chairs nor furniture used at chair height, such as tables for eating and writing,' and 'only in China did people sit upright on chairs' (Jackson and Jaffer 2004: 251, 256). Direct contact was not only with new goods, but with different ways of living. As with the design styles, these functional differences in furniture traditions eventually resulted in mutual influence abroad as well as at home: when 'Joris van Spilbergen went to Kandy in 1602 he was surprised to find that the king's great hall was "furnished with Spanish chairs and a table, where everything appeared to be in the Christian style"' (ibid.: 257).

As Riello argues, 'all of these artefacts, in different ways, are materialisations of the connections that characterised the early modern world' (2017: 34). And we therefore need to understand intra- and extra-European trade in relation to one another. Antwerp's geographical and commercial position, for instance, meant that it functioned in the mid-sixteenth century as 'an important mediator of Italian (material) culture in northern Europe' (Baatsen, Blondé and De Staelen: 438). In the fifteenth century, tin-glazed earthenware was imported from Spain and Italy but, by the sixteenth century, local craftsmen began to produce majolica and à-la-façon-de-Venise glass in Antwerp itself (Figure 4.3). Whilst the endogenous trade in majolica grew in Antwerp through the later sixteenth and early seventeenth centuries, by 1630 there was 'a collapse which can probably best be explained by the enormous success of porcelain that was

FIGURE 4.3: Dutch majolica bowl, late-sixteenth–early-seventeenth centuries, St. George's Street, Canterbury. Canterbury Archaeological Trust, F93 0.22 SG85. © Canterbury Archaeological Trust.

imported by the Dutch' in increasingly large numbers from the start of the seventeenth century. The success of these imports 'drove majolica producers almost desperate, as is evidenced by their inclination to imitate Chinese porcelain as much as possible' (ibid.: 441). Popularity needs to be seen in relative terms.

The level of remove of an individual household from the processes by which the objects with which its rooms were filled had come to be in the country must to some extent have defined the quality of the exoticism which it was felt to bring with it. We know that Thomas Puckering, for instance, bought a 'China-work fruit-table' in London in April 1620 for 44s., and that when he died in 1637, he owned 'twoe basons and Ewers of Counterfeyt China stuffe', 'one little eight square Indian paynted table wth a standerd [stand?]' and 'an Indian rounde voyder[14] and a knife partly guilt a douzin of Indian banquettinge dishes', amongst other objects with exotic potential (Merry and Richardson 2012: 159, 305, 310). These objects comprise both furniture and smaller, more decorative goods, and he is able to tell the genuine imports from the European copies.

The relationship between the raw materials and the design value of objects was also changing across this period, partly as a result of exposure to different aesthetics through trade. Blondé, Stabel, Stobart and Van Damme (2006) find that Majolica and crystal glass signalled a fundamental shift in patterns of consumption in early modern Antwerp: rather than effectively storing money in goods whose value lay in their raw materials (their intrinsic qualities), as had been the case up to this period, householders began to purchase domestic items that were valued for the superiority of their design and their decorative qualities, but did not necessarily have a lasting economic worth. This was particularly obvious in tablewares – so-called 'old luxuries' like silver and pewter items across Europe were, in various quantities, substituted by so-called 'new luxuries' like glass and majolica. These alternative, less durable items demanded ingenuity and knowledge to produce them as, like the Eastern objects, they were fashioned through complex manufacturing processes. But what they also needed was a type of cultured urban skill in order to use them effectively: their fragility and the near impossibility of mending them meant they needed to be handled with refinement or they would be broken beyond use or repair. And, at the same time, they required owners whose cultural skills were adequate to the intellectual sophistication and often classical narrative displayed in their decoration. In addition to familiarity with a generalized Italian Renaissance aesthetic, Baatsen, Blondé and De Staelen remind us that, 'Especially istoriato-majolica served well in dispersing knowledge of ancient history and mythology' (2016: 436) – these were objects decorated with narratives with considerable cultural capital. In the choice of such decoration, its owners advertised their skills of appreciation, and in its use they invited the demonstration of complementary proficiencies in their guests. Using these objects was partly an intellectual matter – they offered both visual impact (surface) and cultural engagement (depth) (ibid.).[15]

In the course of the period we consider here, then, ideas about the design and manufacture of furniture and furnishings were changing rapidly. Processes of making were learned in the places in which imports had been valued, and the objects produced became symbols of something rather more complex than their exotic provenance: they became hybrids of foreign and native style. Broad shifts, from old luxuries with intrinsic worth to more disposable, fashionable goods with a strong aesthetic appeal, and the ability of those lower down the social scale to purchase more of the kind of goods which drew aesthetic attention to themselves, meant that the contemporary eye would light on different objects in the rooms described here from the start of the period to the end. It was these aesthetic, rather than functional, changes that characterized this period.

If we want to understand the influence that furniture and furnishings had on daily life and identity, we need to go beyond knowing what rooms contained. We need to think about the relative visual impact and functional relationship of objects *in situ*, for instance, Florentine acquai – fittings that 'rose nearly to the ceiling' – and the brass ewers and basins, maiolica and glass objects which surrounded them because they were needed to make the acquai function (Preyer 2006: 38–9). We also need to consider the relationship between furniture, furnishings and other types of fixed surface decoration panelling and glasswork. The 10th Earl of Ormond, for instance, dealt directly with Sir Thomas Gresham for the panelling and glasswork for his Irish houses. Based in Antwerp as royal agent to the Netherlands, Gresham had direct access to the most fashionable decorative designs (Fenlon 2011: 141–68). The interplay between size and detail, immovable fittings and movable objects, feeds into our sense of how houses were negotiated, and how the eye might move around them. We need to consider what it felt like to sit in a Spanish chair (upholstered in leather and with armrests, symmetrical in design and meticulous in workmanship) in the *neercamere* of an Antwerp house, whilst others were involved in less prestigious social occasions in similar chairs in the back room or kitchen and, just perhaps, in the knowledge, gained through diplomatic contacts, that the court in Kandy were similarly seated. Knowledge of provenance combined with a sense of who else owned similar objects and where they were used defined attitudes to furniture, as did the age of the objects, the method of their purchase and their possible association with rites of passage.

The material dynamic of display and concealment that furniture enables – objects storing other objects away for ritual moments and familial changes in the future – can also be read metaphorically: some of these things showed their age and provenance deliberately, through the inscription of messages or coats of arms, or with the addition of a qualifying phrase in will or inventory; but others remain silent, the full history of their relationship with house and family lost with the memories of their original owners and users. Looking at furniture and furnishings in this period necessitates careful attention to their quiet but insistent communication of relative prominence within the early modern home.

CHAPTER FIVE

Home and Work

JANE WHITTLE

Pieter Brueghel the Younger's painting of *c.* 1620, retrospectively titled *The Visit to the Farm*, depicts the interior of an early-seventeenth-century farmhouse in the southern Low Countries (Figure 5.1). It reveals a large space full of people and alive with activity. As well as the three wealthy visitors, there are seven adults and three children. Four of the adults are certainly engaged in work activities: there is a woman watching the pot and caring for children, a man who appears to be carving a wooden bowl, and a man and women churning butter in the background. Another woman leans through the door, perhaps on an errand, a man is sitting at the table eating, and another talks to the guests and receives the gift of a sugar loaf. This is a genre painting: not necessarily a realistic depiction of any particular farmhouse, household or moment in time. It is perhaps intentionally humorous and quaint in suggesting such a wide range of people and activities could be found in one room of a moderately wealthy early-seventeenth-century farm. Yet, this humour surely rests on the ordinary nature of the scene, only slightly exaggerated for an elite audience of art consumers. Much like the household advice books of the same period, the painting crams every possible type of activity and household member in a scene of home-life. The people include men and women, adults and children, residents and guests, and almost certainly, kin, servants and neighbours. The activities include work and leisure, production and consumption and care for the family alongside work producing goods.

In the modern world, we go 'out to work': home and work are separated. The domestic house has become a sanctuary from work, a place of leisure and consumption, and a private space for the family alone. Before 1650, the dwelling house had none of these connotations. It was not privileged as a place

FIGURE 5.1: *The Visit to the Farm* by Pieter Brueghel the Younger, c. 1620. © Heritage Images/Getty Images.

of leisure, it was not especially private and, most of all, the house was not separate from work and the wider economy. It is commonplace to state that the home was a place of work in pre-industrial societies, but far less often have the full implications of this statement been explored. What did it mean to live in your workplace, to work in your living space, to manage your household as a business? The lack of separation between home and work in the period before 1650 also requires historians to think carefully about what they mean by 'work' and where different work activities were actually carried out.

The following chapter is divided into four sections, each exploring a different way of approaching the topic of work within the home. The first considers the household as a business and an economy. The original meaning of 'economy' was management of the household, and this meaning was still current in the period 1450–1650. Historians and social scientists have discussed the 'household economy', examining how family and business considerations were intertwined in preindustrial societies. There is a danger with the household economy approach, however, that all members of the household are seen as having the same interests and experiences. The next two sections address this issue. Section two examines the gender division of labour within the home, looking particularly at the role of husband and wife. Late medieval and early modern advice literature on marriage, household management and farming repeatedly asserted that men and women should have different work roles: the man's duties were primarily outside, about the farm or other business, while the woman should take charge of the house and work indoors. Despite the uniformity of this message, actual work patterns provide little evidence of any such rigid division. In exploring these issues, gender historians have provided the most detailed accounts available of the types of work that were actually carried out in particular households. The third section turns to paid workers within the home. One of the most striking characteristics of society in this period was the presence of large numbers of servants and apprentices who lived with their employers, receiving food and accommodation as well as a cash wage. For the duration of their contracts, they were subsumed within the households in which they worked and, legally and colloquially, considered to be part of the family. The final section turns to the house itself, and considers the extent to which the presence of work activities shaped the physical structure of the house. Where was work located spatially within the home? How did this affect the division between public and private space? How did the need for work-spaces influence architectural change? Of all the topics discussed, this has been least explored in previous studies.

THE HOUSEHOLD AS AN ECONOMY

The Le Stranges of Hunstanton in Norfolk were a wealthy gentry family who kept a detailed set of household accounts in the first half of the seventeenth century. In 1619, the resident family consisted of Sir Hamon and Lady Alice Le Strange and their two youngest children, Elizabeth and Roger. Two older sons, Nicholas and Hamon jun. were away at school for much of the year. Within the household, the family were outnumbered by their sixteen resident servants who worked around the house and farm. The Le Stranges' income of around £2,000 a year came mainly from rents, but also from the sale of wool, timber and grain from their estate. Feeding the household was in itself, a major enterprise. They kept a dairy of twenty cows, which allowed the household to be self-sufficient in butter and cheese; 39 swine were kept, providing all the household's pork and bacon; mutton came from the 69 'kitchen sheep'. Wheat and rye was baked into brown bread for servants and other workers. Barley was used to brew the household's beer, which was consumed at an average of 175 gallons a week. Fruit and vegetables came from garden and orchards. The household was not self-sufficient in food, however, as well as luxuries like wine, sugar, spices and dried fruit, local products such as fine white bread, eggs and beef were also purchased. Wealthy gentry households have been studied as an expression of status and political power, but the Le Strange household accounts remind us that they were also complex businesses. This household was by far the largest employer in the local economy. It was managed very largely by Lady Alice, who kept the accounts and ran the home farm, while her husband acted as an MP and JP, pursued legal cases and oversaw the rebuilding of their house (Whittle 2011; Whittle and Griffiths 2012).

Of course, the Le Stranges' household was not typical, falling into the wealthiest top 2 percent of the English population (Wrightson 1982: 24). But their records also offer a window on the economies of households much lower down the social scale. Richard Wix of neighbouring Heacham in Norfolk was a village thatcher. When he died in 1628, his movable goods were listed in a probate inventory and valued at £11 12s. Wix worked regularly for the Le Stranges. He earned 6d. a day as a thatcher; when there was no thatching to be done, they paid him 4d. a day for agricultural work such as hay-making and threshing corn. The Le Stranges occasionally also employed his wife, Anne Wix. Over one year (1619), she was paid a total of 11s. 4d. for knitting hose and stockings on various occasions, and did one day's agricultural labour harvesting peas. Their son earned wages, too, working regularly for the Le Stranges in 1620: he earned 2d. a day for bird-scaring and other agricultural tasks. The Wix family lived in a small house of two rooms and a loft, with a single hearth. As well as their wage income, they rented some land and farmed on a small scale. In the winter of 1628, they had unthreshed barley worth 10s. stored in the house, and owned two cows, a bullock, a calf, eight pigs, six geese and four hens. It was not only Richard but also Anne Wix who had multiple sources of income. She had wool and hemp worth £1 ready for spinning; and cheese and butter valued at 5s. The Wixes illustrate the mixed economy followed by many poorer rural households in this period, making a living from farming, wage labour, craft skills and textile production (see Figure 5.2; Whittle 2011; Whittle and Griffiths 2012).

Modern definitions of work assume both a physical separation of home and work and also a clear difference between work in the economy, which generates income, and domestic work or housework which is unpaid and orientated towards the care of the family. Early economic thought did not make these distinctions. From ancient Greece onwards, the economy was understood first and foremost as the economy of the household. Discussions of the economy imagined the household as a self-sufficient farm, carefully managed for the benefit current and future family members. The national economy was seen as nothing more than an agglomeration of these households. These ideas originated in the writings of Aristotle and Xenophon. Xenophon's work, the *Treatise of Households*, was translated into English in 1534, and this conception of the household as both *an* economy and *the* economy remained influential until the late eighteenth century. Thus, in early modern thought, as in that of the ancient world, there was no separation between the household and economy, or

HOME AND WORK 107

FIGURE 5.2: Preparing food for the winter, December, from the Golf book by the workshop of Simon Bening, 1520–30. British Library add MS 24098 f29v, p. 1. © The British Library.

between home and work. All work was undertaken to provide for and reproduce the family, and took place in and around the home in which that family lived (Gray 2000; Muldrew 1998: 158).

In a self-sufficient farming household such as that imagined by Xenophon, there is little separation between production and consumption. Food, clothing and housing are produced in the home and farm for the same family that then used or consumed them. But this was far from the reality of most European households that existed in 1450, let alone 1650. Rural households of all levels of wealth were likely to produce some of their own food, but they were not self-sufficient. By 1500, an estimated 6 percent of the European population lived in towns of over 10,000 people (Wrigley 1987: 176), where self-provisioning was rarely possible. Houses were built by specialist craftsmen and cloth production had already become an international industry (Jenkins 2003). Nonetheless, it remained true that the most people lived and worked as part of a household economy. Property – house, land and business capital (tools and trading stock) – was managed by the married couple who headed the household, and were passed on to their children. The wealth needed to sustain the family was generated by the work of family members and their employees using that property. For these reasons, not just ancient and early modern thinkers, but also historians and social scientists, have elaborated on the idea of the household economy.

Four early-twentieth-century theorists offer helpful frameworks for thinking about the household as an economic unit or business. Perhaps the most influential is the Russian economist A.V. Chayanov's *Theory of Peasant Economy* (1986) first published in 1925. Chayanov's key insight was that where the family provided the sole form of labour for a particular enterprise (a 'labour family' or 'peasant farm'), that enterprise followed a different economic logic to a capitalist enterprise. In particular, the family had the capacity to 'self-exploit' and survive under circumstances in which a capitalist enterprise, relying on wage labour and making a profit, would go bankrupt. This was because the aim of the peasant farm was long-term survival. Chayanov's work was based on the detailed analysis of the late-nineteenth- and early-twentieth-century peasantry in Russia, where very little wage labour existed and limited production for the market took place. This hampers the direct application of his ideas to Western Europe in the period 1450–1650, which was more heavily commercialized even at that date. Nonetheless, his central point that the fusion of work and family interests in a single household affected the economic choices made by that household is an important one.

Max Weber's discussion of different types of household economy in his unfinished work *Economy and Society* leads to similar conclusions. For Weber, the classic household economy was based on pooled resources: family members provided labour and shared rights to property and wealth. However, unlike

Chayanov, Weber thought that households of this type were compatible with wage labour and production for the market. Elite households, such as the Le Stranges', might employ large numbers of workers and engage in large-scale market production, but their aim was still 'want satisfaction' rather than profit, and the family retained joint claims on the property and wealth. From fourteenth-century Florence onwards, a new type of organization, the firm or enterprise developed. What distinguished the firm from the classic household economy was not the spatial separation of home and work, but rather contractual relationships driven by profit-making motives, which allowed non-family members to be included as partners and some family members to be excluded. In the firm, work, investment and profits were linked to individual partners, rather than the family (Weber 1968: 376–83; Emigh 2001).

Alice Clark, the pioneering historian of women's work, also considered commercialization from the perspective of the family economy. She suggested three ways in which the household might organize the work of production. In 'domestic industry', goods are produced directly for the use of the family; in 'family industry', the family worked together to produce goods for the market; while in 'capitalist industry', the family worked for wages, which were paid to individuals rather than the family (Clark [1919] 1982: 6–7). For Clark, the individualism of capitalist industry marks the end of the household economy. Chayanov, Weber and Clark all suggested that different types of economy could coexist in any particular time period or region. Clark even suggested that particular households might engage in more than one of her types of 'industry'. Together, these ideas suggest a model that can be applied to late medieval and early modern households: they were partly self-sufficient but also involved in market transactions, buying and selling goods and labour; and the aim of the household economy was to generate wealth for the survival of the family over time, rather than individual profit.

While Chayanov, Weber and Clark described societies where the household was the main economic unit and location of production, they were not particularly concerned with the types of work that took place within the home. An important characteristic of pre-industrial households is that productive work (making goods) is not separated from reproductive work (maintaining and caring for the house and family). Yet, historians and social scientists have tended to assume a sharp distinction can be drawn between these two types of work, the first of which is seen as part of the wider economy, and the second of which is not. As we have seen, descriptions of the household economy from the ancient and early modern world drew no such distinction: productive and reproductive work was seen as equally necessary for the survival of the family household. The desire to separate these two types of work comes from modern economic thought and social norms, which belittles or ignores the value of unpaid reproductive work within the home, mostly undertaken by women, to wider society and the economy. Here, the economist Margaret Reid provides a helpful approach in her 1934 book, *Economics of Household Production*. Reid suggested that researchers should apply a 'third-party criterion' to work within the home: any work that could be replaced with purchased goods or paid services, should be considered part of the economy as a whole. Her ideas were adopted by the United Nations in 1993 as a means of calculating the value of unpaid women's work and work on peasant farms as part of gross national product (GNP) (Wood 1997). The approach is also useful for historians. Most work in late medieval and early modern society was unpaid and carried out in or for the household. It is almost impossible to draw a distinction between work intended to generate an income and work that directly supported the family (crops grown in the field or chickens in the yard could be intended for both purposes). Yet, monetary values were often attached to all types of household and farm work in the form of wages offered to servants. The work of the best paid male and female servants were described as equivalent to that of a husbandman or farmer who managed a farm, or a housewife or farmer's wife who managed the household.

GENDER AND WORK WITHIN THE HOME

Early modern commentators saw work as strongly gendered and divided work spatially, locating women's work in the home and men's work outside (Romano 1996; Gray 2000; Schmidt 2011). Early modern farming advice books emphasize this division, while also providing detailed descriptions of women's work around the farm. The English translation of Charles Éstienne's *Maison Rustique, or the Countrey Farme* states that: 'the woman is acquitted of field matters, in as much as she is tied to matters within the house and base court ... [just] as the husband is tied to do what concerneth him, ... all the businesses of the field' (1616: 51). Nonetheless, the significance of the farming housewife's role is emphasized by the long list of tasks for which she had responsibility. In France, Éstienne suggests that:

> Country women look unto the things necessary and requisite about kine [milk cows], calves, hogs, pigs, pigeons, geese, ducks, peacocks, hens, pheasants, and other sorts of beasts, as well for the feeding of them as for the milking of them: making of butter and cheese ... Furthermore they have the charge of the oven and cellar: and we leave the handling of hemp unto them likewise; as also the care of making webs [weaving], of looking to the clipping of sheep, of keeping their fleeces, of spinning and combing of wool to make cloth to clothe the family, of ordering of the kitchen garden, and keeping of the fruits, herbs, roots, and seeds: and moreover, of watching and attending the bees.
>
> —1616: 51–2

Gervase Markham's *The English Housewife* (1615) offered advice on medical care, gardening, cookery, distilling, making textiles, dairying, malting, brewing and baking. The list in Fitzherbert's *Book of Husbandry* (1523) is even more extensive. In addition to the tasks listed above, he notes that the wife should clean the house, care for children, send corn and malt to the mill and check that the miller does not cheat her, and 'go or ride to the market to sell butter, cheese, eggs, . . . hens, pigs, geese and all types of grain, and also to buy the sorts of things necessary for the household' (Goldberg 1995: 167–8). It is important to remember that this wide range of tasks is what was commonly meant by housewifery or the work of the housewife in this period, not just cooking, cleaning and child-care as we imagine today. In fact, advice books rarely bother to note some of the more routine tasks that women seem to have taken care of, such as collecting water and fuel or doing laundry.

Advice books offer an idealized, contradictory and limited view of work activities. They outline work tasks of a large mixed farm, but say nothing about urban households, or the household economies of labourers and craftsmen in the countryside. The rest of this section pieces together evidence from other documents and existing studies to offer a glimpse of routine household tasks, the division of labour in agriculture, types of occupations, the urban household, and the extent to which husband and wife worked together in the household economy.

Routine tasks, those that had to be carried out every day or at regular intervals throughout the year, were most commonly done by women and children. The majority of houses lacked an internal water supply: water had to be collected outside. Records of accidental death from sixteenth-century Sussex in England record young girls and 'spinsters' (probably female servants) using buckets and pots to draw water from wells, ponds and streams. Often, the water was described as near the house or even in the garden. For instance, Elizabeth Chamber, 'spinster', 'went down to a pit in John Freeland's garden . . . with 2 buckets in her hands', while a woman sent her daughter, Margery Wells, 'to a pit near her house . . . to fetch water'. Susan Duncke was only 5 years old when she went 'out to a pit near the house of John Duncke, her father, with a stone pot to fetch water from the pit' (Hunnisett 1996: 54). In France, Roche notes that: 'a strong sociability surrounded the well, where the village women assembled at least twice a day, this being the first and last task of their daily routine' (2000: 148). The same was true in cities where aqueducts transported clean water to communal fountains, as in Rome and Paris (Sarti 2002: 115).

Washing clothes was an exclusively female occupation. For most people, laundry was done in a communal site by a well or river. Another case from Sussex described Joan Hassilden of Henfield, aged 14, who 'had finished washing linen in the accustomed washing-place in the stream near the mill at

Henfield' but slipped when going to fill one last pail of water (Hunnisett 1996: 256). A 1561 court deposition from Devon, England, records the 18-year-old yeoman's daughter, doing the laundry by a village well for several hours. She took the opportunity to arrange marriage with her suitor, without her parents' knowledge. Other tasks took women further afield. Grain can be stored for a year or more, but flour gets stale or tainted, so women regularly took grain to the local mill to be made into flour. A Sussex case describes Joan Brecher, who 'was returning home from Etchingham mill', walking on the bank of the river, 'carrying a small sack of flour on her head', when she slipped and drowned. The accident happened at Bugsell, just over a kilometre from the mill (ibid.: 27). Journeys to market were even longer. In Essex, Flather found the men and women travelled up to 16 kilometres to market, although dairywomen from the south and east of the county regularly rode 24 kilometres into London to sell butter and cheese during the summer (Flather 2013: 354–5).

The presence of these regular out-of-house activities in women's routines undermine arguments that suggest women's work was only located in the house, or that their responsibilities for preparing meals and caring for children limited their movement. There is little evidence that cooking meals took up a great deal of time, as it largely consisted of boiling a mixture of grain, vegetables and perhaps a little meat, in a large metal pot over the fire. A study of 2,400 work tasks from court depositions in South-West England found many examples of pots boiling over the fire unattended, but very few of people actually preparing food for the pot. What did take time was food-processing: baking bread, brewing beer, making butter and cheese, butchering and salting meat. These activities differed from meal preparation because they were aimed at preparing products for sale as well preserving food for future consumption (Whittle 2005a).

Historians are only starting to explore the practicalities of childcare. With regard to childcare in seventeenth- and eighteenth-century Sweden, Oja notes that 'mothers did most of the actual toil and were responsible for finding strategies to combine childcare with other duties' (2015: 77). Young babies might require quite intensive care: in the late fifteenth-century 'Ballad of the Tyrannical Husband', the wife complains 'my sleep is but small' because 'I lie all night awake with our child' (Goldberg 1995: 169). In Sweden, in the summer, small children were 'hung up in cradles close to where people were making hay or herding cattle' (Oja 2015: 89); Hanawalt also notes babies being taken into the fields in medieval England (1986: 176–7). Most babies were watched over, but in small and poor households that was not always possible, judging from the accidents that occurred (ibid.: 176). Children were most likely to come to harm from the age they became mobile until they were old enough to follow either parent on their work routines. Young children were often cared for by servants, siblings and neighbours, or as James Collins notes for seventeenth-century

France, 'someone who was less critical to the economic survival of the household than the adult women' (1989: 442; also see Figure 5.3). They often played outside rather than inside the home (Hunnisett 1996). From around the age of five, boys began to accompany their fathers and girls their mothers, first watching and then working in the tasks of the household and farm (Hanawalt 1986: 157–8).

The actual gender division of labour varied a great deal, even in particular types of production such as agriculture. Rebecca Jean Emigh, describing the economy of Tuscan smallholders in fifteenth-century Italy, found that women were more likely to specialize in the production of wine and olives for the market, while men were more involved in grain production (2000: 125). Mercedes Borrero Fernández, studying the countryside around Seville, Spain, in the same period, found a more complex arrangement. Here, small peasant

FIGURE 5.3: The holy family at work from the Hours of Catherine of Cleves, c. 1435–60. The Hours of Catherine of Cleves MS M.917, pp. 146–9. © Morgan Library and Museum, New York.

farms specialized in viticulture, while large estates produced grain and olives. As the peasants' farms were too small to provide adequately for a family's subsistence, both men and women worked for wages at certain times of the year on the large estates. In winter and early spring, the men worked on the estates, maintaining the olive trees and ploughing the cereal fields, while women worked on the peasant farms digging and hoeing around the vines. In July and August, the men went to work in the grain harvest, but returned to their own farms in September to harvest the grapes. Then, from November to December, the women left home to harvest the olives on the estates, while the men worked on their home farms pruning the vines (Fernández 1998: 14–15). In Essex, England, men ploughed the fields from September to November and in January and February for autumn and spring sown crops. Women spent the winter closer to home, tending livestock, and carding and spinning wool. At other times of the year, women worked in the fields, however (Flather 2013: 351). Some work was done just by women, such as weeding crops in the spring and early summer and gleaning after the harvest. Harvesting hay involved men and women in different tasks: men mowed the hay with a scythe, while women 'made hay', turning it to dry in the sun. Only in the corn harvest did men and women work side by side (Roberts 1979).

Not everyone in the countryside was a farmer. An analysis of 1,616 male occupations, recorded in court cases from villages and small towns in sixteenth-century Norfolk, England, demonstrates that only 44 percent of men were described as yeomen or husbandmen – that is, in charge of running their own farm (Whittle 2000: 236). Another 30 percent of men were described as labourers, indicating they worked for wages as their main source of income. Most, but not all of these men would have worked in agriculture on other people's land, although they might have some land or livestock. Almost a quarter, 23 percent, were specialist craftsmen or tradesmen such as weavers, tailors, shoemakers, smiths, building craftsmen, butchers, grocers or merchants. De Vries found a similar variety in Holland. For instance, in 1514, in the village of Leyderdorp just outside Leiden, out of 50 householders, 26 were farmers, 6 were bakers, 4 innkeepers and 20 common labourers; while in 1562, in Ouderkerk, the majority of the 158 householders were dairy farmers, but 41 households were headed by craftsmen, sailors and day labourers (de Vries 1974: 64–7).

Occupations tend to be recorded only for the male head of household. Probate inventories list movable goods owned at the time of death, which can be used to reconstruct the range of work activities followed by particular households. Hermann Rebel's study of 867 probate inventories from Upper Austria found that the ratio of those involved in agriculture to those engaged primarily in industries and crafts was 3:2 in the sixteenth and early seventeenth century. However, many households had mixed economies: 287 households showed evidence of farming alone, but 115 farmers had diversified into craft production and another 52 specialized in transport services (Rebel 1983: 57–73). A sample of just over 2,000 English probate inventories showed that 64 percent of commercial farmers in Kent and 47 percent in Cornwall engaged in some form of by-employment in 1600–29 (Overton, Whittle, Dean and Hann 2004: 67–8). So, the rural economy was a diversified one, and that diversity reached inside particular households.

Martha Howell, following Tilly and Scott, draws a distinction between the rural household which was 'a family subsistence unit' and the urban household which produced for 'sale in the market place' (Howell 1986a: 28; Tilly and Scott 1987: 22). This contrast is overdrawn: most rural households were not primarily concerned with producing for their own consumption, even if they did produce some of their own food. Urban households might have been more market orientated, but also engaged in some subsistence production (such as keeping cows and pigs) except in the largest towns. Nonetheless, the occupational structure of towns was markedly different from that of villages, with an emphasis on crafts, trades and professions rather than farming. There were sharp differences of wealth between the wealthiest merchants and more humble craftsmen. As in the countryside, there was also a large population of wage earners. In her classic study of Lyon, France, Natalie Zemon Davis (1982) describes the gender division of labour in the urban economy. It was normal in the sixteenth century for apprenticeship and entry into the skilled crafts to be restricted to men. Daughters went into service or were trained informally at home. Wives helped husbands in their trades or, if that was not possible, worked for wages to supplement the family income. As widows, women often continued their husband's business, hiring journeymen and apprentices to carry out the men's work (also Collins 1989: 464).

Davis followed Alice Clark in presenting the family economy of craftsmen and tradesmen as a unified enterprise with husband and wife working in a single occupation whenever possible. Clark states that: 'in every business there are certain operations that can conveniently be performed by women, and when carried on at home within the compass of family life, the work of a trade was naturally sorted out between husband and wife' ([1919] 1982: 294). Tilly and Scott considered that 'the married couple was the "simple community of work, the elementary unit" in the preindustrial household' (1987: 43). The wife's role assisting her husband was seen as a consequence of urban guilds excluding women from apprenticeships. Widows' knowledge of crafts and trades was evident from the number of widows who continued to train apprentices and run businesses after the death of their husbands. For example, a comparison between the inventory of Humfry Holwill, a weaver from Uffculme, Devon, who died in 1613, with that of his widow, Florence Holwill, who died in 1624, shows many similarities. Humfry had three looms and three spinning wheels listed in his inventory, as well as four lengths of finished cloth. He also had hay, two cows, a pig and butter and cheese. We might expect Florence to have continued keeping cows and making cheese, a common form of women's work. But instead, during her widowhood, Florence abandoned farming and concentrated her household economy on weaving, a task which was not undertaken by women in Devon. She had two looms and one piece of new cloth in her house when she died, so must have employed journeymen or apprentices (Wyatt 1997: 39, 47).

Yet, many households deviated from this model of a unified business. In some households, husband and wife engaged in separate but complementary trades. For instance, butchers' wives were often chandlers, making candles from animal fat – a by-product of butchering (McIntosh 2005: 192). Merchants' wives might be silk women, trading in small silk goods, as in the case of Alice Barnham, wife of Francis Barnham of London, whose enterprise is so vividly reconstructed by Lena Cowen Orlin (2007). There were many men who worked for wages in other people's houses, such as building workers or journeymen in the crafts. There were also men who went to sea, as sailors and fishermen. Their wives could not assist or accompany them. Instead, they worked for wages, or as street vendors, or ran small businesses of their own. Clark saw wage-earning households of this type as a sign of the advent of capitalism, individualizing work and destroying the family economy. But these patterns of work had existed since the medieval period and should be recognized as one of many types of preindustrial household economy.

Recent research increasingly emphasizes the presence of households where husbands and wives followed different occupations, out of choice as well as necessity. Collins notes that: 'in sixteenth-century Rouen, 20 out of 36 linen merchants were women, not all widows carrying out their husband's trade, as one might expect, but for the most part single women or working wives' whose husbands had different occupations (1989: 455). In some large cities such as Cologne, there were separate guilds for women's occupations (Howell 1986a: 124). Alex Shepard, using evidence from English church courts, found many married women who claimed to live by their own labour or by separate means from their husband (Shepard 2015: 159–60). Similar evidence can be found when probate inventories for both husband and widow survive (Whittle 2014). Robert Biddle was a shoemaker in Stratford-upon-Avon, England, who died in 1597. His wife, Joan Biddle, was a brewer: her brewing equipment was listed in his inventory as well as hers, made when she died in 1614. Robert and Joan lived on Sheep Street, near the centre of the town, in a house leased from the corporation. The inventory and surviving architectural evidence from the town indicate that the Biddles' house was timber-framed with plaster infill, three stories high, with one front room and one back room on each floor. The ground floor consisted of a hall: their main living room, decorated with painted cloths and warmed by a hearth which also had pot hooks for cooking, and the kitchen, which Joan used for brewing. Upstairs was a parlour with a table and the best bed, and three more bed chambers. One of the attic chambers contained a spinning wheel and mustard mill, perhaps kept there for storage. Behind the house was a stable, a yard, a buttery and Robert's shoemaking workshop. The workshop was not listed in Joan's inventory: it is likely she had leased it out after his death, perhaps to another shoemaker (Jones 2002: 172–4, 285–7). The market town of Stratford-upon-Avon is particularly rich in examples of women following their own trades during the seventeenth century: as well as Joan Biddle, Alice Ainge, the wife of a butcher, was also a brewer; while Mary Edwards, Jane Tomlins and Elizabeth Palmer, whose husbands were a yeoman, tailor and blacksmith, were all maltsters (Whittle 2014: 295).

PAID WORKERS AND THE HOME

In October 1602, Richard Button a journeyman clothier from Cranbrook in Kent, was questioned about an illegal hunting expedition which had occurred the previous Saturday night. He described how he had spent the evening, first in the house of John Weller senior, an innkeeper (presumably drinking) until 9 p.m., then at his brother's house in Cranbrook, 'where he laid down in a bed in a chamber' (perhaps sleeping off the effects of the drinking), before returning home to the house of his master, the clothier John Weller junior. There, he shared a bed chamber with five other men. One of his room-mates, Alexander Weller junior, also gave evidence. Alexander was John Weller's younger brother, aged 22 at the time of the case. He shared a bed with William Reynolds and James Waters, both apprentices, while Richard Button shared another bed with two other apprentices, Richard Cramton and Thomas Kidder. On the night in question, he went to bed at 9 p.m., but was woken when Button came in at 2 a.m. On the orders of his master, Button called Reynolds to go outside and remove a cloth from the tenter-rack where it was being stretched, in case it was stolen, and then went to sleep. When questioned about the mud on his stockings, Alexander said the stockings belonged to James Waters, who had been out driving some of his master's bullocks to water at 6 p.m. the previous evening (Knafla 1994: 176). Thus, it seems likely that the household of John Weller junior included not only John and his wife and children, and perhaps one or two female servants, but also six young men who worked in his cloth workshop and on his farm.

One of the most striking differences between modern households and those between 1450 and 1650 is that the historic households often contained live-in workers: servants and apprentices (Whittle 2017). Early modern servants should not be imagined as equivalent to nineteenth-century domestic servants. They did whatever work needed doing in the household economy: that might include cooking, cleaning and childcare, but also agricultural tasks and other forms of production (Figure 5.4). Servants were workers who lived with their employer and were paid largely with food and accommodation, usually with the addition to a small cash wage and sometimes clothing. They were normally employed for six months or a year at a time. Apprenticeships were a slightly different arrangement. The family of the apprentice paid a premium to the master or mistress for providing training in a specialist craft, and the apprentice lived and worked in a master's household for a longer period: usually seven years. The majority of servants and apprentices fell into the same demographic group: they were young unmarried people aged between their mid-teens and late twenties.

FIGURE 5.4: *The Egg Seller* by Joachim Beuckelaer, 1563–84. Wikimedia Commons, public domain.

In the language of the time, servants and apprentices were part of the family (Tadmor 1996). Household advice manuals assumed these workers would be present and described their subservient position, similar to that of children, at the beck and call of their master and mistress. Their subservience was enforced by law, which placed servants and apprentices under the legal guardianship and control of their master (or mistress in a female-headed household). At its worst, the relationship between servants and employer could be claustrophobic and abusive. Court records document servants who were beaten, raped, starved and denied their wages. At its best, however, servants did seem to have become part of the family. Not only did many servants receive bequests in their employer's wills, but servants who had the misfortune to die young typically also left bequests to their employers. Some servants worked in particular households for ten years or more, despite the fact they were free to leave and find employment elsewhere.

Servants and apprentices are found across Europe from at least the late medieval period onwards. England's Poll Tax returns of 1377–81, record servants as between 7 percent and 25 percent of the taxed population (aged over 14) in rural England and between 6 and 30 percent in towns (Goldberg 1992: 370–1; Poos 1991: 187). They continued to be numerous in the early modern period, for instance in the parish of Ealing, 13 kilometres outside London, servants made up 24 percent of the total population in 1599, although this was an unusually high due to the number of wealthy households just outside the capital (Whittle 2005a: 59). In early seventeenth-century Kent, 15 percent of probate accounts record wages owing to servants (ibid.: 55). Servants were 13 percent of the population of the Danish island of Moen in 1645, and 6 percent of the population of the village of Montplaisant in southern France in 1644 (Laslett 1977: 32–3). In Upper Austria, Rebel found that 56 percent of households in the rural parish of Berndorf contained servants in 1649 and 34 percent of Dorfbeuern's in 1648 (Rebel 1983: 48), while Poska found that 28 percent of households in the Galician parish of Souto de Vigo had servants in 1587 (2005: 59). For Venice, Romano notes that 33–43 percent of households employed servants in the 1590s (1996: 112). The ratio of male to female servants varied. Male servants often (but not always) outnumbered female servants in the countryside, while women outnumbered men in towns where men often entered apprenticeship rather than service. Venice was an exception, where large numbers of male servants were employed as a mark of status, as happened in the households of the gentry and aristocracy across Europe (ibid.).

Servants and apprentices became part of the household economy and had to be accommodated in the house. Small farms in northern England typically employed one female servant if any. Roger Alderson of Grinton in Swaledale, North Yorkshire, left a milk cow to his servant, Katherine Alderson, when he made his will in the mid-sixteenth century. As she shared his surname, it is possible Katherine was related to Roger; however, Roger described her simply as 'my servant'. He also left bequests to his wife and children, so he was not without close family. Sixteenth-century probate inventories indicate a very basic living environment in Swaledale's upland farms, with no houses surviving to the present day. Most dwellings consisted of a single living room, and inventories demonstrate that the majority of movable wealth consisted of livestock rather than domestic goods. It seems likely that Katherine helped to care for cows and sheep, milking and making cheese and butter, as well as spinning wool: the main elements of the local economy, although she may also have helped care for the family's children. She would have slept in the same room as the rest of the family. Sarah Thompson, a Kent widow who died in 1645 was wealthier than Roger Alderson, but, with seven children under the age of eleven, must have needed help with childcare. She also employed one female servant. Nevertheless, Sarah's inventory also records cattle, horses, cows, sheep, pigs and husbandry equipment worth £80, indicating that there was also farming work to be done (Whittle 2005a: 65).

Wealthier households, like that of the Kent clothier John Weller, could be numerically dominated by servants and apprentices. Robert Loder, a prosperous farmer in Berkshire, England, in the early seventeenth century, employed five servants, three men and two women, to run his farm and household in the 1610s. He had a wife and a growing family of three young children, but the adults in the house were mostly employees. While Loder's male servants worked in arable agriculture and carted produce to market, the female servants made malt, milked cows, and picked and sold fruit, for instance travelling to market every day when cherries were in season (Whittle 2005b). Henry Best, a minor gentleman who ran a large farm in Yorkshire, describes employing eight servants, six men and two women, in his farming memorandum book. He built a new nine-roomed house of three stories in the 1630s (Woodward 1984). Even with this space, given he had six children of his own, it seems likely some of the male servants slept in the barns rather than the house itself. A steadily increasing proportion of Kent houses recorded in probate inventories had at least one bedroom described as a 'servants' chamber', growing from 6 percent in the early seventeenth century to 21 percent in the early eighteenth (Overton 2004: 125). More commonly, however, servants shared rooms and even beds, with not only other servants but family members (Flather 2007), as happened in the Weller household.

THE HOUSE AS A PLACE OF WORK

In his memoirs, the wealthy Devon farmer, Robert Furse, recorded the extensive improvements he made to his manor house, Moorshead in Dean Prior, Devon, in the second half of the sixteenth century. Furse enlarged his hall, sealed it (that is, added a ceiling) and glazed the windows, as well as adding a porch. He turned the kitchen into a parlour and built a new kitchen. He also added numerous specialist rooms and buildings to accommodate work activities: a dairy, a cart-house, a rebuilt and enlarged bake-house with a new oven, a new barn and a cider house (Travers 2010: 72–3). The house no longer survives, but mid-twentieth century drawings show a long, rectangular farm house of two stories, one room in depth, built of stone, with the large barn and service wing adjoining it at right angles. It was certainly larger than most Devon farms, but its vernacular style and the fact it was primarily a working farm set it apart from the houses of the county gentry. The house asserted Furze's status as a prosperous farmer, rather than any pretensions to higher status.

The history of preindustrial work located within the physical structure of the house is still very largely unwritten. A lot is known about the types of work people did, and a fair amount about whether it was carried out inside or outside, but economic historians have shown little interest in where exactly work was carried out, in relation to the houses people actually occupied. There is a rich specialist literature by archaeologists and architectural historians about the ordinary or vernacular buildings of the late medieval and early modern period. Unfortunately, this tends to be very regionally specific. As a result, the following section only considers the case of England, but suggests avenues future research might pursue in other European regions.

The typical English house of the late medieval period, occupied by anyone from the gentry to humble husbandmen, was a hall house. The archaeologist, Matthew Johnson (1993b), has emphasized the openness of these houses. The main room or hall, was a large double-heighted space, open to the rafters. At its centre lay an open hearth, without a chimney. The windows were unglazed, and open to the elements. The main door typically entered directly into the hall, and faced the back door, allowing people to see right through the house. This is, more or less, the type of house we see illustrated in the Brueghel painting. The ease with which people (and animals) passed from inside to outside, house to farm, indicates a closer relationship between the house and farm than later dwelling houses allowed. In some regions, houses were shared with the farm animals. In the long-houses of medieval and early modern Devon and Cornwall, cattle were housed in a 'shippon' on one side of the entry cross-passage, while the hall was located on the other (Alcock 2015: 15). Examples of small 'mixed' farmhouses, where people and livestock shared a single room were still found in parts of France in the nineteenth and early twentieth century (Chapelot and Fossier 1985: 223–38).

In sixteenth-century England, vernacular houses underwent significant changes. In 1577, William Harrison's *Description of England* noted 'the multitude of chimneys lately erected' and 'the great amendment of lodging' ([1577] 1698, 1994: 240). W.G. Hoskins expanded on these observations, arguing that a 'Great

Rebuilding' of rural England took place between 1570 and 1640 (1953: 44). New chimneys allowed not only the addition of window glazing, but also the hall to be sealed over to create more upstairs rooms. Specialist kitchens were added to many houses for the first time. It is hard to find an example of a wealthy English farmer who did not rebuild or remodel his farmhouse in this period. Robert Loder in Berkshire, noted in his farm accounts 'the money laid out about my chimney', with payments to the masons for building it, as well as the cost of making stairs, a new window, ceilings and plastering, all in 1618 (Fussell 1936: 157). Henry Best in Yorkshire built a completely new house out of brick.

Maurice Barley notes that 'the multiplication on service rooms in the yeoman's house was the most striking development of the first half of the seventeenth century' (1967: 741). Service rooms, such as the kitchen, milk-house, bake-house, malt-house, brew-house and wash-house, were specialist work spaces. Gervase Markham included a diagram 'model of a plain country man's house' in his 1613 book *The English Husbandman* (Figure 5.5). It was a large 'H'-shaped building, with the hall forming the central axis between two substantial wings. The south wing was devoted to non-work activities but the ground floor of the north wing was devoted solely to service rooms, containing a buttery, larder, kitchen, dairy and milk-house. The popularity of service rooms is also evident in probate inventories. A sample of over one thousand

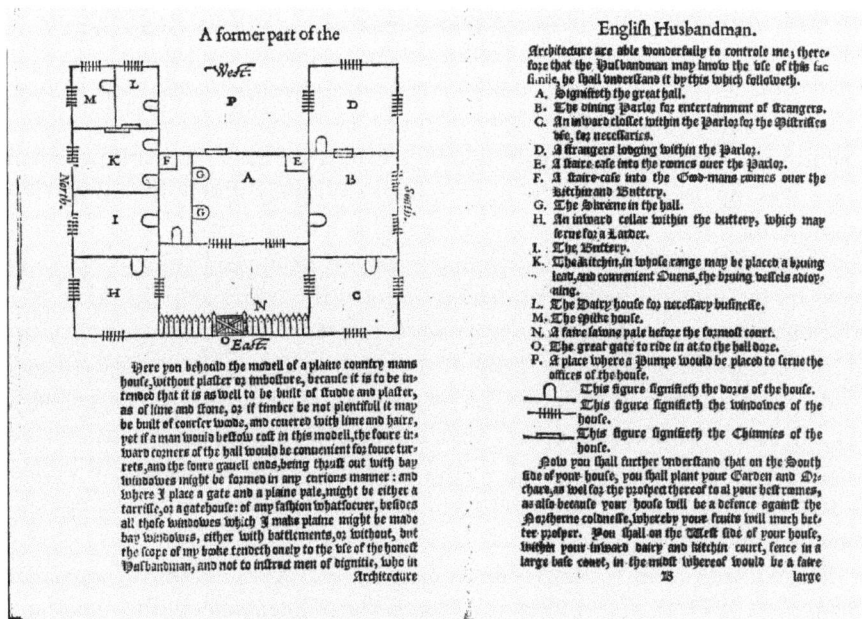

FIGURE 5.5: House plan from Gervase Markham's *English Husbandman*, 1613. Early English Books Online (EEBO), public domain.

probate inventories from early seventeenth-century Kent reveal that by that date 48 percent of houses had a kitchen and 46 percent at least one other service room, 35 percent had a milk-house and 10 percent a brew-house. Urban houses experienced similar trends. Large open halls were sealed over and the number of rooms increased. The houses of middling and wealthy town-dwellers saw the proliferation of service rooms. As we have seen, the house of Robert Biddle, a shoemaker in Stratford upon Avon, had a kitchen, buttery, stable and workshop. The house of Thomas Bird, a wealthy tailor and draper in central Exeter contained a kitchen, buttery, milk chamber, working shop, cloth shop, wool shop and stable, as well as hall, parlour, gallery and four bedchambers when he died in 1577 (Osborne 2016: 340–5).

Barley explains the proliferation of service rooms in terms of the desire for a more comfortable living space: 'men and their families wished to have some rooms for use not cluttered with churns, tubs and other utensils' (1967: 741). He considered it natural for people to want separate spaces for work and leisure within their home. Yet, it is significant that changes in English vernacular architecture prioritized workspaces in at least an equal degree to living spaces. How did these changes affect work and living patterns within the house? Did a new kitchen mean that the housewife was demoted from her position at the centre of house, by the hearth in the middle of the hall, into a back room away from the main social interactions? Or did the centre of the house move with her, leaving the hall as a moribund space stripped of its activities and purpose (Pennell 2016: 133–5)? Certainly, by the eighteenth century, in many houses the hall was simply an entrance space where the stairs are located, as it is in houses today. Or is it wrong to see women's work as centred on the kitchen in the first place? The limited evidence available about how room spaces were used in this period suggests flexible and fluid patterns of use. We have seen that Joan Biddle used her kitchen for a commercial brewing enterprise, but the household still had pot hooks by the hearth in their hall so that family meals could be prepared there. Nor was it always women who cooked, a quarter session case from Knook in Wiltshire, in 1622, records a man who not only stole and butchered a sheep for his family to eat, but 'put part thereof into the pot over the fire to make broth and some provision for his wife being great with child and three children which remained upon his charges'. Kitchens were not only used for food production. Pennell (ibid.) notes that kitchens were the common location of weapons in most houses: the coroners' inquests for Somerset in 1591 record one John Gaylarde, who was standing by the fire in his master's kitchen, cleaning a gun, when it went off by mistake.

While specialist work rooms were becoming more common, they were by no means ubiquitous in the early seventeenth century. Barnard Tucker was a weaver-farmer from Uffculme in Devon whose movable goods in his probate inventory were valued at just over £68 when he died in 1613, only two years after marriage. He and his wife, Joan, had one young child and another on the way, but the household was certainly larger than this. Not only did it contain three beds, but there was too much work to be done by a married couple alone, particularly with one young child and the wife pregnant. Men's work is evident from two weaving looms, wheat sown in the fields, hay in the barn; women's work from a spinning wheel, two milk cows, a pig and poultry, flitches of bacon, cheeses and two brewing vats; there was also a flock of 52 sheep to be cared for (Figure 5.6). It is likely the couple employed at least one male apprentice weaver, and a female servant to do house and farm work. The Tuckers lived in a well-furnished but relatively small house of four or five rooms. Although it is not possible to link the inventory to any particular house, a number of houses survive in Uffculme from this period. They have thick walls of cob (clay with straw) on a base of stone-rubble and are roofed with thatch. The Tuckers' house had two downstairs rooms. The main living room, the hall, was used for dining, leisure and cooking: as this was the only room with a hearth it was probably used for brewing as well. The other downstairs room, the buttery, was typically used for storage and food preparation in farmhouses but in the Tucker household

FIGURE 5.6: *A Woman Spinning* by Adriaen van Ostade, 1652. © The Hulton Archive/Getty Images.

was a cloth-making workshop. It contained two looms and a spinning wheel, in addition to storage vessels and the brewing vats. Upstairs were 'the chambers', two or perhaps three rooms contained the beds and chests of clothing and linen. These rooms were also used for storing cheeses and newly woven cloth (Whittle 2011; Wyatt 1997). There is little evidence of specialist workspaces: all the rooms had a number of functions. Nor is there any evidence of architectural difference between the houses of weaver-farmers and those who made a living from farming alone in Uffculme.

Barnard Tucker's house was typical of weavers in rural Devon, where no weaving workshops are evident in surviving inventories before the second half of the seventeenth century. In rural Kent, however, out of thirty inventories which mentioned looms in the first half the seventeenth century, in twenty-seven cases the looms located in a specialist workshop, although two were in a hall and one in a barn. Urban weavers also seem to have had specialist workshops within which to work their looms from an early date. John Dysell was a poor weaver from Oxford, whose inventory was made in 1587. He lived in a three-room house with a hall containing a table and seating, decorated with a single painted cloth; a chamber that combined as a bedroom and cooking area, and a 'shop' which contained only his '2 narrow looms with their appurtenances'. The looms were his most valuable possessions, worth £2 out of a total inventory value of £3 18s. 8d. (Havinden 1965: 250). Exeter weavers also had 'shops' containing looms as part of their dwelling houses in the late sixteenth century (Crocker 2016: 83, 187).

CONCLUSION

While the advice literature presents a simple dichotomous model of men outside and women inside, actual households and patterns of work show every possible variation. Each household economy had its own relationship to the home. Shops and workshops for selling and making goods were often integral to the dwelling house. On the other hand, many goods were sold at market stalls or by street sellers, taking the work away from the home. Just as farmers used the farm house as their headquarters, but were often absent working in the fields or travelling to market, so merchants were based at home, but were often away on business. Given that many women earned wages or followed their own trades, it cannot be assumed urban women were tied to the house any more than rural women were. The important difference with the modern world was not that all work was located in the home, but that there was rarely an alternative work-building that people travelled to each day. Either people worked in a house (their own or someone else's) or they worked outside. Men and women did both.

The late medieval and early modern house was a much more porous space than modern houses. Routine tasks spilled out of the house in the case of collecting water and doing washing. Farm animals might be housed inside with people. Other animals wandered into the house despite not belonging there. Hanawalt (1986) notes accidents in medieval England caused by chickens lifting burning embers from the open hearth, while sixteenth-century coroners' rolls record the consequences of pigs entering kitchens. Nor were houses necessarily places of privacy. Not only were walls often flimsy and conversations easily overheard, as emphasized in Orlin's (2007) study of late-sixteenth-century London, but people were frequently invited into each other's houses to do business. A Devon court case records a woman who 'came into the house of Maud Leighe' in the village of Sidbury, 'to buy a cheese': this must have been one among very many small commercial transactions which took place every day in the English countryside. And this was aside from the many thousands of people who ran retail shops, inns and taverns, or offered lodgings in their homes.

Before the late eighteenth century, 'the economy' was the household economy. The home was the expected location of work and business. There is some indication, however, that an increasing architectural division was taking place within the home between specialist work spaces and rooms intended for sleep, leisure and socializing. When wealthy farmers rebuilt or modernized their houses in the late sixteenth and early seventeenth centuries, they incorporated numerous service rooms: kitchens, dairies, brew-houses and bake-houses intended for specialist work activities. In areas of textile production, weaving workshops became more common. But these changes were patchy, and probate inventories suggest a pattern of mixed usage, and great variation locally and regionally. More research is needed to place patterns of work within the house, and examine how this changed and varied in the centuries before work was removed from home, before we can fully understand the place of work in the late medieval and early modern house.

CHAPTER SIX

Gender and Home

AMANDA FLATHER

Gender and home were intimately linked in Renaissance theoretical constructions of patriarchal order (Sommerville 1995). Despite fiercely fought confessional conflicts during the Reformation, Catholic and Protestant theologians all agreed that order in families, and by extension within wider society, required adherence to a classical doctrine that assigned a public role to men and confined women within the domestic sphere. The principle was simply summarized by the Spanish Catholic theologian, Fray Luis, when he asserted that 'just as men are made for public things, so women are made to be shut away' and by the English puritan preacher, Henry Smith, who declared that husbands and wives should see themselves as like the cock and the dam: 'the cock flyeth abroad to bring in and the dam sitteth upon the nest to keep all at home' (Smith 1591: 43; Léon [1583] 1999: 219). Within this system, the roles and spaces of the husband and wife were clear and distinct. The husband and master was required to wield absolute dominion over the house and household and take charge of 'public' affairs, which included the fields, business and the holding of political office. The wife had to be subject and obedient to him, focusing her attention solely upon the ordering of the house.

The ideology rested on a definition of the 'natural' characteristics of women and men derived from classical thought, Christian ideology and contemporary science and medicine that determined that women were physically, emotionally and morally weaker than men and were best suited to staying at home. Puritan divines were especially exercised by the dangers of female freedom. Thomas Gataker (1620: sig. F4) was one amongst many clergymen who warned that, 'Where the wife be not subject to her husband, to let him rule all the household, especially outward affaires; if she will make against him, and seeke to have her own wayes, there will be doing and undoing. Things will go backward, the house will come to ruine.' But Catholic commentators and popular axioms echoed these themes. A Provencal proverb stated that: 'The household is going very badly when the hen plays the cock,' and a Catalonian adage asserted: 'Neither trousers for the woman nor skirts for the man (Segalen 1984: 128, 156–7).

Historians have long argued that this rhetoric of 'spheres' was very powerful, but it was an ideal that was not a perfect framework for the organization of human affairs in the sixteenth and seventeenth centuries. While women were excluded from legal, political and religious positions of power in Renaissance society, there was no rigorous segregation of the sexes for everyday activities. During the period between 1450 and 1650, there were some shifts in the organization of the domestic interiors of middling and elite groups from hall-based houses to specialized rooms in most parts of Europe, as Chapters 3 and 5 have explained, and some scholars have suggested that these architectural improvements led to significant changes in the ways that homes were controlled and relations between the people who lived in them. As specialized service areas proliferated, women and servants were ousted from the 'front', 'public' living spaces of the hall and parlour and relegated, marginalized and 'privatized' to the 'back' spaces of the kitchen and service areas around the yard. Homes were increasingly segregated with respect to gender and status and the consequence, it is argued, was a progressive marginalization and subordination of women's authority and influence within and beyond the domestic sphere (Johnson 1996: 163–6).

Newer research based on different sources that has attempted to recover spatial experience has revealed a more complex reality. Specialization of space did occur and, by the seventeenth century, many houses had single-function rooms like kitchens on the ground floor and bedchambers on upper levels (see Chapter 3). But the demands of work and housewifery, especially in ordinary one- or two-roomed homes, meant that segregation of space was rarely possible or practical. Apprentices, servants, masters, mistresses, their children, neighbours and customers coexisted and went about their daily tasks without strict patterns of spatial segregation or control (Flather 2007: 39–74; Chojnacka 2001: 125–8). In Spain, for instance, where women in respectable households were meant to be sheltered from the street, they were in constant communication with the world beyond the house through their servants. A good example is a case involving Don Fernando de Aguilar in Ecija in 1612. One man was objected to as a witness, because 'he had dealings with a black woman who nursed some of Don Fernando's children . . . and he is in the service of a kinsman of the said Don Fernando, for which reason he has regular entry into Don Fernando's house' (Casey 1999: 212). Elite Mediterranean women were probably confined at home but they were few in number. Northern aristocratic families cared little about restricting their women and ordinary families in all regions could not afford to keep women at home (ibid.; Chojnacka: 2001). Renaissance marriages were economic partnerships, characterized by interdependence and companionship. Studies of marriage and masculinity have also highlighted the ways in which household work strategies blurred boundaries between male and female spheres of activity and the importance of the home as a space of work for both men and women (Shepard: 2003). Depending on occupation, there could be considerable overlap in terms of the tasks and spaces in which male and female work was performed.

Yet, a lack of segregation within Renaissance homes does not mean that there is not still much to know about the relationship between gender and the domestic interior. Studies of different spaces in modern societies have shown how they can be gendered, even when they are shared, through perception, experience and use. These theoretical contributions have helpfully suggested that spaces are social as well as material, conceptual as well as physical and inseparable from issues of power of one kind or another (Massey 1994: 185–6). They suggest that analysis of the organization of the integration of the activities of men and women within domestic spaces that were shared in everyday social practice can offer important insights into the operation of gender as a social force in Renaissance culture.

It is, of course, important to recognize complexities and variations of household form. Homes contained complex and variable groups of people in shifting association to one another. Spatial and social relationships altered according to levels of wealth, location, age and occupation. They also varied along with the time of day, season of the year, the life cycle and because of economic or demographic crises. Home meant something different for adult women in Perigord in southern France, for example, where a new wife might live with her mother-in-law, than in England where families tended to be simpler, and encompassed one married couple, children and probably servants and a wife was answerable to no one but her husband (O'Day 1994: 171; Wrightson 1982: 44–5). In addition, more households in most regions of Europe and North America included servants of both sexes than had previously been assumed, emphasizing that an understanding of the influence of gender on experience of home requires not just a consideration of women and men, but also an analysis of the spatial relationships between and among the different individuals of both sexes of varying age and status who lived together under one roof (Sarti 2005a).

Yet, despite these complexities, the home was the most important arena in Renaissance society in all regions within which crucial distinctions between the relative roles and status of different categories of men and women were organized and defined on the basis of age, marital and social status. An understanding of the ways in which different types of men and women experienced and used the homes that they shared can expose how gender intersected with the other hierarchies that ordered the domestic world in ways that complicate the polarized picture of relations between men and women presented by prescriptive literature and subsequently by historians who have relied upon it.

This chapter explores the intersection between prescription and these more messy realities of the spatial organization of the integration of the activities of daily domestic life. Focusing on English sources but drawing where possible on comparative evidence from Europe and North America, it examines the influence of gender on patterns of control of early modern homes and on the organization of domestic spaces for the everyday activities of eating and sleeping that required the sharing of space by household members. It argues that when we look more closely at the organization, even of small houses belonging to ordinary people, we find that spatial use and organization did reflect and reinforce social stratification. But gender was only one amongst a range of social factors that competed to determine experience of the family home.

CONTROL

To properly understand the influence of gender on patterns of control of the Renaissance home the legal context must first be considered. Men were meant to be responsible for overall domestic management and their prerogative of control was recognized in law. Women and men in Renaissance society were in a different legal position with respect to the properties in which they lived because laws pertaining to property ownership were highly gendered in this period. Wives in England were perhaps the most disadvantaged because there, according to common law, a married woman was termed a *feme covert*, which meant that, upon marriage, her legal identity was subsumed by her husband and thereafter she had no legally enforceable rights of ownership of the property in which she lived (Sommerville 1995: 97–105). Admittedly, this was not the whole story. Equity and ecclesiastical law in England moderated and protected the interests of some wealthy married women against these common law disadvantages. Their families made settlements that protected personal property that women had brought to the marriage (Erickson 1993). Women were also in a better position in some areas of Roman law – Spain and France, for example, because property brought to the marriage became community property and wives could make wills to dispose of their own property. Portuguese women enjoyed equal inheritance rights with men and, in Galicia, daughters inherited their parent's property in exchange for care in old age (Poska 2005: 112–24). Scholars have also found that in Sweden, Spanish and Portuguese America, and Virginia, women used a variety of local institutions and customs that gave them substantial legal and proprietary rights. But, broadly speaking, while some women were able to manipulate their own property holdings when married, the houses in which they lived were legally controlled by the husband (Warner 2013: 228). The English proverb that stated that an Englishman's home was his castle was essentially correct. A married woman's legal position in Renaissance society was rarely equal to that of her husband. The house in which she lived was literally *his* (Coke 1651: 221–3).

The male head of household also had legal power to exercise control over his wife's access to and use of the home in several ways. He could use a measure of violence to enforce obedience. He could expel his wife from her house if she committed or was suspected to have committed adultery. For example, William Collins turned his wife Isobel out of doors, after her alleged extramarital affair and William Wheeler of South Weald expelled his wife because she 'used such company that he liked not of, and he often warned her to forbear and she would not' (Emmison 1973: 163; ERO/D/ABD2). By the end of the period, English law also established a limited right to chastise a wife by confinement if a husband believed his wife kept 'bad company' or was being extravagant. Women did not possess comparable legal powers to limit their husband's autonomy or to put away unfaithful husbands, although they could seek a separation, if extreme cruelty could be proved (Foyster 2002: 42–6). This unequal power between spouses was graphically displayed in cases of domestic abuse, where the advantages possessed by husbands in terms of their physical strength, their property rights and their legal entitlement to control and to discipline the movements of their wives meant that they held the balance of power in conflicts over control. It was always the wife who was thrown out. For example, a Sussex villager inflicted cruelty and humiliation on his wife by locking her out of the house while he had sex with their maid in the marital bed, and thereafter relegated his wife to a spare room (Capp 2003: 92). Robert Jordan, tallow chandler of Barking, threw his wife, Sarah, out of the house after the birth of their first child (LMA/DL/C/254: 140v), and another violent and unfaithful husband, John Hayward, moved his mistress into his house and forced his wife, Dorothy, out in 1644 (ERO/Q/SBa 2/56).

Yet, while the basic assumption governing the organization of the early modern home, underpinning attitudes and backed by law, was that absolute authority was invested in male household heads, the 'sovereign' power of the male householder was never absolute and mitigated by a variety of legal, social, cultural and economic factors. Ideals were undermined, first by demographic facts. Roughly 20 percent of households in large cities such as London and Geneva, parts of rural Spain, small towns in France and North America were headed by widows or single women, who exercised full legal authority over their homes and their resources (Wall 1981: 303–17; Bennett and Froide 1999). In some regions of Italy, south-western Germany and Scandinavia, the property rights of single women and widows were circumscribed, but in England, colonial North America, Spain, Portugal, the Low Countries and France, single women and widows were endowed with the capacity to own and control the properties in which they lived and to take legal action to defend those rights in court (Warner 2013: 228).

The reality that the majority of people in pre-modern society did not own their own homes also created problems for the patriarchal model. The type of tenure agreed with a landlord had a significant effect on the ability of a householder to control access to his own home. Copyhold tenants, for example, in sixteenth-century England, were more insecure than leaseholders, and their contracts could be terminated at the will of their landlord with very little notice, so that even those men who seemed relatively well set up in life might have to move around a great deal (O'Day 1994: 136). But gender could have a part to play in this. A study of serfdom in areas of Bohemia has shown that manorial courts were far more likely to evict female tenants than male. Although 4 percent of the tenants were widowed women, they were the subject of 15 percent of the eviction cases. And while male tenants were mainly evicted for serious offences such as disobedience to their lord, female tenants were evicted for debt or for no discernible reason (Ogilvie 2000: 986). Of course, men and women lacking money or property lived even more insecure lives. Without regular income, many poor people of both sexes slept on the street or in an outhouse. Alternatively they might take a room in an alehouse or lodging house for a night if they earned the money to pay for it. But the complicities of gender and class are also apparent here, in that single or widowed women represented a significant proportion of the lodgers, sub-tenants and homeless in large cities and towns (Sarti 2002: 13; Baer 2000: 13–39).

Even in more stable families, the ideal of absolute male authority was undermined by moral and political stress on the importance of the ordered household for social and political stability which blurred boundaries between public and private power. The borders of early modern houses had considerable social, legal, metaphysical and gendered significance, and legal regulations limited official intervention into household affairs (Wilson 2013: 4–10). But belief in the patriarchal family as the bedrock of social order meant that the internal affairs of households were considered to be a matter of legitimate 'public' interest, which meant that in Renaissance society, the male head did not have absolute autonomy and control over the organization of his household any more than did his wife. The Church, the state, the law and local community had an interest in organizing the relationships within the home and intervened actively to maintain them. The extent of community surveillance varied according to status, region and local economic and population structures. In England, it was perfectly permissible for neighbours to spy through windows or cracks in walls to secure proof of sexual misdoings, if conditions were considered serious or blatant enough. There were also a range of circumstances in which the secular and ecclesiastical courts were permitted to enter privately owned domestic spaces without the consent of the owner. Suspicion of illegal activities taking place in a private dwelling might prompt official intervention. The constable was also permitted to make forcible entry if he had cause to suspect that the crime of adultery or fornication was being committed inside the house. Justices of the Peace could issue warrants to constables empowering them to enter houses and arrest 'all nightwalkers', especially those keeping 'suspicious company' at night-time. State officials could intervene in domestic relations in extreme cases of marital cruelty or disharmony on the grounds that the peace of the neighbourhood was being disrupted (Amussen 1988: 34–66; Casey 1999: 192–220; Hardwick 2010: 86–9). For example, in Neuchatel, in 1604, David Tissot Robert was imprisoned for three days because he spent his money on drink while his wife and children starved (Watt 1992: 150–1).

Gendered patterns of authority within the home were also complicated by systems of day-to-day domestic management. The position of the wife was always contradictory, since, according to law and ideology, she was a partner, manager and dependent, powerful in relation to her subordinates while owing subjection and obedience to her husband. One of the most influential Catholic theorists on marriage, the Spanish Dominican Vicente Mexia, in his *Salutary Instruction on the State of Marriage* (1566), argued forcefully that: 'the wife was not a slave or servant, but a free woman, lady of the house, and estate and goods and whatever he has, with the one obligation of obeying him' (Kamen 2000: 162). Protestant conduct books also revealed a tension between their insistence on male authority and their acceptance that, within the family, the wife exercised a joint authority over children and servants. The English Puritan, William Gouge, asserted that wives and mistresses were 'joint governors' with husbands and masters 'over all the inferiors' and that husbands and wives, masters and mistresses should exercise authority over subordinate children and servants of both sexes (1622: 485).

In these texts, the home was not represented simply as a school of female subordination; it was also constructed as an arena of female government. Entrenched within the elite and popular mind was a belief that the proper government of the household depended upon the maintenance of three hierarchies: gender, age and marital status. Husbands ruled over wives; masters *and* mistresses ruled over servants and fathers *and* mothers over children. The hierarchy of gender was only one in a complex configuration of obligations that ordered the family home. Male moralists set out a division of 'duties' that assigned responsibility and considerable authority to married women with regard to control of their domestic spaces. Oliver Serres, the seventeenth-century French author of an agricultural manual, explained that: 'The affairs of the fields belong to the husband, those of the house to the wife' (Collins 1989: 441). Domestic female authority was also sanctioned by popular culture. Men who interfered with day-to-day domestic duties were derided as 'cotqueens'. Inversion ballads like *The Woman to the Plow and the Man to the Hen-Roost* depict the chaos that ensued when a man meddled in domestic management (Mendelson and Crawford 1998: 205).

In reality, roles were not so polarized and men and women were both involved in management of the home but in different ways and to different degrees. Men were assumed to be in overall charge. Indeed, recent studies of men and masculinity have demonstrated how the house and home contributed to men's social and gender identities. Stable financial administration as well as maintenance of domestic authority provided a means by which middling sort men could claim status and citizenship in the wider world (Shepard 2003; Foyster 1999b; Hardwick 2010: 91). It is difficult to establish how far these manly values of domesticity were shared across the social spectrum but it seems that similar qualities were prized amongst the English gentry (Rothery and French 2012: 120). Studies of gender and consumption have shown that the home was an important symbol of the wealth, taste and values by which elite men were judged by their peers (Fletcher 1995). While some women were involved in architectural projects, more often men took control of the design and commissioning of building work. For example, the seventeenth-century English gentleman, Hamon Le Strange, controlled the expenditure for rebuilding and remodelling the family house, which was an important symbol of his status and masculine authority. He left responsibility for control of domestic accounts and supply of the day-to-day needs of the household to his wife, Alice (Whittle and Griffiths 2012: 203–9).

Interconnected but complimentary managerial roles can be discerned at all social levels. Men took charge of broader responsibilities but the day-to-day management of the home was largely left to women. While the duty could be a heavy burden, it also offered wives a degree of domestic power, especially where it involved control over finances. Responsibilities were most complex in large and wealthy households, where married women controlled the purchase and storage of vast quantities of food, clothing, linen and sometimes furniture as well as the supervision of servants (Whittle and Griffiths 2012). But lower down the social scale, in manufacturing trades, for example, it was often the wife who ran the retail side of the enterprise while her husband worked in the workshop. She also kept the books and even collected the debts (Figure 6.1). Business accounts show that record-keeping was often left to the wives or sometimes daughters of merchants (Howell 1986a: 200). An example is Magdalena, the wife of Balthasar Paumgartner, a wealthy sixteenth-century merchant from Nuremburg. While her husband was away buying textiles and other goods in Italy and selling them at Frankfurt fairs, Magdalena became his book-keeper, distributor and collection agency (Ozment 1986: 72–3). Farmers' wives were also often financial managers, who kept charge of family money and were responsible for the discharge of household bills. William Stout, who grew up on a small estate in the north-west of England in the late seventeenth century,

FIGURE 6.1: *The Account Keeper* by Nicolaes Maes (1634–93), Dutch, 1656. Museum Purchase 72:1950. © Saint Louis Art Museum, Museum Purchase 72:1950.

recalls that his industrious mother was 'not only fully imployed in housewifery but in dressing their corn for the market, and also in the fields in hay and corn harvests, along with our father and our servants'. She also added to the estate through land investment while her husband was alive ([1665–1752] 1967: 68). Married women in urban and rural areas were also active in the credit market both as creditors and debtors, selling and buying plots of land in the land market, renting land and houses, and in various other business transactions (Macfarlane 1976: 266, 267, 272; Hardwick 2010: 94).

Wherever the men of the family had to work away from home, the domestic power of women was likely to be relatively emphasized. This has been observed in Galicia, for example, where the seasonal migration of the male population was a feature of social and economic life, and the home and its land was run by the women (Poska 2005). Several studies of elite households in Northern and Southern Europe have also shown that because husbands were often away from home on political or commercial business, their wives were left to manage the estate (Moody 1998; Dewald 2015). In these circumstances, a wife was expected to be an expert not only in the management of the household, including the domestic accounts, the procurement of food and clothing and the direction of servants as well as the care of children, but she might also have to handle complex business affairs on behalf of her husband. In extraordinary circumstances such as war, the wife was the natural substitute for her husband. For example, while the Norfolk gentleman, Thomas Knyvett, was kept away from home by the exigencies of civil war in the 1640s, he told his wife, 'I know I cannot have a better steward than thyselfe to manage our affaiers' (Schofield 1949: 110). But even in more everyday circumstances, women often took charge of household accounts. For example, the sixteenth-century French nobleman, Jean de Parthenay-Larchevesque, was widely admired for his industry and business acumen but he was quite happy to leave the management of his household and its financial affairs to his wife (Dewald 2015: 145).

Where servants were part of the household, women's authority was also reinforced. While the master was legally responsible for subordinates, married women took day-to-day charge of their management and supervision. Mistresses decided when servants would be sent on errands or ordered to stay indoors. They also had the right and the obligation to administer physical correction to enforce obedience. Distinctions in corporal punishment of maidservants and man-servants were recommended in so far as several writers expressed the view that it was fitting for the 'master' to correct men-servants and the mistress to 'correct' maidservants. But impropriety did not equate with lesser authority, and treatises on domestic government repeatedly restated the principle that obedience, reverence and respect were due in equal measure to 'masters, mistresses and dames' (Dod and Cleaver 1612: sig. Z1). Legal records also confirm that women were not only willing to beat their servants, sometimes for the most minor of misdemeanours, but that some were fully capable of cruelty (Ulrich 1980: 187). A pamphlet of 1680 records the case of Sarah Bell, brought to trial at the Chelmsford Assizes for the murder of her twelve-year-old servant. She had apparently thrown a knife at her, 'the girl having crossed her, in not performing a message she had sent her on' (ERO/Ass 35/12/4).

Mistresses as well as masters also carefully policed the demeanour of their servants and punished them if they showed disrespect. Rules of gesture were taken very seriously in Renaissance society as a means of expressing and enforcing age and status hierarchies. Inappropriate demeanour was regarded as a serious sign of insubordination and punished severely, even in relatively modest middling-sort homes (Bremmer and Roodenurg 1991; Braddick 2009;

Walter 2009). For example, in the mid-seventeenth century, the apprentice felt-maker and Quaker, Richard Davies, apparently enjoyed a 'close friendship' with his employers until he took up the Quaker style of comportment and refuted conventional forms of deference, upon which his mistress 'broke his head' and threatened to murder him (Southall 1899: 23).

Parenthood was also central to married women's authority. Children were expected to show respect, duty and obedience through bodily behaviour that acknowledged their mother's superior age and rank. Elizabeth the Countess of Falkland continued to kneel before her mother when speaking to her, even into adulthood, despite rising above her in social rank and though she was always considered to be an 'ill-kneeler and worse riser' (Hewitt and Pinchbeck 1969: 18). Women were also responsible for day-to-day discipline and while relationships between mothers and children were often affectionate, control could also be quite brutal. In 1605, 12-year-old Thomas Haskins, told the borough court of Colchester that:

> yesternight a little before the fyer begann in Mr. Osborn's Barne . . . John Rudlande called to this exa[minan]t he beinge playeinge by the fyreside in his mother's howse, and asked him if he wolde go with him onto the ffeildes and this ex[aminan]t tolde him that he durst not goe for if his mother cam home and founde him abroad she woulde beat him.
>
> —ERO/D/B5 Sb2/6: 139

The levels of control described in these cases were a manifestation of a domestic spatial and social system that reflected and reinforced not simply the subordination of female to male, but also of one age to another. Yet, children were positioned very differently in relation to their parents than were servants to their masters and mistresses. Servants experienced more immediately than children the sense of home as a threat rather than a refuge because their position within the household hierarchy was so much more unstable and insecure. Because they had no title to property and the customary verbal agreements which served as servants' contracts were difficult to enforce, they were frequently violated and servants were simply turned 'out of doors'. Apprentices were in a stronger position because their indenture agreements included a guarantee of board and lodging that carried greater legal weight, although there is plentiful evidence that they, too, could be thrown out (Flather 2007: 48–51). Male and female servants were open to this kind of usage but gender did have its part to play in all of this because young female servants were especially vulnerable to eviction if they became pregnant. According to the law, they were not to be turned away but, in many cases, they were, especially if the bastard was their master's child. Susan Lay was a servant in the Beattie household and had sexual relationships with both the father and son of the family, until she became pregnant, when her mistress shipped her off to London to keep her away from the prying eyes of neighbours (ERO/Q/SBa 2/74).

It would be wrong, of course, to imply that servants were entirely passive or confined. Hollar's image of a maidservant with her basket of produce reflects a wide variety of evidence that the demands of work took female as well as male servants out of the house on a daily basis, as Jane Whittle in Chapter 5 of this volume has shown (Figure 6.2). The seventeenth-century Berkshire yeoman farmer, Rober Loder, for example, noted in his account book that his male servants worked in arable agriculture and carted produce to market, while the female servants performed domestic work and also made malt, milked cows and picked and sold fruit, for instance travelling to market every day when cherries were in season (Whittle 2005b). Day-to-day demands and negotiations created a diversity of alliances as well as conflicts between husbands and wives as well as between masters, mistresses and servants. Close relationships could form between servants and their mistresses, who worked side by side for much of the day (Hardwick 2010: 90; Fairchilds 1984: 38–40). The law also gave remedies to servants who were treated cruelly; others simply left. Servants who stayed did not always accept close supervision with obedience or submission. Women, in particular, often received violent threats from male subordinates, which may have been expressions of resistance by young men against a complex system of gendered domestic power that rendered them relatively powerless.

Trade and manufacturing businesses, in particular, demanded that men and women frequently worked side by side in shops attached to houses and this may have caused more friction. For example, one day, when Rachel Skynner of Braintree chastised her servant, Thomas Yeldham, for his 'lewdness' while at work in her shop, he 'gave her such a thrust against the shop chest that in her conscience he was the very and only occasion of the death of her child and put her in great peril of death' (ERO/Q/SR 81/47). Edward Barlow had many 'brawls' with his mistress, and the Lancashire apprentice, Roger Lowe, was relieved to leave his master's house to take up residence in his shop, despite its discomfort, because of his mistress's 'pestilential nature' (Sachse 1938: 119; Capp 2003: 165–6). Feckless servants could prove even more of a threat to competent management than disobedient ones. Dishonest servants were quick to exploit opportunities for petty pilfering. The German servant, Barbara Jager, for example, routinely stole 'salt, lard, bread, flour and sausages' from her employers and sold them on to buy 'caps and bodices' for herself as well as drinks for soldiers and journeymen with whom she flirted (Rublack 1999: 117). The threat that servant theft posed to household security and control was regarded with sufficient seriousness in seventeenth-century Paris that the law specified that thieving servants were to be hanged in their master's doorway (Fairchilds 1984: 72–3).

Domestic power was always fragile and mitigated by a complex combination of obligations and conditions. But consideration of how spatial arrangements

FIGURE 6.2:*The Kitchen Maid* by Wenceslas Hollar (1607–77), date unknown. Wikimedia Commons, public domain.

offered servants opportunities for agency or resistance to patterns of domestic authority needs to be balanced against circumstances when they experienced their houses as arenas of direct power. In matters of household government, wives and mistresses as well as masters had power to control the use and organization of their own homes in ways that the servants and children they supervised could not.

EATING

Eating arrangements also reflected and reinforced hierarchical distinctions between household members who shared the same home but experienced and

FIGURE 6.3: *The Prayer Before the Meal* by Jan Steen, 1660. Wikimedia Commons, public domain.

perceived it differently. Eating together was regarded in Renaissance society as a defining activity for the expression of family unity. It was, as Jack Goody has commented, 'the domestic household writ large' (1982: 204; and Figure 6.3). The meal table marked out the boundaries of belonging to the household. A husband was expected to provide adequate provision for his wife and children (Wrightson 1982: 90, 108). Bed and board formed part of the contractual arrangement between apprentices and masters; and servants lived and ate in the homes where they worked (Kussmaul 1981: 40). But eating also had an undoubted importance in Renaissance society for the marking-out of social difference (Mennell 1985; Sabean 1984; Goody 1982). Even in small homes, where space and material possessions were shared, decisions about who prepared the meal, where they ate it, what they ate and how much, were laden with symbolic meanings that expressed complex gender and generational hierarchies spatially.

In the sixteenth and seventeenth centuries, food preparation was a gendered activity. Men worked as cooks in wealthy aristocratic households and in commercial kitchens in inns and taverns. But, at home, cooking was organized and performed by women, whether as mistresses of the household or as servants. Nonetheless, the spaces in which food was prepared were not gendered in any explicit way. While cooking had moved from the hall to the kitchen in many homes by the late sixteenth century, these rooms remained firmly multifunctional and used by men and women. Perception and experience of home may therefore have been different because of the different activities of the different sexes but a sexual division of labour did not necessarily mean that space was segregated or that women were marginalized by their work (Pennell 2016: 12; Whittle 2011: 147).

Where a person ate their meal was an important means of differentiating status but traditions varied in the way that they articulated assumptions about gender. In the Basque country, women were not allowed to sit at the householder's table and in some parts of northern Germany men ate their meal sitting down, while women and children remained standing to eat, near to the fire and after the man had finished his meal. In other northern areas, women and men sat at the same table but on opposite sides and arranged in hierarchical order (Sarti 2002: 155). Age and status more than gender determined place in several districts of rural France, where the master sat at the head of the table with his wife by his side; then came the children ranged in order of their ages, then the oldest of the ploughboys, other male servants and finally the two female servants who sat at the foot of the table under the direct gaze of the mistress (O'Day 1994: 186). Court evidence also suggests that, in England, dining arrangements gave symbolic expression to a married woman's superior position in the household hierarchy as wife and mistress. Witnesses who gave evidence in support of Jane Lillington, whose status as wife or servant was at issue, emphasized that she 'sat at the upper end of the table and carved as mistress of the family' (Meldrum 2000: 163). As spheres of life began to separate out and families acquired more rooms and more furniture, wives ate together with their husband and children at the 'upper' table, at times joined by an employee who was considered to be of the same social standing, while servants and apprentices of lower rank sat at a 'lower' table, sometimes in a separate room (Sarti 2002: 156).

It was also assumed in Renaissance culture that social factors influenced what people ate and how much. According to English prescriptive literature, the key determinants were status, age and 'place'. Conduct writers advised that the subordinate position of servants and children in relation to *both* household governors should be reflected and reinforced by their lesser quantity and quality of food (Sommerville 1995: 35). In practice, it seems that male and female servants were often treated well and consumed the same food as their employers.

Robert Loder, for example, a Berkshire yeoman farmer, in trying to prove to himself that keeping servants was too costly, adopted the assumption that each member of the household, including his five servants, ate equal shares of the food purchased and consumed similar quantities of candles and firewood (Kussmaul 1981: 40). On the other hand, evidence from a wide variety of sources, shows how differences within the household hierarchy could be marked out and enforced by the allocation of different qualities and quantities of food according to rank. In Italy, for example, the expression *vina da famiglia* was widely used in the Renaissance period for the inferior-quality wine provided for domestic staff (Sarti 2002: 170). We also find that, in England, in 1656, Edward Barlow noticed that in the household of his prospective employer, apprentices were seated at the same table as the family, but at the lower end. They were given pudding without suet and plums, and meat of poorer quality (Barlow [1659–1703] 1934: 20). On the other hand, the accounts of a seventeenth-century London baker listed the following weekly costs for consumption that allocated most food for the household head and his wife but more provisions for his servants than for his children. Of the total outgoings of £6. 10s. of the establishment, £2. 9s. went on food at 5s. a head for the baker and his wife, 4s. a head for the helpers (journeymen, apprentices and maids) and 2s. for their children (Laslett 1965: 1).

In some circumstances, though, patterns of consumption also expose complex interrelations of gender and class. Marital cases suggest that while wives could be deprived of food by abusive spouses, they expected to be given a quantity and quality of food that reflected their husband's rank and their superior 'place' within the household hierarchy. A good example is the case brought by Margaret Percy against her husband for cruelty and adultery in 1590. She presented the court with evidence of economic hardship as well as physical brutality and complained that he left her 'in very bare estate for provision and forbidding the butcher to let her have any meat' (Gowing 1996: 224). Another abused wife protested that her husband forced her to eat 'bread and chese', complaining, 'can't you eat that as well as the children?' She replied, 'No . . . I want a bit of meat' (Earle 1994: 245). But working women and girls were frequently given less food than men and boys. An ordinance from south-west Germany, in 1550, notes that male agricultural workers were to be fed meat and other foods twice a day, and women only vegetables, soup and bread. Only men were to be provided with wine; women were given milk and water. (Wiesner Hanks 2000: 108). In poorer households, wives may have deliberately given themselves smaller portions of food, so that their husbands, whose wages were higher, could continue working. Popular culture implies that husbands generally expected and received the best and most food. An inversion of the expected gender order during the family meal was a favourite device deployed by ballad writers to depict loss of male control: the married man's complaint that, 'Of every several dish of meat, she'll surely be first taster, And I am glad to pick the bones, *she is so much my master*,' implies that the normal expectation was that husbands had preferential access to the household meal and the wife ate what was left over (Mendelson and Crawford 1998: 263).

SLEEPING

The organization of sleep was also a means of differentiating status and demonstrating power. The mistress and the master slept in the best and most comfortable bed, and increasingly, depending on the size and wealth of the household, in a separate room. The difference in the positions of husbands and wives was exposed, though, in cases of marital conflict when women were most often displaced. When Vincent Bernard was charged with mistreating his wife, Margaret DelaVergne, included amongst the complaints was the accusation that he did not want to put up with her sleeping in his bed and made her sleep in the servant's bed (Hardwick 2010: 88).

The unfortunate consequences of the fight between the Rector of Alphamstone and his wife, as reported to the court of quarter sessions in 1572, offers another vivid example of the enforcement of gender hierarchy in the allocation of space for sleep. It appears that the household only had three beds. After an argument, the Rector remained in the best bed and his wife was forced to take the second, displacing their son, Symond Callye, who joined their maidservant, Joan Rayner, in the third bed. Joan was forced to sleep with Symond from two weeks before Christmas to Candlemas, and, 'not having the feare of God before her eyes, being overcome with the entyceing and alurement of the same younge man, consenting to his wicked demand, is now become with child by the same Symond' (ERO/Q/SR 79/5).

The example of Symond and Joan provides evidence of the lack of ability of individuals of lower status to exercise control over the spaces that they used for sleep. Very often, a combination of age, rank and gender determined the bed on which a person slept. The subordinate status of servants, apprentices and to a lesser extent children of both sexes in the hierarchies of 'place' and age could be signified by the order and quality of beds assigned to them. Experience varied, of course, according to the rank of the servant and the size and wealth of the household. Some footmen and senior female servants in elite households were provided with separate rooms and feather beds (Richardson 2010: 98–9; Whittle and Griffiths 2012: 134). Many 'gentlemen' apprentices, too, had their own chambers and those who could afford it sometimes rented a room separately from their master's house (Earle 1989: 103). But lower-rank servants were often allocated the third, fourth or fifth 'best' or 'worst' 'flock' or 'boorded bedd steddles'. Alternatively, they might be expected to sleep on 'trundle' or 'truckle beds', low beds on wheels that could be stored under larger beds during the day. They were also relegated to sleep in dark, damp garrets or basements, or on boarded beds in the chambers over service rooms, which were sometimes separated from the main dwelling house (Flather 2007: 69–70). We learn in a deposition given by Thomas Jones in 1620, for example, that while he was a servant to William and Isobel Collins of Halstead, he lay in a chamber outside the main house, directly over the cheese house from where, he alleged, he could spy on his mistress through cracks in the floorboards, as she conducted her adulterous affair in the outhouse below (ERO/D/ABD 1). That bedrooms hardly existed for servants in many rural homes is suggested by the confession made by Susan Newman to the borough court in Colchester in December 1654. She accidentally set fire to her master's barn when she was startled by a cat and knocked over a candle, while she was 'about the makeing her masters servants bed in the same barne' (ERO/DB5 Sb2/9: 95v).

Servants' sleeping arrangements tended to be more temporary than their superiors'; they were required to move whenever their master and mistresses commanded them. Many apprentices did not have bedrooms at all and were required to sleep on truckle beds in their masters' shops so that they could serve customers late into the evening. William Stout, apprenticed to a Lancaster grocer in 1679, recorded that he and his fellow apprentices were obliged to 'have a bed in the shop' because they were 'called up at all times of the night' to serve customers (Stout [1665–1752] 1967: 13; Sachse 1938: 6).

The subordinate status of servants was further signified by the order and manner in which they retired to sleep. There was an expectation that servants should wait up until their employers came home at night, to warm their beds and light them to their chamber. A servant in the Chauveau family in seventeenth-century Paris said that if she went to sleep before her master and mistress, she was woken up to see to their needs (Hardwick 2010: 90). Most masters and mistresses expected their servants to wait up for them, to warm their beds and guide them by candlelight to their chambers. William Winter, apprentice to John Sumner of Barking, explained that one Sunday about eleven o'clock at night, his master came home late and he immediately 'waited upon him up to his Chamber doore and att the doore gave him a candle' before he 'went his way in order to goe to bedd.' Elizabeth Pepys expected help with undressing and Samuel became disgruntled if his boy did not help him to bed (LMA/DL/C/245: 398v; Latham and Matthews 1970–83, vol. 8: 200).

The sleeping quarters of servants and children were also often more crowded than the bedchambers of their superiors. In seventeenth-century Paris, children often slept two or three to a bed even in quite prosperous homes (Pardailhe-Galabrun 1991: 73–83). It was also common practice for servants to share a bed with the children. In 1592, Mary Clarke, maidservant to Rebecca Purcas of Thaxted, informed the court of quarter sessions that she shared a bed with 'one child of thirteen years of age' (ERO/Q/SR 124/59: 60).

Occasionally, details emerge about the sleeping arrangements of elderly or sick relatives that expose their liminal status within the household. It seems that old age or dependence granted few privileges to individuals when it came to the allocation of space for sleep. Indeed, it seems to have consigned men and women to a position similar to children and servants. We find, for example, that George Hayward's elderly father slept in a chamber with a female servant and the children, while his son and daughter-in-law slept in a separate room upstairs (ERO/Q/SBa 2/56). Another unfortunate example is the ailing sister-in-law of Robert Fleate, a glover of Colchester, who shared a bed with his three children, while he and his wife slept in comfort in the room next door (ERO/DB5 Sb2/2).

Many individuals in better-off households slept in overcrowded conditions. For the most part, gender had less of an influence on these arrangements than age, status and place, although some distinctions can be discerned between the experiences of male and female servants in that maidservants more often slept in the same chamber as their masters and mistresses (ERO/Q/SBa 2/56). By the seventeenth century, these arrangements had begun to change and, where possible, single-sex and separate sleeping accommodation was provided for servants wherever possible or practical (see Chapter 5). In some cases, though, these arrangements were regarded as unsatisfactory. In Paris by the seventeenth century, it seems that distinctions were expected to be observed in the sleeping arrangements of servants and older family members. A witness supporting a complaint by Jeanne Chauveau against mistreatment by her step-mother, Isobel Dubois, included amongst instances of wrong treatment that: 'Dubois made Chauveau sleep with her servants' (Hardwick 2010: 88). But even if servants slept separately, they rarely, if ever, possessed a key to the room in which they slept and so could not develop the sense of privacy that their employers began to enjoy in more affluent Renaissance homes. The only space over which almost all servants had control was a lockable box, in which they kept their personal possessions. Lack of autonomy and control made young female servants extremely accessible to masters who could sexually assault them. So, young women like Dorothy Baker, for example, whose master, Mr Kemp, 'would locke her up at night to have his pleasure of hir', were left vulnerable to the violence that habitually characterized their experience of domestic life (ERO/DB5 Sb2/6: 72).

CONCLUSION

Even though Renaissance houses were not organized according to systems of segregation in any sort of straightforward or binary way, the home was an arena that still resonated with power and symbolism that had complex and contradictory meanings for women in different locations and of different occupation, age and class. Hierarchical distinctions between men and women, masters and servants, old and young were expressed and enforced by the way that space was used for eating and sleeping, and the manner in which it was controlled. But married women were by no means excluded from power within this spatial system. In the extremes of marital breakdown, their inferior position in relation to their husband with respect to control over the homes in which they lived was starkly expressed. Yet, in most other contexts, patriarchal authority was less prominent and there is little evidence of heavy-handed husbandly control. Indeed, while the authority of the mistress did not carry the legal, institutional and social weight of her husband, the difference between her position in relation to the servants and children whom she supervised was stark. Responsibility for daily management of domestic space did bring with it a good deal of autonomy and de facto powers of control, which meant that the home was not only and simply an arena in which married women were victims of patriarchy. They were active agents as well.

CHAPTER SEVEN

Hospitality and Home

PAULA HOHTI ERICHSEN

In his poem, 'Veglia carnevalesca', the sixteenth-century Italian writer and the son of a Bolognese blacksmith, Giulio Cesare Croce, provides a dynamic picture of an evening's domestic social gathering. Describing the processes and actions that were associated with hospitality, he demonstrates how, at the beginning of the party, the house is in full motion. The host and his servants are busy, as they bring chairs for the guests, moving them close to the fireplace and further away from the fire; they bring lights and food into the room and place more firewood on the fire, while the host greets the arriving guests (Croce 1620: 3r–v). The short text conveys the excitement and, perhaps even the anxiety of the host, as he attempts to master the preparations of the event and make his guests as comfortable as possible.

Croce's poem did not grow out of just his personal experience and fascination with domestic social entertainment. The importance of home-based hospitality gained prominence in the lives of Europeans in the Renaissance period, resulting in a growing range of social activities at home that ranged from formal business negotiations to informal evening gatherings, games, theatrical and music performances, and elaborate wedding banquets and childbirth receptions (Ajmar-Wollheim and Dennis 2006; Preyer 1999; Hohti 2010a; Cohen and Cohen 2001–2; Kent 1987).

The importance of hospitality in the Renaissance period, together with the varied forms of social entertainment at home, was also reflected in the ways in which the home was arranged, furnished and decorated. On the occasion of an important family event, reception rooms and even private spaces were turned into festive spaces by setting portable tables and benches, and displaying art works, wall hangings, tablecloths, elaborate candle-stands, silverware and other family valuables in the house (Thornton and Syson 2001; Ajmar-Wollheim and Dennis 2006; Goldthwaite 1993 and 1987; Jardin 1996).

The wide range of new cultural practices, together with the range of material objects that were associated with domestic sociability, made hospitality at home in fifteenth and sixteenth-century Europe a socially and culturally significant activity and a defining feature of Renaissance culture, that was invested not only with expectations of entertainment and friendliness, but also with sets of socially and culturally defined ideals and rules about behaviour and decorum.

THE SOCIAL AND CULTURAL SIGNIFICANCE OF HOSPITALITY

In his treatise written in 1490s, the Renaissance humanist, Giovanni Pontano, outlined hospitality as one of the five important social virtues of spending money (Liefkes 2006: 254; Lindow 2007: 110).

Pontano's concern for social activity and entertainment at home was not just simply to enjoy informal evening gatherings or elaborate meals in a familiar and friendly atmosphere with relatives, friends and acquaintances. Instead, dinners, banquets, games, theatre performances, poem recitals and other social occasions that were organized at home were tied to the social ideals of the time, and played a key role in the construction and cultivation of the family's social life and public identity.

The social significance of hospitality was especially important for the wealthy European elites, because the ability to host guests was associated closely with family honour and reputation (Heal 1990). Contemporary sources demonstrate the extent to which status, power and success of families was measured by their capacity to invite, entertain and impress guests. The Italian writer and fencing master, Torquato Alessandri, for example, articulated the strong connection between nobility and hospitality, stating that anyone who wished to be legitimately and honourably called with the title of 'gentleman' should have 'a large well-furnished house always open to guests' (Guerzoni, 2011: 30). Giovanni Rucellaio, borrowing from Cisero, emphasized the duty of the gentleman of honour to treat guests with generosity: 'In the house of a rich man,' he said, 'numerous guests should be received and they should be treated in a sumptuous manner; if one did otherwise the great house would be a dishonour to the owner' (Preyer 1999: 362).

Stories of good hosts were circulated in contemporary literature and letters. In 1523, the Venetian ambassadors praised their compatriot, Cardinal Cornelio, for always having a house full of Roman gentlemen. 'Not a week goes by,' they said, 'without two or three cardinals dining at his table, on two or three occasions' (Fletcher 2015; Lindow 2007: 102). Similar compliments were expressed in England, where George Abbot, the future Archbishop of Canterbury, praised the Earl of Dorset in his funeral sermon for 'keeping a great house' and 'providing generous entertainments' (Heal 1990: 6, 23, 156).

Although social and cultural associations between hospitality and honour were most pronounced among the leading families of the European elites, the significance attributed to generous hospitality transcended social boundaries, extending all the way to ordinary European artisans, small-scale traders and labourers, in both the city and the countryside. Several archival records and literary commentaries suggest that at least the wealthier sections of society further down the social scale shared the belief that keeping a household, even a modest establishment, involved giving and openness within one's capacities. In England, generous behaviour and hospitality were often outlined as one of the prime virtues for artisans and farmers. A farmer argues in John Norden's *The Surveior's Dialogue* (1607), for example, that his 'sort' had traditionally maintained 'good houses and hospitality', lamenting only that rising rents now imposed limitations on this behaviour (Heal 1990: 377; Norden 1607 :13). According to one Thomas Fuller, the good yeoman 'is bountifull both to strangers and poore people' and keeps a table that has 'good honest food' (Heal 1990: 377; Fuller 1642: 117). As among the ruling elites, good hosts were well regarded in the community. An old farmer was complimented in the 1650s as an example of good behaviour for all the rest of his kind in Devonshire and Cornwall, because a feast was celebrated at his house in the company of the poor, and all were seated 'at the upper end of the table and [everyone] had good cheer and free welcome' (Heal 1990: 377). Some popular social occasions, such as the wedding celebrated at Joan Colby's house, made such an impression on the guests that a detailed account of the feast was provided by a witness still nineteen years after the event (ibid.: 370).

The social significance associated with hospitality at various levels of society made the private house an object of public gaze. Neighbours often gathered on the street, watching not only the guests as they arrived in the house through the narrow streets, but also how they were greeted by the host, what kinds of garments the hosts were wearing and how the house was set up for the occasion. Sometimes, crowds of spectators stood outside grand houses, trying to get a glimpse of the elaborate displays and service of food, to the extent that occasionally special measures had to be taken to control the crowds (Waddy 1990: 57).

The social and public importance attached to home-based hospitality made the boundary between the domestic and the public flexible and subject to conflicting pressures, transforming the home, during social occasions, to an open and socially and culturally contested site, whose status and social and cultural meanings had to be constantly negotiated and redefined between family and friends, relatives, neighbours, business partners, political allies, enemies and others who visited the house (Cohen and Cohen 2001–2: 71; Ajmar-Wollheim 2006: 207).

HOSPITALITY, HOME AND IDENTITY

Home as a site for hospitality in the Renaissance period had an important symbolic significance; it provided the immediate framework within which the family's reputation and status was determined and evaluated. Several Renaissance authors compared the house tp the 'face' of the family, suggesting that the family's house not only stood for, but embodied the family's reputation, qualities, character and social status (Fortini Brown 2000: 304–17; Frigo 1985: 122; Cohen and Cohen 2001–2: 70; also Heal 1990: 6–7). In his treatise on architecture, Filarete, for example, compares the variety of domestic buildings to men: 'Buildings are made in the image of men ... You never see buildings ... that are exactly alike ... some are big, some are small, some are in the middle, some are beautiful, some are less beautiful, some are ugly, and some are very ugly, just like men' (Ajmar-Wollheim and Dennis 2006: 12). The association between the family and its dwelling was reinforced by terminology. The Italian term *casa* for the house, for example, as Thomas and Elizabeth Cohen have pointed out, referred not only to the physical structure of the building but also to its occupants, including the family, kin and the household (Cohen and Cohen 2001–2: 65).

The analogy between the family status and the quality of its dwelling was extended in the Renaissance period to include furnishings, interior decoration and other material possessions as well. Household goods, from chests and sculptures to textile decorations and silverware, embodied the family's honour, status and pride, and contributed to creating a sense of hierarchy between those individuals, groups and communities who owned, used and saw them.

The arrangement of the home was crucial, especially during hospitable occasions, because house visits made the interior and the furnishings visible to the public. 'Worthy and elegant furnishings and abundant ornaments,' says Pontano, bring 'pleasure and prestige to the owner of the house, when they are seen by the many whom frequent his house' (Lindow 2007: 110–11). The importance of sumptuous decorations in social occasions of Renaissance men and women becomes evident in several writings. In his memoranda, Giovanni Rucellai, for example, describes in detail the 'very beautiful furnishings' that accompanied the celebrations of his son Bernardo's marriage to Nannina de' Medici in June 1466. The ornamental objects, ranging from a richly decorated sideboard to various types of tapestries and wall hangings displaying the arms of the Medici and Rucellai families, were seen by several hundred onlookers, including 'kinsmen, friends and neighbours' (ibid.: 103).

As ideas of how status could be reflected by the dwelling families lived in spread and became common, the family house and its interior became a subject of debate. Several advice manuals were produced in the Renaissance period to provide instructions on how to set up dining rooms, corridors and chambers for social occasions. Alberti, writing on Vitruvian lines, for example, emphasized the importance of decoration in the house, stating that:

it is preferable to make the parts that are particularly public or are intended principally to welcome guests, such as a façade, vestibule and so on, as handsome as possible. Although I may think that any excess must be censured, yet I feel that those who spend so much on the bulk of their buildings that they cannot afford to adorn them deserve even greater censure than those who overspend slightly on ornament.

—[1443–52] 1988: 292–93

The importance of adornment and household decorations was also emphasized in English works, such as in Henry Wotton's *The Elements of Architecture* (1624). He writes:

Every Mans Proper Mansion House and Home,' he writes, 'being the Theater of his Hospitality, the Seate of Selfe-fruition, the Comfortablest part of his owne Life, the Noblest of his Sonnes inheritance, a kinde of private Princedome; Nay, to the Possessors thereof, an Epitomie of the whole World; may well deserve by these Attributes, according to the degree of the Master, to be decently and delightfully adorned.

—Heal 1990: 6; Wotton [1624] 1903: 15

HOME AND THE VISUAL DISPLAY OF HONOUR

Since hospitality and social events at home were, in part, designed to impress and amaze the visitors who were connected to the family by social, economic or political reasons, it was important to prepare the home well for social events (Thornton 1991: 13). Rich households were decorated with carefully designed cultural signs, including tapestries, wall hangings, painted and carved chests, sideboards and cornices that were, in the Venetian writer Francesco Sansovino's words, 'loaded with gold' (Fortini Brown 2000: 296). Often, heads of households themselves supervised the appropriate display of their private spaces in order to satisfy culturally determined requirements for luxury and good taste. The Florentine ruler, Piero de Medici, for example, had his chamber prepared 'in a manner worthy of emperors and queens, for the great unconquered fighter, with a canopy of silk with fringed curtains, and on the bed a cover of Alexandrian velvet, embroidered with silver and fine gold' (Lindow 2007: 108).

Visitors were often taken around the house to view the art works, expensive furnishings and other family valuables that were put on display during house visits, demonstrating how important it was to make family possessions visible to the public eye. Describing in a letter addressed to the Milanese duke, Francesco Sforza, the visit of his 15-year-old son, Galeazzo Maria Sforza, at Cosimo de' Medici's palace on his way to meet Pope Pius II in 1459, the counsellor, Niccolo' de Carissimi, for example, recalled how, after dinner, the young prince Galeazzo and his entourage were invited on a tour to the noblest parts of the palace, including 'the studies, chapels, halls, chambers, and garden'. He further noted that all of these spaces were: 'constructed and decorated with admirable mastery, decorated on every side with gold and fine marbles, with carvings and sculpture in relief, with pictures and inlays done in perspective by the most accomplished and perfect masters even to the very benches and floors of the house' (Lindow 2007: 108; see also Ajmar-Wollheim 2006: 209).

Surviving letters and descriptions, written by impressed guests who admired a range of household ornaments and material possessions in chambers, studies and halls when they were visiting wealthy households, provide valuable evidence of how decorations in the house were perceived by guests. After his visit to the Florentine palace, Galeazzo Maria Sforza wrote a letter to his mother, praising:

> the tapestry decorations, chests of inestimable workmanship and value, noble sculptures, design of infinite kinds as well as of priceless silver – the most beautiful I may ever have seen, or believe it possible to see. For, to tell of this house, for whomever might want worthily to discuss it and describe its parts, not my tongue, not the space of one day, and not of one month, but many . . . would be necessary.
>
> —Hatfield 1970: 232

In a similar tone, the Bolognese humanist, Giovanni Sabadino degli Arienti, praised the features of the Ferrarese palace of Belfiore, recalling that, 'all the rooms of this palace take light from glassed windows. The joy of seeing the ornaments of the delicate and splendid beds and coverings makes this habitation appear like an earthy paradise' (Lindow 2007: 108–9). Both of these accounts convey a sense of a genuine amazement at the richness of the interior.

Although wealthy Europeans demonstrated great interest in the material splendour of their homes, the importance attached to the public display of the private home and elaborate family possessions was not exclusive to cultural centres such as Florence, Rome, Paris or London. In Scandinavia, rulers and heads of noble households furnished their estates by the second half of the sixteenth century in the continental style. Interest in the European style of hospitality and ceremonial behaviour becomes evident from works such as the *Oeconomia*, written in the 1580s by the Swedish councillor, Peter Brahe ([1585] 1971). Writing instructions to the young noblemen, the author emphasized how important it was for young noblemen to go abroad and learn about foreign customs and people, including how they organize feasts and ceremonies (Pylkkänen 1956:19). Even in as remote places as Finland, then a part of the Swedish kingdom, extensive decoration schemes were introduced to present the princely interiors in Renaissance style during weddings and other social occasions. The interiors were furnished with oriental rugs, Flemish-figured tapestries representing classical subjects, art works and libraries containing classic works in Greek and Latin (Hausen 1909; Pylkkänen 1956: 4–5).

Such emblems of wealth and good taste had a profound influence on how hierarchies were created and understood. However, ideas associated with domestic luxury and material display in the Renaissance period became widespread and extended beyond the wealthy ruling families and aristocracy. The inventory of 1604 of Francesco Vrins, a Flemish merchant, for example, demonstrates that it was important for the businessman to appear cultivated, learned and international through the display of his furnishings. He had no less than twenty-two paintings and a large, framed *mappamondo* on his walls. In addition, his corridors and reception rooms were furnished with a wide range of cultural status symbols, such as a credenza, a harpsichord, a mirror with an ebony frame, a large gilded lantern, two tables, nineteen chairs and twenty-two stools and benches (Fortini Brown 2000: 311; da Castiglione 1554).

Renaissance sources suggest that similar furnishings were displayed in households even further down the social scale. According to the Italian sculptor and architect, Sansovino, there was no one in sixteenth-century Venice 'with a furnished abode so poor who does not have walnut chests and bedsteads, green woollen wall hangings, rugs, pewter and copper vessels, gold chains, silver forks and rings, such is the constitution of the city' (Allerston 1998: 33). Although economic hardship and, sometimes deliberate, cultural resistance to the aristocratic mode of consumption imposed limitations on material abundance and hospitality at the lower social levels, sixteenth-century inventories of artisans convey an increasing sense of refinement associated with the most public areas of their house where the material props could be seen by visitors. By the mid-sixteenth century, it was relatively common to find the artisans' reception room (*sala*) decorated with objects that were characteristic of the general way of living in urban houses, such as wooden cornices, *spalliera* hangings that were placed behind the dining table, as well as paintings, small statues of saints and portrait busts (CDP/733/273, 1549: 6r–v; CDP/733/215, 1549: 1r; CDP/746/457, 1551: 2r; Penny 2006; Hohti 2010b). Some artisan families, such as the Sienese barber Cesario di Albertino, had various ornamental elements to provide a decorative appearance of the reception room, including three 'beautiful' lacquered vases, an elaborate gilded, rectangular mirror and a roundel decorated with coats of arms (Hohti, 2010a). The shoemaker, Girolamo, had placed a credenza in front of an elaborate, framed hanging that included familial coat of arms, and set the 'beautiful, decorated basin' specifically designed for the credenza, mentioned above, on a decorative tablecloth. He also had steps or shelves on which further dinnerware was placed on display, including an ewer, a large plate and other tableware, four candleholders and some lamps that he may have kept in the cupboard below (CDP/725/70, 1547:

1r–v). In Flanders, a moderately well-off Dutch tailor, ter Hoeven, had among his other household goods, five paintings, three tables, and some books, Delft pottery and tiles, seven lace curtains, two mirrors, about twenty chairs and forty-nine napkins, while Andrea Faentino, a Venetian sculptor had several books in his library, including Alberti's treatise on architecture (Sarti 2002: 123; Palumbo-Fossati 1984: 132–4).

This evidence demonstrates not only that the relationship between social rank, domestic space and cultural practices associated with hospitality was complex, but also confirms, as Elizabeth and Thomas Cohen have pointed out, that the codes about honour and propriety, as manifested through refined objects and behaviour within the domestic space, were understood and manipulated by individuals and families across the social spectrum (Cohen and Cohen 2001–2; Hohti 2010b).

HOSPITALITY AND SOCIAL ENTERTAINMENT

Hospitality at home provided an important means to meet friends and celebrate special occasions, but it was also one of the principal means to secure friendships, establish new networks and connections and protect one's reputation and place in the community. Individuals who had fallen out of favour were pitied, because 'few frequented his house and they were men of little consequence ... He remained cold and alone at home, and no one visited him to talk about political affairs – he who used to have his house full of every kinds of person' (Lindow 2007: 102).

In addition to securing one's place in the broader community, hospitality helped to reduce conflicts, express loyalties and maintain good social relations with friends, neighbours, employers and business associates. Many Europeans shared the belief that hospitality could be employed as a means to reduce social conflict and enhance solidarity in communities. This social function of hospitality was seen as so significant that in England, for example, the corporation of York decided to retain its feasts and dinners even during the severe economic crisis in 1557–8, because the 'meeting of neighbours at the said feasts and dinners and there making merry together was a good occasion of continuing and renewing of amity and neighbourly love one with another' (Heal 1990: 303).

Household inventories provide evidence that there was a great deal of socializing in Renaissance homes. One indication of this, noted by material culture historians, is the general evolution of the reception room (called *sala*, *portego*, parlour or hall) in the Renaissance period from a multipurpose functional space into a specialized room furnished for social gatherings and dining. This room functioned as a space where families ate, weddings were celebrated, men got together for drinking and games and women gathered for poem recitals and music (Sarti 2002: 133–4; Heal 1990: 159–61; Palumbo-Fossati 1984: 139). Sometimes, the houses of the rich and influential individuals included several reception rooms that could be set up for large-scale social entertainment. The *portigo* of the Venetian Donado di Michele da Lezze, who lived in the second half of the sixteenth century in the parish of Santa Maria Formosa, included, for example, twenty-four walnut benches, some decorated and some plain, twenty-two chairs, two tables, a walnut credenza, five chests of various types, a copper bucket and three stools (Fortini Brown 2000: 310).

Although houses outside the wealthy ruling elites were rarely large enough to organize events of this magnitude and scale, the cultural shift towards creating domestic spaces that were suited for hospitality and home-based social activity is visible also outside the classes of the wealthy elites. The son of the miniaturist, Cristoforo, called Gasparo Segizzi, who died in Venice in 1576, for example, had a house with two reception rooms, the larger of which was in the principal floor and contained eleven benches as well as a table 'to dine' (Palumbo-Fossati 1984: 138). In Siena, many houses inhabited by craftsmen such as barbers, bakers, innkeepers and shoemakers, included a space specifically designated as *sala*, and listed benches, chairs and a long folding-table 'for dining', as well as a number of embroidered linen towels, tablecloths and linen napkins that were used in dining. Some artisans and shopkeepers also had an ewer and a basin near the dining table on the sideboard, which were used for washing hands before and after the meal (Piponnier 1999: 343). The shopkeeper Benedetto di Bartolomeo's reception room, for example, included a basin and two ewers on the sideboard, covered with a linen tablecloth, while the barber Cesario di Albertino had a bail 'to wash hands' in his *sala* (CDP/684/10, 1532: 3r; CDP/733/240, 1550: 5r).

Raffaella Sarti has noted that, compared with peasant interiors, the urban interior generally appeared rich in furniture and objects that were often new and sophisticated in the early modern period. She highlights especially the visible presence of a large number of chairs, stools, footstools, armchairs, settees and folding tables in homes across social classes as evidence of an increasing home-based social activity in cities like Paris and London; the number of seats, as she demonstrates, is far greater than the inhabitants of these households (2002: 123–4).

The rich evidence concerning the lifestyle and material conditions of both high-ranking as well as ordinary men and women suggests that, although Vitruvius and other classical authors who provided guidance for Renaissance living, insisted that the 'person of common fortune' did not have the need for social space at home because they have a social obligation to visit their superiors, not to receive visitors in their house, hospitality and social events at home were an increasingly common feature of Renaissance everyday life across most social classes.

FORMS OF HOSPITALITY

Hospitality at home in the Renaissance period took many forms, and involved a range of occasions, from the informal entertainment of neighbours, friends and occasional visitors to the public ceremonial occasions organized for important guests. The Sienese, Girolamo Bargagli, provides a long list of different circumstances that demanded visits, which included, for example, visits in case of illness, to present condolences for a death or congratulations for a marriage, a newly acquired dignity or fortune, or to greet someone on their return from a long journey or a military campaign (Ajmar-Wollheim 2006: 208).

The most common occasions for hospitality were the numerous visits that were paid by relatives, friends and other guests who visited the house on various business or social matters in daily life, such as craftsmen, traders, workmen, ambassadors, bailiffs, auditors of land, clerics and travellers. These guests, including 'strangers', were often provided with food, and accommodation in the house while they were performing their tasks. On a typical January day in 1531, for example, one Sir Hugh Hastings, who had a modest household at Norfolk, had one unnamed stranger to dinner and four to supper, as well as three workmen at each meal (Heal 1990: 52). In many places, such as in England and Sweden, large households kept careful records of the guests who visited their homes, including their numbers and the provision of food. The account books reveal that in Häme castle in Finland in 1569, for example, 217 guests altogether dined in the household, of which 173 ate at the governor's table and 44 at the servants' table. These guests included masons, pot-makers, tailors, builders, glass masters, weavers as well as men of high standing, and they were provided with food prepared from ham, fat, butter, beans, cereals, game and different types of fish, depending on the occasion, the season and the rank of the guests (Vilkuna 1998: 238–9 and 250).

In addition to hospitality associated with the daily household economy, the weekly cycle offered many occasions for home-based entertainment. Families invited guests for dinners at home on particular weekdays. Drawing on household accounts, Felicity Heal has shown that Sunday was commonly regarded as a feast day and may have been a particularly favoured day for the reception of visitors. Household books of wealthy English families demonstrate that many families spent more money on food on Sundays than on other days, and it was also the day when meat might be available (Heal 1990: 79).

In addition to dinners, informal evening gatherings, known in Italy as *veglie*, as Marta Ajmar-Wollheim has demonstrated, were also a common aspect of domestic social life and entertainment. These events, organized for friends and neighbours involved playing board-games and cards, singing, drinking, story-telling, dancing and theatrical performances, and might be accompanied by refreshments and candied fruits, almonds or other snacks (Ajmar-Wollheim 2006: 209–15; Dennis 2010). The popularity of such events is demonstrated by the fact that, in the Renaissance period, a number of printed works dedicated to the rules of parlour games appeared on the market. One of the popular editions was, for example, Girolamo Bargagli's *Dialogo de'Giuochi*, published in Siena in 1572, which described the rules for 130 parlour games (Bargagli 1572; Ajmar-Wollheim 2006; Valenti 1992: 261–2).

Home visits in daily life, such as dinners, *veglie* and other evening gatherings organized for friends or neighbours, were often informal and integrated in the activities of the household. But when guests of high rank visited the house, such as ambassadors, princes, magnates, bishops or country gentlemen, hospitality usually involved extravagance and complex rituals. In the letter by Niccolo' Carissimi to the Duke of Milan, referred to above, the Milanese counsellor recalls the ceremonies that surrounded the Galeazzo Maria's visit in Florence. Following the greetings and orations that had taken place in front of the Palazzo Signoria, the young prince continued to the Medici Palace, where he was hosted by Piero di Cosimo. 'I went to and dismounted at the palace of Cosimo,' writes Niccolo,

> and first I found Piero di Cosimo all in state at the top of the first stair, who embraced and kissed the aforesaid Count with great lovingness, and took the hands of and welcomed the whole entourage as pleasingly as he could. Then the aforesaid Count went immediately into the little chapel of the aforesaid Cosimo. He was waiting for him there . . . And he threw himself forwards with reverences, and the said magnificent Cosimo gathered him to his bosom.
>
> —Lindow 2007: 107

The rules of decorum were pronounced and guided the social behaviour of the ruling groups, but assumptions about order, hierarchy and decorum associated with hospitality were also understood at the lower social levels, although they were articulated with slightly different sets of principles. This became evident from an account written by the French gentleman, Jouvin de Rochefort, where he described his visit one evening to an Alpine hut in South Tyrol during his travels around Europe in 1672. The cowherds, embarrassed to have such a noble and well-regarded visitor, tried to make him comfortable by offering him immediately 'the very best of their chairs, namely an upturned basin', and setting the table with the best food they had: with turnips cooked 'in a pot with flour, salt, butter and milk', six eggs, half a cheese, a few pieces of bread, a plate of small fruits and a little 'tasteless wine'. The family sat down on the floor around the table. The head of the family handed over the plate with the eggs and the turnips to the guest. 'I immediately put my hand in,' recalls the gentleman, 'and the rest of the family did the same. No one dared take another until I took one' (Sarti 2002: 148).

FEASTS AND LARGE-SCALE SOCIAL ENTERTAINMENT

The yearly calendar offered several occasions for feasts and generous hospitality. Felicity Heal has demonstrated that the Christmas season in England, especially Christmas Day, the Feast of the Innocents, New Year and Twelfth Night, were favoured by all social classes for grand entertainment, including kin and influential guests so that even among the villagers, 'every family is provided with goose pies, minced pies and ale' (Heal 1990: 71–6 and 355–6). Further down the social scale, among farmers, the feasts of the agricultural year, such as the times of harvest and sheep-shearing, were also important occasions of generosity. Henry Best described in the 1640s the invitation of 'all the work folkes and their wives that helped them that harvest' to a meal of boiled beef, apple pies, hot cakes and ale (ibid.: 357).

The most important and excessive form of hospitality, however, was associated with rites of passage: weddings, christenings and funerals. These public family events, organized for relatives, neighbours and influential guests, represented moments when it was especially important to appear generous and demonstrate social power, good behaviour and powerful family connections. Wedding banquets especially were often elaborate occasions and usually involved the provision of a wide range of food courses within a luxury setting for an extensive number of guests, as well as music and dancing (Figure 7.1).

Other family events, too, such as the birth of a child, were also important occasions of social activity. Mothers and newly born babies were visited in the bed chamber by women of the community who brought gifts, while christenings might involve neighbours, guests and godparents of high rank who might spend 'the whole day, and a good part of the night, in feasting' (ibid.: 61). Sometimes, on the occasion of the birth of the child, the bedroom was turned into a festive space, with food, music and dancing (Figure 7.2).

The importance of generosity on these occasions even at lower social levels becomes evident in one Ralph Josselin's statements. He noted with pride in the celebrations that followed the birth of his eldest child that he 'entertayned my neighbours all about it cost me 6li and 13s 4d at least' (ibid.: 368).

Not even funerals were spared from excessive spending. Burials were often accompanied by elaborate and generous hospitality. We learn that the guests at the funeral of Isabel, the wife of Maurice, Lord Berkeley, who died in Coventry in 1517, were given a 'drinking' with cakes, ale, claret, wafers, sweets, and 'Blanch powder'. At another funeral, that of Lady Katherine Berkeley, held in 1596, it was claimed that just the leftover food was sufficient to feed more than 1,000 poor folk in the afternoon. At lower social levels, the Lancashire Presbyterian minister and a son of a yeoman and builder, Adam Martindale, noted in his diary of the 1650s and 1660s that, when his father died, all the men who came to the house to fetch his father's corpse, including beggars, 'were entertained with good meat, piping hote, and strong ale in great plenty' (ibid.: 82, 120).

FIGURE 7.1: *Marriage Feast at Cana* attributed to Damaskinòs Michele, 1561–70. Museo Correr, Venice. Wikimedia Commons, public domain.

FIGURE 7.2: *The Birth of Caterina Cornaro*, anonymous, Italian, Venice, sixteenth century. © Isabella Stewart Gardner Museum.

The celebrations of marriages and other grand occasions could last for many days. 'For several days,' wrote Vespasiano da Bisticci, following a grand reception in Florence in 1462, 'Piero (de Medici)'s house was like a "corte bandita"' (Preyer 1999: 371). Important events such as weddings were held on a large scale even at lower social levels. Recalling his experience at a popular wedding that he had attended in France, one man named Menetra wrote that, after he had arrived 'just in time to sit down at the table' and enjoyed the meal, toasts, dancing and jokes, 'the wedding feast lasted three days' (Sarti 2002: 72–3). The number of guests was often also high. An attempt was made in England in 1575 to limit the numbers attending the bridal feasts at popular levels to 80 persons (Heal 1990: 370).

Rites of passage were often ritualized occasions that were accompanied with a number of gifts and commemorative objects. Families commissioned a wide range of specialized wares and art objects to celebrate marriages and childbirths, such as 'betrothal goblets', wooden birth-trays and painted roundels, which were often decorated with the family of arms (Musacchio 1999, 2008; Matthews-Grieco 2006: 117). Even ordinary families seem to have valued the custom of commissioning objects and giving gifts at births. Several inventories belonging to ordinary men from artisan classes included objects, whose nature and decoration point to the potential celebratory and ritual function of the objects. The possessions of the Sienese carpenter, Christofano di Bartholomeo, for example, included among other valuables a glass goblet that bore his coat of arms. Many artisans and shopkeepers, from shoemakers to grocers, were also in possession of roundels and other birthware, designated in Italy by the terms *da riscappato* or *da parto*, that were presented as symbolic gifts to the new mother (CDP/722/13, 1546: 1v; CDP/682/38, 1531: 1r; Hohti 2010a: 667).

BANQUETS

Commemorative objects and domestic furnishings, as we have already seen, played a key role in supporting and enforcing the family rituals and events, and were designed to secure the reputation and honour of the host. However, perhaps the most important context for expressing social aspirations and guaranteeing a good reputation among neighbours was to treat the guests with elaborate meals.

Renaissance Italians were already familiar with Christian notions of hospitality, which tended to emphasize the charitable notion of hospitality towards one's neighbours. Although many occasions, such as funerals, involved giving alms and food for the poor, it became more and more important for status-aspiring Renaissance families to create impressive banquets on a lavish scale in order to entertain their social peers, business partners and political allies.

Surviving printed descriptions of festive banquets reveal the luxury associated with the tables on important occasions such as weddings. According to Allen Grieco, festive meals consisted traditionally of a first course and two to three main courses that were prepared using refined ingredients such as candied lemons, walnuts and ginger, sweet wine, biscuits, mixed salads, fresh cream, liver with a red sauce, a wide variety of refined meats, like veal, fish, fowl and partridges, and ended up with a marzipan cake, raw fruit or cheese. In the Renaissance period, however, banquets and upper-class meals underwent an evolution and cookbooks written by cooks such as Cristoforo Messisbugo (1540s) and Bartolomeo Scappi (1570) suggest that, by the 1540s, the number of food courses in houses of the rich could increase to as many as seventeen, including seven to nine dishes for each course (Grieco 2006: 247–50).

The growing luxury at the table was also reflected in the large number of new specialized dinnerware. As the festive meals became more complex in the course of the fifteenth and sixteenth century, new types of wares in growing numbers were needed to get through a meal. In his study of Italian majolica, Richard Goldthwaite has shown that the number of dishes required by high-ranking wealthy families, such as the Este, to get through an extravagant meal grew from a service of about fifty plates, two bowls and four pitchers in the mid-fifteenth century, to close to over four hundred pieces in the late sixteenth century (Goldthwaite 1989: 21).

Sets of sumptuary laws were passed from the fifteenth century onward in a number of European towns to curb the conspicuous display, luxury and excess of the extravagant meals. In Venice, the legislation set a maximum cost per each guest in the 1460s, stating that a maximum of half a ducat per guest could be spent during wedding banquets, with the substantial fine for offenders of 200 ducats. Informants were promised half the fine, and if they were slaves or servants, they were given their freedom as a reward. In the 1470s, in both Venice and Florence, the banquet regulations extended to the number of food courses offered at meals, allowing in Venice only three courses and in Florence only two, one of boiled meat and one of roasted meat (Grieco 2006: 247–8; Fortini Brown 2000: 320).

Although excessive luxury was restricted to the wealthiest sectors of society, banquets organized for kin, friends and neighbours were also central to popular weddings. Describing the celebrations for his sister Caterina's wedding in his *Ricordanze* (1478–1526), the Florentine coppersmith, Bartolomeo Masi, for example, reported that right after the bride had received the ring, more than thirty guests were invited for a banquet, organized on the ground-floor reception room (*salotto*) of his house (Corazzini 1906: 245–6).

Funerals tended to include meals as well. Some surviving testamentary bequests demonstrate that men and women often left money in their wills, in order to have a dinner held at their own funerals. One Robert Robinson, for example, left a large sum of £30 'to be spent upon a dynner . . . amongst my good neighbours, that accompany my body to the buryall'. Robert Jennings, a London draper, left money to his company, not only for a dinner at the time of his funeral, but also for two or three after the event (Heal, 1990: 371–2).

The food offered at popular celebrations was, of course, much less complex than the refined dishes consumed and served among the high-ranking European elites. The most basic meal at the lower social levels consisted of beans, salt, bread, onion and garlic (Grieco 2006: 251). However, wedding banquets, religious holidays and harvest-time feasts were moments of relative abundance among lower social ranks, and provided occasions when even ordinary men and women had a variety of food courses available. One English account claimed that husbandmen 'do exceed after their manner (in feasting); especially at bridals, purifications of women, and such odd meetings . . . it is incredible to tell what meat is consumed and spent' (Heal 1990: 353). The generosity associated with food in popular festive events is suggested also by an account from Yorkshire from around 1640, where some noted that:

> It is usual, in most places, after they get all the pease pulled or the last grain down, to invite all the workfolks and their wives (that helped them that harvest) to supper, and then they have puddings, bacon, or boiled beef, flesh or apple pies, and the cream brought in platters, and every one a spoon; then after they all have hot cakes and ale; for they bake cakes and send for ale against that time: some will cut their cake and put it into the cream, and this feast is called cream-pot, or cream-kit.
>
> —Sarti 2002: 187

According to Felicity Heal, the costs of the food at popular weddings might have been shared by the fathers, and it seems that at least in some rural areas, it was common to finance the wedding by brewing and selling a special ale as a way of raising money towards the hospitality at the wedding. In Scotland, if the couple was poor, social occasions such as christenings were sometimes funded by inviting a great number of people and then having a collection of money to cover the cost of the feast (Heal 1990: 367–76).

Although dinners and drinking connected to popular weddings, childbirths and funerals were sometimes held in taverns, it seems that the homes of urban artisans were sometimes well equipped to organise a banquet of some sort in their house. Pietro, the tailor, for example, had a dining table and seats for thirteen people in his reception room (*sala*), together with fourteen serving bowls, eighteen metal plates, twenty-four drinking or wine glasses, some jugs and a wine-cooler, six large tablecloths, eight linen towels and seventeen napkins, that made it possible to serve food and drink to many guests (CDP/733/273, 1549: 6r–v). He also owned a number of serving dishes of refined quality, including a fine gilded marble bowl, a gilded *all'antica* cup, two gilded knives, one fork and a silver spoon, which allowed him to perform slightly more elaborate dining rituals. Several artisans also owned specialized table ware, such as spittoons, salts, flasks, wine glasses, coolers, carafes and plate racks, some of which were valued pieces and made from fine materials, including novelties such as maiolica and *cristallo* glassware (CDP/746/ 457, 1551: 2r; CDP/733/273, 1549: 6r; CDP/684/10, 1532: 3v). Dinnerware could also be borrowed or rented (Thornton and Syson, 2001).

Sumptuary laws were much more relaxed when it came to lower-class entertainment, for the obvious reason that economic hardship and social status prevented families of modest means from celebrating on a magnificent scale. However, heavy drinking and drunken behaviour at popular feasts were severely condemned by authorities. In England, the Kendal corporation insisted as part of its programme for the reform of the poor in 1575 that there should be no general drinking at churchings. The same authority also tried to limit the consumption of 'bridal-ale' at weddings, ordering that no wedding should be accompanied by general or public drinking before or after the marriage. The severe tone of the orders suggests that popular parties, even funerals, were often characterized by heavy drinking. A few town councils also tried to restrict the wasteful behaviour and superfluous spending of the populace by imposing limits on the sale of bridal-ale, the number of gifts and guests at childbirth celebrations, and the cost of food and drink brought to women lying in childbed, making it forbidden in 1568 for ordinary folk in Leicester to host a feast at any churching (Heal 1990: 366–70).

HIERARCHY AND ORDER

Dining rituals, like other public social occasions at home, were often informed by socially determined rules that were governed by principles of hierarchy and decorum. 'Can there be anything more inappropriate,' asked Giovanni Pontano, 'than watching a peasant drink from a glass ornamented with gems?' (Lindow 2007: 140). In wealthy households, the most important guests were greeted with ceremony and ritual upon entrance in the house, and offered the finest food, the best dinnerware and the most comfortable seats, with backs and velvet or leather coverings. Guests of lower rank ate simpler meals in a separate table and were not invited into the reception room.

Rules of decorum were especially prominent in high-profile occasions marking rites of passage such as births and weddings, and conspicuous dining rituals that were associated with the occasions were closely associated with Renaissance ideals of civility, good table manners and polite conversation. Several works in the Renaissance period were dedicated to social skills and good manners in social situations, providing advice and guidelines to Renaissance elite men and women on how to pay visits or get through social occasions as a host (Ajmar-Wollheim 2006: 208–9).

Celebrations at popular levels of society, including weddings, were generally celebrated in a much more relaxed and informal atmosphere, with men and women mingling freely in a mixed pattern of eating, drinking and dancing (Figure 7.3).

However, a sense of hierarchy and decorum may have occasionally guided the most important social events of the lower-ranking families, too. In the account of the artisan wedding banquet referred to above, organized by the Florentine Masi at his house, the coppersmith records in his diary that more

FIGURE 7.3: Detail of *A Marriage Fete at Bermondsey* (also called *A Wedding Feast at Bermondsey*) attributed to Joris Hoefnagel, *c.* 1569. © The Picture Art Collection/Alamy Images.

than thirty people were seated at the 'first table' (Corazzini 1906: 245–56). However, at least in the village communities, the crucial factor that determined seating or influence of the guests in the feasts may not have been wealth but age, 'so as the younger rich reckoneth it a shame sooner than a grace to step or sit before the elder honest' (Heal 1990: 363).

Hospitality at the lower social levels, then, was partly governed by its own specific rites and customs. Although economic factors explain some of the differences of social practice between social classes, the differing customs and rules of behaviour at social events was also a cultural issue. Sometimes confusion might arise when cultural rules were misunderstood or transgressed. This is well illustrated in a fifteenth-century novella, written by Gentile Sermini (1975). The author tells the story of Mattano, a young man from the countryside. In an attempt to gain social prestige, he sets himself amongst rich men in Abbadia a Isola, a small town outside Siena, and starts spending money on clothing, furnishings and food in the same way as the urban upper-class men of the town. However, Mattano's attempts to impress his social superiors fail. Unaware of the urban cultural etiquette and the type of food he should serve for his upper-class guests, he prepares dishes such as goose, warmed-up cabbage and soup with vast amounts of garlic, all of which were considered unrefined foods in the period. Garlic, in particular, was associated with the lower classes, to the extent that it was called 'the spice of the poor' (Grieco 2006: 251; Hohti 2010a: 663).

Thus, what emerges from the story of young Mattano is that families at each social level were expected to follow the rules and customs of their own social group. However, as we have seen from the rich Renaissance visual and written records that have survived up until our day, the social and cultural significance associated with hospitality was shared across social classes. Domestic social events, from informal evening gatherings to formal wedding celebrations, were not only an important means to meet friends and celebrate rites of passage, but they also provided crucial occasions for people from different ranks to secure solidarities in the broader community of neighbours, relatives, business associates and political allies, among rich and more humble families alike.

The high social importance attached to hospitality by most Renaissance families placed the home at the centre of public attention, making it an important cultural mediator of the host's status, wealth, power and honour. The complex messages that were transmitted and negotiated through the behaviour of the host, supported and enhanced by a wide range of interior decorations, food and the commissioning of commemorative objects, made hospitality and home important social and cultural players in defining what it was like to live and conduct daily life in Renaissance Europe.

CHAPTER EIGHT

Religion and Home

TARA HAMLING

This chapter examines the nature and quality of religious practice within the home over the period 1450–1650, which crucially spans the process of 'long' reformation.[1] Across those areas of Europe where Protestantism took hold, there were profound changes in how people should and could observe their faith in daily life. It is impossible to do justice to the complexity of chronological, regional and social differences in responses to reform, so this chapter offers a broad overview of how the transition from Roman Catholicism to Protestantism altered the practice and experience of religion in the home.[2] At the same time, the discussion emphasizes the enduring quality of traditional temporal and material patterns that embedded religion within everyday domestic life. This subject is a tricky one to study, in part because of the elusive nature of 'private' devotion, by its nature rarely documented (as noted by Foister 2003: 334). Partly for this reason and partly because domestic life has long been considered mundane and lacking in consequence, religion in the home has received far less scholarly attention than public worship. Yet, people in this period observed their faith primarily as an essential, habitual component of their daily lives and religious behaviours were assisted and conditioned by the domestic environment. As an historian of material culture interested in the cultural impact of the Reformation, my core evidence consists of extant buildings and objects. This is an inevitably incomplete and partial record, distorted by a range of historical processes, including contemporary iconoclasm and the vagaries of survival and preservation, but by studying this visual and material evidence in conjunction with a range of textual sources, such as conduct and devotional literature, journals and biographies, it is possible to reconstruct to some extent how domestic religion was formed both theoretically and materially.

The first section of this chapter focuses on patterns of piety within the home, examining the nature and structure of devotional activity and the spaces and objects that facilitated the practice of lived religion. It provides an overview of change over time from the late medieval to the early modern, highlighting a significant degree of continuity in the cyclical rhythms of devotion as well as the use of material props, despite the impact of religious reform. This section focuses mainly on England, treated as representative of the relatively common nature of private devotion across Christian Europe in the late medieval period, before examining the emphasis within Protestant thought on strict observance of household religion. It shows how the process of reformation shifted the focus and emphasis of domestic devotion, creating a balance between personal and collective observance and encouraging more public displays of piety.

The second section focuses on religious practices surrounding the midday meal. Again, the discussion is concerned with Protestant practice, but with a wider geographical range considered through close investigation of a specific genre of family portrait. As Wayne Franits (1986) has established, depictions of the family saying grace before a meal emerged as a particular subcategory of portraiture to express the piety and virtue of individual households. This genre, which was particularly popular in the Protestant Netherlands, exploited the conventions and iconographies of German prints devoted to the spiritual and moral education of children during mealtimes as well as allegorical depictions of the well-ordered household to present idealized representations of families performing prescribed religious behaviours. Franits explains how this genre of portraiture can be understood in relation to the substantial body of conduct literature on household government published in England and the Netherlands in the wake of the Reformation. One particularly detailed version of this genre is examined in order to reconstruct the material environments for domestic religion and thereby establish the importance of objects and images as prompt and guide to spiritual endeavour in the home.

PATTERNS OF PIETY

The routines of early modern life intersected with ritual; daily rhythms and mundane practices were turned to spiritual service and momentary elevation to higher goals. In the later medieval period, the practices of domestic devotion had agency; duty contributed to the credit of good works while holy figures could be called upon to intervene in worldly affairs. Religious reform meant that human action was no longer implicated in the supernatural workings of the divine. Nevertheless, traditional patterns of piety endured while accommodating new emphases, locations and materials.

TIMES FOR DEVOTION

Evidence about how people were supposed to observe religion in their daily lives is provided by the wealth of prescriptive and devotional texts published in print. These commentaries on domestic matters and devotional instructions set out a routine of ideal behaviours and modes of thought corresponding to the time of day and specific activities. While there was an outpouring of these texts following the Reformation, there was already a growing awareness in late medieval society of the need for religious guidance for the domestic household, represented, for example, by Richard Whitford's *A Werke for Housholders*, first published in 1530 and then in several subsequent editions (see Wooding 2014). It was written in simple, direct prose and was clearly meant to have a broad appeal though it, and the wave of similar publications that followed, adopted and adapted strict monastic discipline for the laity. These guides to domestic devotion built on an established pattern of prayer and meditation as set out and supported by the Book of Hours, a collection of texts, prayers and psalms that allowed lay people to incorporate elements of monasticism into their own devotional life (Duffy 2011). These prayer books divided the day into canonical hours, with periods of fixed prayer at regular intervals, from dawn through to bedtime, although with particularly elaborated devotions in the morning and evening. The nature of this devotion was inward and meditative, focusing especially on devotion to the Virgin Mary, sometimes including illustrations of events from her life, such as the Annunciation accompanying Matins and the Nativity for Prime (Figure 8.1).

These books ranged from lavishly decorated illuminated manuscripts commissioned by elite members of society to relatively plain manuscripts with few or no illustrations that catered to a wider market. By around 1500, relatively affordable printed versions were also available to the emerging middling sort. Many books of hours were small and portable, to be carried or worn as a visible sign of piety, as well as to provide ready access to support prayers spaced throughout each day.

The emphasis on Marian devotion expressed in, and represented by, the book of hours made it unacceptable in reformed piety, which emphasized Christ as the only mediator between God and man, although its use was phased out gradually, with evidence that some Protestant owners themselves censored objectionable elements (Duffy 2011: 164, fig. 106). The book of hours also provided a template for reformed prayer books; the medieval book of hours, with its deep marginal illustrations, provided a model for the first authorized Protestant prayer book in England, Richard Day's *A booke of Christian Prayers* printed in 1569 by John Day, with a revised version in 1578 (Figure 8.2).

While Reformed books of prayers shifted the subject of prayers and meditations from devotion to Mary and the Saints to Christ, they maintained much of the former emphasis on prayer at regular fixed intervals throughout the

FIGURE 8.1: Illustration of the Annunciation accompanying Matins, Book of Hours made in Bruges, *c.* 1530–5. Metropolitan Museum of Art, New York, No. 2015.706. © The Metropolitan Museum of Art. Image provided through Open Access for Scholarly Content via the website: www.metmuseum.org.

day, especially to accompany activities in the morning, evening and at mealtimes. The synergy with time of day retained from traditional books of hours can be seen by comparing the morning prayers in the English primer printed by Richard Grafton, printer to King Henry VIII, in 1546, and the book of prayers of 1578:

In the Primer of 1546, the devotions for Prime (at 6 a.m.) includes: 'Felowe of thy fathers light, Lyght of light, & daye moste bright, Christ that chasest away nyghte, And for us to praye aright. Dryve oute darknesse, from our myndes, Dryve away the flocke of findes [fiends], Drousynes take from our eye, That from slothe we may aryse.'	Compares with *A Book of Christian Prayers* 1578, 'A Prayer to be sayd at our first waking': 'O Lord Jesu Christ, which art the greatest of all lights, the only true light, the light from whence springeth the light of day, and the sonne . . . Lord I beseech thee inlighten mine eyes, that I may never slumber in darknes, least my ghostly enemy say at any time, I have prevailed against him.'

FIGURE 8.2: Page from Richard Day, *A Booke of Christian Prayers*, 1578, with woodcut illustrations, including Christ carrying the cross. © The Huntington Library, San Marino, California.

In addition to shifting the emphasis, if not the timing, of personal devotions, religious reform resulted in renewed attention to communal religious observance in the home, creating a balance between personal and collective prayer embedded within daily life. The inculcation of family piety was a particular priority for Protestant theologians. The household was described as 'a little Church, and a little Commonwealth . . . a school wherein the first principles and grounds of government and subjection are learned' (Gouge 1622). Heads of households were expected to lead their families in religious education, discipline and duties, including prayers, Bible reading, catechism and singing psalms (Martin and Ryrie 2012).

According to the influential Elizabethan clergyman, William Perkins, household service of God should combine edification (instruction) and invocation (prayer and thanksgiving) and such service has particular times: morning, 'in which the familie comming together in one place, is to call upon the name of the Lord, before they begin the workes of their callings', and evening, 'because the familie hath seene the blessing of God upon their labours the day before, and now the time or rest draweth on, in which every one is to commend his body and soule into the protection of the Lord'. Besides this, Perkins recommends other times to perform this duty, 'as before and after meales; For meats and drinkes are blessed to the receivers, by the word and prayer' (1609: 6–7).

Printed guides to domestic conduct were bought by the expanding ranks of the middling sort – those householders with patriarchal and administrative authority within their local communities. Nehemiah Wallington, a London woodturner, recorded how he bought a copy of clergyman William Gouge's *Of Domestical Duties* because:

> This year 1622 My Family incressing and how having a wife a child a manservant and a maidservant: and thus having the charge of so many souls I then bought Master Goughes Booke of Domisticall Duties that so every one of us may larne and know our Dutyes and honour God every one in his place where God had sett them, . . .
>
> —Booy 2007: 271–2

and he proceeded to 'draw out' 77 articles for himself to follow and 31 for his family, 'for the Reforming of our lives' (ibid.). Although it is impossible to know if other householders took such instruction to heart to this extent, these texts certainly sold well and were extremely influential culturally, being absorbed and reiterated across genres such as sermons and poetry. Such texts were also influential across geographical boundaries. Willem Teellinck, a Dutch minister, spent nine months staying with friends in Banbury in 1604.[3] He explains how he saw among this English community godly teaching and godly lives to serve as a model for his own life and household. At the heart of this godly community in 1604, in which Teellinck found himself, was John Dod, vicar of Hanwell in Oxfordshire but also preaching in Banbury. In 1598, he had published, with co-author Robert Cleaver from the neighbouring parish of Drayton, the influential *A Godly Form of Householde Government*, which went into several editions and disseminated the stricter Protestant model of household religion and behaviour. Teellinck later produced his own manual on household worship, the *Huysboek* (written in 1618 but not published until 1639), which reflects his experience in England.

Evidence that these ideal patterns influenced actual behaviour more widely is provided by autobiographical and biographical accounts of godly individuals.

The diary kept by Lady Margaret Hoby of Hackness Hall, North Yorkshire, between 1599 and 1605 provides revealing details about her daily devotional routine – a typical entry includes private prayer on rising, prayer before or after dinner and supper, with evening readings with the household (what she variously calls the 'lector' or 'publec praier') before praying privately and then going to bed. These religious behaviours are interspersed with domestic tasks such as winding yarn, preserving quinces, making gingerbread – usually in the afternoon – providing a sense of the interpenetration of domestic labour and devotional practices for women especially. The entry for Saturday, 6 October 1599, provides a sense of the balance between domestic and spiritual needs: she dined and 'after, I wret notes in my testament, then I went to the Granerie, and other places in the house, and so came to examine my selfe and praied : and then I went to supper, and so to the lector, and then to bed' (Moody 1998: 26). There is also a sense here of the patterns of movements between more withdrawn areas of the house, chamber and closet, and the further extremes of service rooms such as the granary.

Further down the social scale, the notebooks of Nehemiah Wallington and Robert Woodford, a Northampton attorney, provide evidence of the religious behaviours and spiritual struggles of members of the literate but occupational middling sort in the first half of the seventeenth century. Both men took seriously their duty to lead household religion to benefit their family and community as well as scrutinizing their own faith and actions for signs of God's grace and mercy. Robert Woodford's diary entry for 28 November 1637 records praying in secret in the morning then being 'greatly affected in publiq prayer in the family' during which he read the 32 and 33 chapters of Genesis to them' (Fielding 2012: 143).

Biographical accounts of individuals furnished another category of godly lives, a genre that disseminated patterns of pious living. Setting out an exemplary model of faith, these 'lives' highlighted the more extreme forms of domestic devotion in order to inspire others. The biography of John Bruen (1560–1625), a Cheshire gentleman, provides an extraordinary level of detail about the practice of religion within his household. According to his biographer, Bruen would devote an hour or two to private prayer after rising early, before ringing the bell to wake the rest of the family and call them together for collective religious duties, starting with prayer, then singing a psalm and reading a chapter of the Bible, ending with a final prayer. This morning routine was repeated every evening after supper but with further instruction from him 'propounding and applying some wholesome doctrine' (Hinde 1641: 40). While the duty of instructing the household fell primarily to the male householder, it was expected that the mistress of the house would support him in this responsibility. Thus, the funeral sermon of Lucy Thornton (d. 1618) praises not just her commitment to her own spiritual duties, but also her role as religious leader within her household: 'In her private familie, praiers morning and evening, reading of the Scriptures, and singing of Psalmes, were never wanting in manie yeeres. Besides, that the Sermons were most carefully rehearsed, servants and children duely enstructed, and manie heavenly speeches by her continually ministred, to the breeding of grace in the hearers' (Mayer 1619: 10).

SPACES FOR DEVOTION

The pattern of daily and weekly devotions required movements within the house. The chapel and closet are the locations generally associated with the practice of domestic religion, but both of these spaces were the domain of the privileged few in gentry houses, at least until the mid-seventeenth century, when members of the middling sort might claim a space of their own in the form of a study or closet (Orlin 2007). In the larger houses of the nobility and gentry, the domestic chapel was the setting for communal worship and could be very grand, indeed – the chapel at The Vyne, a magnificent Tudor mansion in Hampshire contained, according to an inventory of 1541, a lavish appointment of altar-cloths, hangings and plate as well as 'two large tablets of the Pictor of our Lorde', which could have been a form of sculpture or a painting. There was also an embroidered image of 'our Lady'. The textiles included 'crymsen satin, yellow damaske and blue velvet'. The impression is of incredible opulence as much as sanctity (Howard and Wilson 2003: 147–8).

Annabel Ricketts (2007) has shown how the process of reform in England created some original architectural responses to the location and form of domestic chapels. Before the religious changes of the mid-sixteenth century, chapels were usually sited apart from the main body of the house, positioned at the end of a main circulation route or to one side of it. The location of the chapel was emphasized in the exterior architecture and many chapels possessed an external entrance. All this created a sense of isolation and seclusion appropriate to the sacred quality of the (usually) consecrated space. Because reformers disavowed the idea that any space was more sacred than another, the Elizabethan period witnessed a general decline in the use and provision of chapels; some in older buildings were converted to new uses, as storerooms or grand reception rooms, while newly built houses often lacked a chapel. Where chapels were created, they were more integrated within the body of the house. Their location was no longer distinguished in the exterior architecture and the internal arrangement of space was more fluid, with a central core opening out into peripheral areas such as passages and landings (Figure 8.3). This design not only allowed servants easy access to services, but also served to integrate spiritual activities within domestic life, both physically and symbolically. This reflects the Protestant custom of holding services for everyone together, suspending normal duties while the household was at prayer.

FIGURE 8.3: An Elizabethan 'assembly chapel', Hardwick Hall, Derbyshire, 1590–7, an openwork screen separates the upper chapel from the landing. © National Trust Images/Nick Guttridge.

In the 1620s and 1630s, chapel provision rose significantly in response to more conservative forms of Protestantism, sometimes called 'anti-Calvinism' or 'Laudianism'. The location was usually more detached from the main floor plan again, while the reintroduction of exterior architectural features to indicate the location and special status of the chapel now made use of classical forms. These patterns are tied to the practice of consecration, which declined under Elizabeth but revived under the Stuarts. These architectural trends therefore reflect differing positions even with English Protestantism about the need for discreet, specialized spaces for domestic worship.

In lesser houses without chapels and closets, other spaces were utilized for personal and collective devotions. The bedchamber had long been a focus of personal devotion. Morning prayers should, according to most commentators, be 'said at the bedside' (e.g. Bayly 1613). Richard Whitford's discussion of morning and evening prayers, first published in 1530, pointed out the difficulty in following such strict performance of prayer, including calling upon the intercessionary powers of various saints, for ordinary people who 'done lye ii or iii sometime together / and yet in one chamber dyvers beddes and so many in company / if we shulde use these thynges in presence of oure felowes / some would laugh us to scorne and mocke us' (Whitford 1530: sig. Aviiir). Religious practice in the home is often described as 'private devotion', but it is clear that performance of personal prayer was not always private. Robert Woodford seems to have observed private prayer by himself but also with his wife, describing 'some comforts with my wife in private prayer & by my selfe in secret' (Fielding 2012: 145). Finding a space for solitary prayer and spiritual reflection must have been challenging in the busy houses of the middling sort. Nehemiah Wallington records in his notebooks how, as a young man living in his father's house during 1618–19, he would use the 'hie garret', or uppermost attic room, to create personal space for prayer, he also describes using his father's shop: 'I was walking alone in the shope in the darke and meditating the day before as also this night upon the words of Jesus Christ that he [who] looketh aftter a woman and lusteth in his hart after hurr hath commited adultrie in his hart' (Booy 2007: 84, 35).

Following personal devotions, the household was expected to gather together in what Lewis Bayly in *The Practise of Pietie* (first published in 1613, with multiple subsequent editions) describes as 'some convenient room', big enough to accommodate the family and servants. This room might be the hall, parlour or largest first-floor chamber. Despite having a household chapel, John Bruen generally observed family religion in the 'great parlour', after which his servants would pray again together, 'which they generally performed in the kitchen' as they finished their evening chores (Hinde 1641: 35). Similarly, Margaret Hoby would sometimes extend such collective observance by supervising servant's discussion in the kitchen. In one diary entry, after her own 'examination and praier' and reading of the Bible, she 'went into the kicthine, wher Mr Rhodes [minister and household chaplain] and my selfe had som speech with the poore and Ignorant of the som princeples of religion' (Moody 1998: 9). Presumably, this instruction in the kitchen made use of the preparation time before supper.

Hinde tells us that John Bruen made use of many different places both inside and outside for his own private prayer and meditation. Inside, 'Hee had variety of Closets, Studies, Chambers and other convenient rooms . . . and if he went abroad he had his Gardens, Orchards, Arbours, Groves, Woods and Fields, Walkes and Shades' (Hinde 1641: 157). According to Samuel Clarke, in his *Godly Lives*, Lady Alice Lucy (*c.* 1594–1648) of Charlecote in Warwickshire (who, as an invalid was confined to home) used her own movements through domestic space and, more specifically, the thresholds of rooms as a trigger or prompt to perform the religious duty of spontaneous prayer or meditation. He records: 'It was observed that she never removed out of one Room into an other, but she used some short Ejaculations, with lifting up her Eyes and hands to God' (Clarke 1683: 141).

TOOLS FOR DEVOTION

According to his biographer, Bruen provided Bibles for his household – one in the parlour and one in the great hall, where it could be readily accessed by servants. Nehemiah Wallington's father had similarly provided a Bible in the 'folk's chamber' (servants' bedchamber) of his London townhouse, which the young Nehemiah went up to 'and tooke the Bibel and geathered out all the judgments of God which were threatened against the wicked and laid them to my own selfe: for I had written them out in a pce of paper' (Booy 2007: 33).

The provision and ready access to Bibles in ordinary peoples' homes from the mid-sixteenth century marks one of the most significant changes in lived religion over the period covered by this volume. The transition from personal, meditative internalized prayer supported by a book of hours, rosary and a range of small devotional artefacts such as figurines of saints, to Bible-based reading and reflection is a fundamental part of the story of how the impact of reform changed the practice and experience of religion in the home.[4] The extent and pace of this transformation has, however, been overstated in many standard accounts. It is arguable how far religious artworks had permeated the domestic sphere outside elite households prior to the Reformation because access to such objects was restricted by cost. Susan Foister (1981) found that artworks such as pictures, alabasters and other sculpture occurred in only about 10 percent of inventories surviving in The National Archive (TNA), Richmond, for the period c. 1480–c. 1580, reflecting the possessions of the wealthier members of society in the southern counties and London. Only some of these items were religious in nature, and ownership of such items was likely even more restricted in less prosperous areas of the country.

However, in these houses of the wealthier middling sort, religious images came in a wide range of media, from painted hangings to glass and alabaster (Foister 1981). The cult of John the Baptist was particularly popular in the late fifteenth century, represented by numerous alabaster panels in the Victoria and Albert Museum, London (V&A) (Figure 8.4).

Foister (ibid.: 278) found that alabaster heads of John the Baptist occur frequently in inventories of the more prosperous southerners in the period up to 1520, sometimes with a cloth. These heads were usually kept in one of the main living rooms, which raises the question of how far devotional items were displayed in 'fixed' locations in the home. That items were sometimes associated with a cloth suggests that they were out on display, perhaps in the form of a simulated shrine. Visual evidence suggests items might have been kept stored away in cupboards. Jeanne Nuechterlein has noted how some fifteenth-century Netherlandish scenes of the Virgin at prayer show her 'kneeling in front of a cupboard built into the wall, partly open to reveal books, scrolls, vessels, or rosaries: clearly the Madonna keeps her religious paraphernalia shut in the

FIGURE 8.4: *Head of St John the Baptist*, English, fifteenth century, carved and painted alabaster panel, V&A Museum No. A.164-1946. © Victoria and Albert Museum.

cupboard until she brings them out for her devotions' (2005: 78). However, one Netherlandish painting of the Annunciation shows an indulgence woodcut of St Christopher pinned to the chimney-mantel, which presumably reflects actual practice (Aston 2003: 71).

Painted, carved and stone images of the Virgin Mary, Christ and popular saints such as John the Baptist, St Barbara and St Catherine were probably always restricted socially but cheaper figurines made from pipe clay and cast from moulds were exported from Germany on mass and were affordable to a much wider section of society. A late-fifteenth-century pipeclay figurine of the Virgin Mary carrying the infant Jesus Christ in the British Museum is just 6.5 cm in height (Figure 8.5).

FIGURE 8.5: Virgin and Child, fifteenth century, pipe-clay statuette. British Museum No. 1855,0512.17. © Trustees of the British Museum.

A similar, broken figurine in lead alloy found in North Lincolnshire suggests the popularity of these miniature figures that could presumably be carried on the person as well as used in the home as a focus for petitionary prayer.[5] Images in the homes of ordinary people in the late medieval period were therefore likely small scale and portable. Again, it is not clear how far these cheaper images were set up in a fixed location for worship but their small size invites touch and holding. It is thought that these figurines were particularly popular with women (Gilchrist 2012: 156). This idea is supported by the lack of such items found on the wreck of the *Mary Rose* warship, which sank in 1545.

These images of holy figures that had attracted cults of devotion in the late medieval Church were denounced by reformers as examples of idolatry – misdirected worship to false idols created by man. The visitation articles of

Elizabeth I of 1559 ordered the clergy to purge such images from parish worship but also to see that they were removed from private homes of parishioners, asking: 'Whether you know any that keep in their houses undefaced any images, tables, pictures, paintings, or other monuments of feigned and false miracles, pilgrimages, idolatry and superstition, and do adore them, and especially such as have been set up in churches, chapels, or oratories' (Frere 1910).

These articles make clear that location was a key concern in determining what constituted an idol, so that images 'set up' in special places such as chapels or oratories required defacing. There has been a great deal of attention focused on iconoclasm in scholarship of the period (e.g. Phillips 1974; Aston 1988, 2015). But given that few houses had a chapel, and that ownership of pictures and paintings was limited even in the upper levels of society, it is questionable how far a wholesale purge of ordinary homes was necessary, let alone feasible. It is likely that people made their own amendments to devotional tools to conform to the new situation; there is evidence of printed prayers being redacted or defaced to remove objectionable elements (Duffy 1992: fig. 85; Watt 1991: fig. 9). Moreover, narratives of destruction and loss neglect evidence for an expansion rather than reduction in the presence of images and objects in ordinary people's homes. Religious reform coincided with economic and social change, resulting in an increase in the wealthier middling sort who could afford to invest in domestic building and furnishings, including objects with religious content. It is clear, therefore, that the practice of reformed religion in the home continued to embrace the use of images and objects as support and guide to faith, although with important shifts in media and subject matter, from three-dimensional sculptures of holy figures to narrative representations of scriptural subjects. There was also a fundamental change in how people were supposed to engage with devotional objects. Reformers argued that salvation was secured solely through faith in Christ, which rendered petitionary prayers to saints mediated through material things not only redundant, but also idolatrous. This meant that devotional objects should no longer serve as a focus for worship, mediating honour and solicitations offered to holy figures, but they could be used as reminders of spiritual matters and as prompts to meditation.

Thus, the reception rooms in sixteenth- and seventeenth-century houses were often decorated with biblical texts and imagery to display the pious identity of the household as well as to reflect and support religious activities taking place in these spaces (Hamling 2010). Given that Protestant advice emphasized morning and evening Bible readings, prayer and psalm singing, the emergence in the later sixteenth and early seventeenth century of a widespread fashion for pious texts incorporated within wall decoration is a striking example of the connections between domestic decoration and household religious practice. While this kind of wall decoration tends to follow common trends in design, with inscriptions written in framed cartouches within a frieze at the top of the wall, there is great variety in the range of texts employed showing the personal choices of the patron in picking out biblical passages with particular resonance for him and his family in the same way he would select appropriate readings for the household (Hamling and Richardson 2017). Many texts painted on walls are taken from Proverbs, with its bite-size admonitionary wisdoms offering particularly convenient content in nature and form to translate into decoration.

Among the hundreds of examples of such wall writing, just a few examples give a flavour of their content and range. At Calico House in Newnham, Kent, which was remodelled in the first decade of the seventeenth century by a wealthy yeoman, Stephen Hulkes, a room on the first floor was decorated across all four walls with imitation panelling and a frieze above containing texts, now fragmentary (Figure 8.6). The texts presented verses from Proverbs 4 and the

FIGURE 8.6: Wall painting with biblical texts, Calico House, Newnham, Kent, c. 1600–17. © English Heritage.

wording indicates that the inscriptions followed the Bishops' Bible of 1568. The intact fragments (as underlined) suggest that the frieze gave verses 1–4:

> <u>Heare O ye</u> chyldren a fatherly instruction, & take good heede, that ye may learne understanding | For I have geven you a good doctrine, forsake not ye my lawe | For when I my selfe was my fathers deare sonne, <u>and tenderly beloved of my mother</u> | <u>He taught me also sayinge, let thyne heart receave my wordes</u>, kepe my <u>commaundementes and thou shalt lyve</u>.

Similarly fragmentary wall paintings recorded in a first-floor room of a farmhouse in Piccotts End, Hemel Hempstead, include inscriptions at frieze level quoting Proverbs 10:27 and 29 as given in the Geneva Bible: 'The feare of the Lord increaseath thy dayes: but the yeres of the wicked shalbe diminished' and 'The way of the Lord is strength to the upright man: but fear shall be for the workers of iniquity.'[6] Above the fireplace in a ground-floor room in one of the cottages on the High Street, of Much Hadham, Hertfordshire is the inscription referencing Proverbs 31, 30: 'Favour is deceitful and / Beauty is vanity / But a woman that / Feareth the Lord, she/ Shall be praised.'

In addition to wall paintings with religious texts, homes in Protestant England were often decorated with scenes from the Bible, especially from the Old Testament. Such decoration served to exhibit the piety of the owner and his household as well as providing an appropriate atmosphere and setting for daily religious observance. Some of the most common subjects, and their relevance in contemporary theology, are discussed below.

THE FAMILY SAYING GRACE

This second section of the chapter focuses on religious behaviours around mealtimes. Eating was considered an especially fraught activity because it indulged the bodily appetite and could lead to the sin of gluttony. In addition to mitigating such indulgence, the coming together of the family for mealtimes provided a particularly useful opportunity for religious instruction and discipline. The spiritual significance of the family meal and shifts in emphasis over the process of reform in the sixteenth century have been treated in detail recently, and forms part of a growing scholarship on the nature and practice of domestic devotion in early modern Europe (Morrall 2002; Ryrie 2013).

The following discussion uses the visual evidence of a particular genre of family portraiture which emerged in the sixteenth century to establish the devotional quality of mealtimes and the spaces in which dining took place. It works out from a particularly rich example of this tradition of showing the family 'saying grace before the meal', providing a series of annotations to comment on the significance of the decorated items depicted within the painting. The portrait depicts the Family of Hans Conrad Bodmer, attributed to Heinrich Sulzer and dated 1643, which Andrew Morrall has identified as representing 'the full development of a specifically Protestant ideal of the well-tempered home but in much more schematic form' (2007: 114 pl. 5).[7] The painting shows Bodmer, a Burgermeister of Zurich, with his wife and family arranged around a huge dining table (Figure 8.7). In addition to Bodmer and his wife at the head of the table, facing the viewer, twelve offspring are arranged neatly around three sides of the table, while another child tends an infant in a cradle on the right. Two servants are also depicted; one is busy cooking in the kitchen and another carries into the room a dish of food. All those at table are depicted as engaged in prayer, with hands pressed together.

It is significant that the family is depicted engaged in the particular activity of the daily meal, or at least in pious preparation for it. As Morrall observes: 'In choosing specifically to be portrayed during the saying of grace, in a manner that recalls the prototypical meal of the Last Supper, the family members demonstrate – and memorialise – their collective piety' (ibid.). In keeping with

FIGURE 8.7: *The Family of Hans Conrad Bodmer*, attributed to Heinrich Sulzer 1643. Schweizer Nationalmuseum: DEP-3721, Photo: DIG-1773. © Gemälde.

the Protestant emphasis on constant self-examination and moderation, eating (along with other forms of bodily activity) was loaded with moral and spiritual significance. In order to prevent indulgence in bodily appetite and abuse of God's bounty, householders were advised to regulate behaviour and thought at mealtimes by reading from the Bible as well as praying beforehand and with further prayers of thanksgiving, possibly with the singing of psalms, after. Appropriate subject matter for individual meditation during meals was detailed in a range of devotional guides. The pivotal importance of the midday meal in the daily devotions of the family explains why this particular portrait convention proved popular with families concerned to communicate their commitment to the ideal of good governance and godliness.

What is extraordinary about the Bodmer portrait compared to others in the genre is the degree of attention given to the wide range of fixtures and furnishings in this extremely well-appointed room. Morrall (ibid.) has pointed out how the surrounding furnishings speak to a particular ethical attitude and the aims of a reformist cultural ideal. The ornament of these significant domestic *loci* reflected the character and interests of the family, constructing and expressing forms of social and religious identity as they would wish to be seen by others. Yet, these fixtures and furnishings were also experienced repeatedly on a daily basis by members of the family and the images they displayed could be instrumental in providing exemplars to regulate behaviour while encouraging reflection on specific points of Christian doctrine. The sections below examine how the kinds of decorative furnishings depicted in this painting were used to communicate wealth, position and piety not only as symbolic representations in paintings, but also as active material agents within households to inform thought and behaviour.

SPACES FOR DINING

In beginning an analysis of the interior furnishings in the Bodmer portrait, the first question to consider is: where in the house is this daily activity taking place? By the second half of the sixteenth century, it was becoming increasingly common in larger houses for families to dine away from the main living space in a ground-floor withdrawing room or best first-floor chamber (Sarti 2002). The exact location of this principal room within the floor plan varied according to urban and rural models and region, but wall decoration in these larger rooms sometimes refers to this dining function and its spiritual associations.

On the wall to the far left of the Bodmer portrait is a tablet with a written inscription, which reminds the family that God tests his children even in the comfort of the living room and refers to the saving sacrifice of Christ.[8] Displaying religious texts on walls was apparently common as interior decoration and might take the form of painted inscriptions or printed materials. Such texts often exhibit biblical passages or prayers. Despite the more humble status of the individuals depicted, Jan Steen's painting of a family praying before their meal (1660) shows a text hung prominently behind the table in a similar manner to the Bodmer portrait. Loosely adapted from Proverbs 30: 7–9, it translates as: 'Three things I desire and no more / Above all to love God the Father / Not to covet an abundance of riches / But to desire what the wisest prayed for / An honest life in this vale / In these three all is based.'[9] As described above, in England and Scotland in the second half of the sixteenth century, there was a widespread fashion for painting inscriptions directly on the wall surface (Bath 2003; Davies 2008). This permanent addition to the fabric of house interiors represents a considerable commitment to the content in relation to the expected use of space. An explicit link made between the function of the room and its decoration is established by recently uncovered paintings in a ground-floor room at Cowside Farmstead, Langstrothdale, North Yorkshire, with the texts: 'Whether ye eat, or drink or whatsoever ye do do all to the glory of God [I] Cor[inthians] X: 31' and 'Better is a dinner of herbs where love is than a stalled ox and hatred therewith Pro[verbs] XV: Cha[pter] 17 ver[se].'[10] An emphasis on Christian charity in the context of dining is represented by the depiction of the Rich Man and the beggar Lazarus from Luke 16: 19–31, in work of 1580 at Pittleworth Manor in Hampshire.[11] The decoration includes two scenes from the Parable of Dives and Lazarus, illustrating Luke chapter 16, depicted on either side of the Royal Arms of Queen Elizabeth I.

The parable of Dives and Lazarus seems a particularly fitting subject for depiction in a domestic setting, reflecting the use of the room for dining, and serving as a reminder of the responsibilities of householders to provide charity to the poor. But the subject also alluded to death and judgement, serving as a warning of dire consequences resulting from negligence in this duty. As Tessa Watt has observed in relation to the Pittleworth paintings: 'The image of the poor beggar functioned much like a skull on the desk, which warned one in the fullness of life to be thinking of death. In fact, such a memento mori appears as a moral text on another wall in the same room: "Thus lyving all ways dred wee death and diing life wee doughte"' (1991: 208–9). This suggests a high degree of sophistication in the choice of supposedly 'decorative' subject matter, which utilizes themes and imagery centring on scenes of everyday domestic activity, while simultaneously providing a reminder of Christian values in the context of death and judgement.

The story of the Prodigal Son was a common subject for depiction in fixed and moveable decorative arts, such as wall painting and cushion covers, throughout Europe. Although they differed on points of theological interpretation, the story could appeal to both Catholics and Protestants, as its primary message was God's willingness to forgive sin (Haeger 1986). Thus, Flemish tapestry cushion covers with scenes from the story were copied by workshops based in London in the later sixteenth century.[12] The popularity of the Prodigal Son for a Protestant audience was probably due to the fact that it was flexible in the purposes it served (Watt 1991: 204). It combined a moral warning against indulgence in the pleasures of the flesh with more profound spiritual meanings. Godly literature elaborated on the original meaning of the parable as an example of God's mercy in forgiving remorseful sinners. As Samuel Gardiner explains in his address, 'To the Religious Reader', in his book *The Portraitur of the Prodigal Sonne*: 'The spirit speaketh evidently throughout this whole discourse how as the Lord is just in punishing of sinners: so is hee as mercifull unto those that doe repent' (1599: sig. A4v). To what extent the pictorial vivacity of scenes of feasting and whoring was enjoyed over and above contemplation of the moral and spiritual meanings of the parable is not clear. Other biblical subjects depicted in pictorial form in English wall painting include, among others, Adam and Eve, Abraham Sacrificing Isaac and the story of Joseph. These stories are multilayered, in that they could offer exemplars or anti-exemplars for didactic purposes but were also commonly deployed in exegesis to illustrate God's mysterious plan of election. While the Bodmer's walls are not painted with biblical scenes, it is possible that this family would have been familiar with similar work on the exterior of houses, such as the famous extant example of the Adam and Eve mural dated 1647 on the exterior of a house in Ardez in Switzerland.

In any case, these biblical stories were also depicted in items *on* the dinner table. Moving now to the table in the Bodmer portrait, its white linen tablecloth might itself have been embellished with biblical scenes such as the two spies carrying grapes out of Canaan, representing the bounty of the Promised Land and fulfilment of God's commitment to His chosen people (see the example dated 1550–99 in the V&A Museum No. T.45-1910). The table also has ample provision of tableware, an item in the far-right corner, in front of Bodmer's wife, appears to be a stoneware tankard. Stoneware developed in the Rhineland at the end of the thirteenth century and as a hard, non-porous ceramic, was ideal for domestic use (Gaimster 1997).

By the sixteenth century, various workshops operating in Cologne, Frechen, Siegburg and Raeren were producing for export elaborate wares applied with moulded decoration, often with mythological or biblical scenes, based on contemporary engravings. These wares were no longer primarily utilitarian but a luxury commodity and sign of status. Morrall (2002) has established how ceramic vessels in sixteenth-century Northern Europe responded to 'the increased ritualization of dining habits, so that their presence would reinforce the aura of piety expected of the household and, more specifically, the quasi-sacramental commensality accorded the family meal'. He identifies pots with politically charged, confessional content as well as vessels with moralizing inscriptions and highlights one striking ewer with scenes of Lot and his Daughters and Noah and his Sons as a warning against the dangers of drink. Many other extant ceramic items demonstrate how the subject matter of tableware could mirror the activities taking place around it but with a clear moral message. A small stoneware tankard in the

Museum of London is decorated with applied panels in low relief, depicting scenes from the parable of the Rich Man and Lazarus, and has been dated as 1525–50.[13] Other examples date from the 1570s to the 1590s, including one dated 1572 with scenes from the parable of the Prodigal Son.[14] A stoneware jug in the collections of the Shakespeare Birthplace Trust depicts the Feast of Herod, with John the Baptist's decapitated head being presented to Herod on a platter. In depicting a scene associated with grand feasting, the jug, which probably held ale, sets up a comparison between indulging bodily appetites and John's rejection of worldly luxuries, while as the precursor of Christ, John's death prefigures His coming sacrifice.[15] A white stoneware tankard of the mid-sixteenth century in the Metropolitan Museum, New York, has graphic scenes of Adam and Eve's expulsion from the Garden of Eden, with a scene of the Last Judgement.[16] In this manner, these prestigious tableware items were not only admonitory but could direct the mind to spiritual concerns during periods of (potentially excessive) bodily indulgence.

FOCAL POINTS

The source of heat is a natural focal point within domestic rooms. In the Bodmer portrait, the large ceramic stove in the corner of the room attracts notice with its relief and painted decoration. Stoves built from interconnecting ceramic tiles developed in the fifteenth century and became widespread in the colder climates of Central and Northern Europe, from Germany, Austria and Switzerland, eastwards to Hungary and Poland, and throughout the Baltic regions and Scandinavia. Tiles for stoves were also exported to England and the Netherlands but appear never to have been widely used in these areas. Early tile-stoves were initially restricted to the greater royal and ecclesiastical houses, but they became increasingly used in the houses of wealthy citizens (Gaimster, Goffin and Blackmore 1990). Although essentially free-standing, the stove would be positioned against a wall containing openings to connect to a stoke-hole and flue at its rear. This allowed the stove to be stoked directly from an adjacent room, and for fumes to be extracted so that the main heated room was smoke-free and clean. To draw attention to this agent of warmth and comfort, the front surfaces had relief-moulded decoration enhanced with coloured lead glazes or had painted tin-glazed decoration. Morrall (2007: 114) has identified that the stove in the Bodmer portrait is decorated with a series of Cardinal and Theological Virtues: visible are Justice, Prudence, Faith and Hope. He argues that the imagery of the Virtues 'was deeply bound up with the aims of a reformist cultural ideal: with the ordination of civility, the control of appetite, the transformation of nature by breeding and piety; even, in a sense, a means of Grace' (ibid.).

Another kind of embellished stove was made from cast iron. These consisted of iron plates bolted together as a free-standing box-shaped structure to contain the burning fuel. While ceramic stoves have attracted academic notice due to their sheer magnificence, iron stoves, with their plain monochrome appearance, have been largely overlooked despite their rich pictorial character. Designs for iron stoves very often depicted biblical subjects. Used from the 1530s onwards, most of the more sophisticated examples date from the later sixteenth and early seventeenth centuries. An early publication by Henry Mercer dedicated to the origins and development of the decorated iron stoves of Pennsylvanian Germans in colonial America identifies the range of Bible subjects that were the most popular and widely spread of all stove designs in sixteenth-century Germany (Mercer 1914: 18–19). Those taken from the Old Testament largely cohere around familial themes and/or themes of salvation and deliverance, such as Adam and Eve, Abraham and Isaac, Lot and his daughters, Joseph and his brothers.

One sixteenth-century German stove plate featured in Mercer's book depicts, once again, the parable of the Rich Man and Lazarus (ibid.: 21 pl. 17). The central portion is dedicated to a scene of the Rich man and his wife seated at table with two guests in what looks to be a garden pavilion. They are being entertained by a band of musicians set behind them, and a jester. Below them, under a balcony, Lazarus lies on the ground in rags, holding a crutch and a bowl for food. As the dogs lick his sores, a finely dressed servant brandishes a whip to drive him away. An inscription spells out the essence of the story: DER. ARMER. BEGERT. VON. DEM. RICHEN. ZO. SPISEN (The poor man asks to eat at the rich man's table). On the left-hand side of the composition, two smaller scenes show the deaths of the two men: the Rich man upon his bed along with a devilish beast to take his soul to hell, while angels attend to the dying Lazarus, beneath. At the top right-hand side of the composition, Lazarus is shown at peace and comforted by the King of Heaven, while the rich man is depicted in the flames of hell. As with the Pittleworth paintings mentioned above, these stark reminders of death and judgement might seem out of place in a lavishly decorated dining space but serve as a necessary reminder of the transience of worldly pleasures. The impact of the image of the rich man burning in hell must have been enhanced by feeling the heat from the stove, adding another sensory dimension to inform pious response.

According to Mercer, the most popular of all biblical patterns among the poorer classes in Germany, often copied and repeated, was the Marriage Feast at Cana, when Christ turned water into wine. An extant example is in the V&A, London. Dated *c.* 1600, it depicts twelve fashionably dressed figures arranged around a table laden with food and tableware, in the foreground are six flagons (Figure 8.8).

Christ and his followers dressed in simple robes are to the right of the party. An inscription at the base identifies the subject: HISTORIA.VON.DER. HOCHZEIT. ZU CANA IN GALILEA.JOHAN.2. It is not hard to see why this subject, with its message of divine intervention to ensure sufficient provision, might have appealed to families of more modest means.

FIGURE 8.8: Marriage Feast at Cana, German, *c.* 1600, stove plate, cast iron. V&A Museum No. 319-1897. © Victoria and Albert Museum.

In regions of Europe where fireplaces provided heating, the area of the hearth and chimneybreast were similarly embellished with biblical imagery. Cast-iron firebacks were made in the same way as stove plates and served as an allied art form in countries that relied on chimneys rather than stoves as the main source of heat; they protected the back of chimneys and reflected heat back into the room. As domestic buildings increasingly incorporated chimneys, these allied functional accessories were in demand and gradually the plain iron plates came to be embellished with imagery. For England, the most ornate examples tend to date to the middle part of the seventeenth century and production was mainly in the south-eastern counties, so the fashion was probably concentrated in this area. Several extant examples have biblical subject matter, including depictions of Adam and Eve and the Sacrifice of Isaac (Hodgkinson 2010: 173–4). These two iconographies were by far the most popular as a subject for interior decoration more widely. This can be explained by their significance in representing the essence of the Christian scheme of sin and salvation. Adam and Eve eating the forbidden fruit was synonymous with the concept of sin, while the image of Abraham about to sacrifice his son Isaac, as an Old Testament prefiguration of the Crucifixion, represented obedience and redemption (Hamling 2015). These two scenes are often found decorating the area of the chimneybreast in England. Examples include Adam and Eve standing either side of the Tree of Knowledge at the centre of a carved wooden over-mantel dating from *c*. 1620 in a second-floor chamber of 90 High Street in Oxford, England. A scene of Abraham sacrificing Isaac is at the centre of a magnificent chimneypiece, which is the focal point of the plasterwork decoration dated 1623 in the great chamber at Boston Manor in Brentford, Middlesex. Another example in carved woodwork, dating probably from the 1620s, is in a town house in Salisbury, Wiltshire (Hamling 2010: figs 94, 152).

These particular iconographies as conventionally represented contain insufficient information to narrate the whole story, rather the particular scenes – taking the forbidden fruit from the Tree of Knowledge and the moment of angelic intervention to halt Abraham's hand – evoked stories that were already familiar in verbal and visual form. Sometimes the theological significance of these Old Testament stories as typological prefigurations is made explicit by their pairing with scenes representing the fulfilment of God's promise through Christ. A barrel-vaulted plasterwork ceiling dated 1620, in what was the main first-floor chamber of a town house in Barnstaple, Devon, incorporates in roundel cartouches scenes of Adam and Eve and the Sacrifice of Isaac alongside the Annunciation and Nativity (Figure 8.9).

FIGURE 8.9: Section of barrel-vaulted plasterwork ceiling at 62 Boutport Street, Barnstaple, Devon, *c*. 1620, including scenes of The Nativity (*top left*) and The Annunciation (*top right*). © Tara Hamling.

Very similar images with this 'synoptic' quality can be seen in the Bodmer painting, but depicted in painted sections of glass set in the window. Four scenes are represented: Adam and Eve, Cain Killing Abel, the Sacrifice of Isaac and Jacob's Ladder. The type of glass decoration depicted in the Bodmer portrait probably reflects the new form of enamel painting, rather than the stained glass of the medieval period. This direct painting of larger pieces of glass emerged in the mid-sixteenth century due to improvements in glass and paint technology.

To the right of the Bodmer's window, on a shelf, is a display of plate, possibly in painted ceramic. On the other side of the room, in the pediment above the doorway to the kitchen, are three brass dishes of a form commonly decorated with biblical scenes as the central motif. The production of brass bowls was centred in Nuremberg in the fifteenth and sixteenth centuries but there were other centres in Northern Europe and techniques and styles were widely copied well into the seventeenth century. These dishes were display pieces, but with practical utility for washing hands after a meal. Several dishes depict the two spies carrying grapes out of Canaan (Figure 8.10).[17]

Once again, the theme of nourishment in connection with divine providence is applied as decoration to an object that would be experienced in the specific context of domestic victualing. Thus, spiritual reminders were always at hand, quite literally in this case.

FIGURE 8.10: The Spies of Canaan, German, sixteenth century, brass dish hammered in relief. V&A Museum No. M.129-1937. © Victoria and Albert Museum.

FURNITURE

Finally, we turn to the furniture depicted in the Bodmer portrait. Large items of furniture were a considerable investment, often acquired at the point of marriage or the establishment of a house, and were understood as part of the material inheritance of the property (Hamling 2013). Apart from the table, which occupies the middle and majority of the room and must be depicted with exaggerated proportions and solidity, the other major item of furniture depicted in the room is a buffet, or sideboard, with either an upper shelved section or separate shelves attached to the wall.

As Julie De Groot has observed in relation to sixteenth-century Bruges, the way in which cupboards were positioned and juxtaposed with other objects, such as paintings and candles, could amount to a form of domestic altar.[18] This arrangement can be seen in the family portrait of 1602 by Gortzius Geldorp, where a large cupboard in the background resembles an altar with its white cloth and candles; it is set alongside a framed painting of the Crucifixion on the adjoining wall.[19] Yet, increasingly in the seventeenth century, cupboards also came to be embellished with carved imagery to incorporate biblical subject matter within the design. For example, a seventeenth-century *buffetkast* in the Sint-Janshospital (Memlingmuseum) is adorned with carved scenes of the Annunciation and Nativity in rectangular panels in the upper section, while in the lower, larger section, and set within roundels, are scenes of Cain and Abel Sacrificing to God and Cain killing Abel. These two scenes together represent the mystery of God's covenant with His chosen people in accepting the *younger* son's sacrifice, resulting in Cain's jealous rage and sealing his reprobation.

While buffets were intended primarily to support and display objects, other forms of storage furniture were designed to stow and secure valuable items, especially linen. While the items themselves were out of view, the sheer bulk and scale of large cupboards such as the Dutch *beeldenkast* proclaimed the quantity and quality of the goods housed within. These cupboards were therefore an important showpiece and were embellished with a profusion of imagery. A famous painting by Peter De Hooch depicts the centrality of the *beeldenkast* to the household, both in terms of its physical location in the *voorsael* – the main reception room and hub of the ground floor – and as the locus of a core domestic activity, with two women carefully putting away pressed linen.[20] The Cardinal and Theological Virtues were commonly depicted as supporters or as the main subject of these extravagant Dutch carved oak cupboards. These female personifications embodied the virtues expected of those charged with the maintenance of domestic linen. A lavish Beeldenkast dated 1622 in the Metropolitan Museum includes six large representations of Virtues, with six scenes from the story of Joseph on the cupboard fronts (Figure 8.11).

In addition, there are smaller representations of David playing his harp and Samson and Delilah, with a tiny identifying inscription, which suggests the need

FIGURE 8.11: Cupboard (Beeldenkast), Dutch, dated 1622, oak, Metropolitan Museum of Art, New York, No. 64.81. © The Metropolitan Museum of Art. Image provided through Open Access for Scholarly Content via the website: www.metmuseum.org.

for close viewing. Like the parable of the Prodigal Son, the story of Joseph combines great dramatic and visual potential with familial subject matter and spiritual symbolism. The story charts the abuse and betrayal of Joseph at the hands of his own brothers, his various tribulations as a slave, his stellar rise to fame and fortune, his reunion with his family and his forgiveness of their sins against him. Key moments in the narrative, such as Joseph being cast into the well and the attempted seduction of Joseph by Potiphar's wife, illustrated the mortal vices of covetous siblings and adulterous wives. However, the essential meaning of the story in Protestant literature was to praise Joseph as a model of godly behaviour, and as an Old Testament parallel or 'type' of episodes from the life of Christ.[21] Once again, the story contains the essential themes of faith, endurance of trials and eventual deliverance. Thus, while the placement of these huge decorated cupboards reflected their role as a practical hub for the daily routines involved in servicing domestic life, their decoration can be understood as central to the construction of the pious household; in extending the moral and religious education of communal Bible reading and associated devotions, these images could act to reinforce and bolster understanding and thereby ensure compliance with Protestant ideals of the well-governed household.

CONCLUSION

This chapter has outlined how religion in the home was practised and experienced temporally and materially; devotion was embedded in the structure of the day and within domestic spaces that were decorated and furnished to prompt and support devotional routines. The period 1450–1650 straddles the transformative religious reforms of the first half of the sixteenth century. Reform is often characterized as a sudden and wholesale shift from the sensory and material practices of Roman Catholic devotion to a plain Protestant piety, focused entirely on reading and hearing the Word. In reality, change was far more complex, gradual and socially gradated, involving material processes of purging, editing, adapting and redirecting. Wealthier Protestant families still expressed and experienced their faith through external means and the home remained the primary site of daily devotional life, but gone were the friendly yet revered images of saints to be held, kissed and prayed to. Protestant domestic devotion looked instead to edifying extracts and examples from scripture to inform and shape mindfulness of sin and salvation. Scripture was writ large on the walls of many Protestant houses, but it was an inherently material form of address.

NOTES

Chapter 1

1. In 1581, Richard Mulcaster, headmaster of Merchant Taylors' School in London, had declared the householder as 'the appointer of his owne circumstance, and his house is his castle' (Mulcaster 1581: 225); see also the first example in *The Oxford Dictionary of English Proverbs*: 'h. étienne, *Stage of Popish Toys*, tr. G. N. 88 [The English papists owe it to the Queen that] youre house is youre Castell' (1948), 308.
2. My thanks to David Fairer for this insight and phrase, as well as for the Foakes reference below. Throughout the writing of this essay, I have owed thanks to the suggestions, corrections and interpretations of many friends and colleagues, in particular Paul Hunter, Clare Kinney, Elizabeth Fowler and David Gies, as well as Albert Braunmuller, Alan Cameron, Anne Cameron, Lynn Strongin Dodds, Kate Glover, Dan Kinney, Deidre Lynch, Katharine Maus, the late Russ McDonald and Lena Cowen Orlin.
3. See *OEP* (1948), 308, with examples from Dickens and Heath.
4. The etymology of 'home' in the *The Oxford English Dictionary*, Second Edition, ed. John Simpson and Edmund Weiner [*OED*] (Oxford: Clarendon Press, 1989), suggests it is a *bit* more complicated than that.
5. Even in German, the phrases replicating the use of the English 'home' tend to employ the word for 'house': 'a loving home' = 'ein liebeolles Zuhause'; 'away from home' = 'von zu Hause weg'; available online (and accessed 1 June 2017), respectively: https://collinsdictionary.com/us/dictionary/english-german/home; https://collinsdictionary.com/us/dictionary/english-french/home; https://collinsdictionary.com/us/dictionary/english-spanish/home; and https://collinsdictionary.com/us/dictionary/english-italian/home.
6. William Shakespeare, *The Comedy of Errors*, ed. Matthew Steggle, at Internet Shakespeare (1623a), available online: http://internetshakespeare.uvic.ca/doc/Err_F1/scene/2.1/ (accessed 5 June 2017).

7. William Shakespeare, *Two Gentlemen of Verona*, ed. Melissa Walter, at Internet Shakespeare (1623d), available online: http://internetshakespeare.uvic.ca/doc/TGV_F1/scene/1.1/ (accessed 5 June 2017).
8. William Shakespeare, *King John*, ed. Michael Best, at Internet Shakespeare (1623b), available online: http://internetshakespeare.uvic.ca/doc/Jn_F1/scene/2.1/ (accessed 5 June 2017).
9. E.g., 'The Latemest Day', no. 29, *c*. 1275: 'Al hit wolle agon— / His lond & his hus & his hom—', see Carleton Brown, ed., 'The Latemest Day', no. 29, in *English Lyrics of the XIIIth Century* (Oxford: Clarendon Press, 1962), 50.
10. Rybczynski oversimplifies for dramatic effect. There were, of course, the establishments of the solid burghers and guildsmen and craftsmen in the small towns even before the Black Death. My thanks to Clare Kinney. But historians agree on noticeable historical differences, and I tap into those.
11. Hoskins's argument has been contested in details but not in fundamentals. See Robert Machin, 'The Great Rebuilding: A Reassessment', *Past and Present*, 77 (1977): 33–56, and Lena Cowen Orlin's summary of the debate in her *Locating Privacy in Tudor London* (Oxford: Oxford University Press, 2007), 66–70.
12. For a lovely study of Renaissance gardens, see Rebecca Bushnell, *Green Desire: Imagining Early Modern English Gardens* (Ithaca, NY, and London: Cornell University Press, 2003).
13. William Shakespeare, *The Merry Wives of Windsor*, ed. Helen Ostovich, at Internet Shakespeare (1623c), available online: http://internetshakespeare.uvic.ca/doc/Wiv_F1/scene/1.4/ (accessed 3 August 2017).
14. As Clare Kinney reminds me, in early modern literature, the domestic spaces in the 'lower' genres of pastoral or fabliaux are generally thingier. *The Miller's Tale*, for example, gives us a world of 'wonderful tangibility: it is a universe full of highly specific objects, kneading troughs and tubs, plowshares, heavy doors, hotcakes, a pair of shoes with a latticed window pattern cut out in them. The narrative gives us real sense of architectural space' (from her ENGL 3810 lecture at the University of Virginia).
15. I have modernized the thorn (þ) and have regularized the italicized letters within words, but I prefer the richer orthography and the original verse of Furnivall's transcriptions ('Make þou no þer cate ne hond / Thi felow at þou tabull round') to the modernizations of both in Edith Rickert's 1908 edition, *The Babees' Book: Medieval Manners for the Young: Done into Modern English from Dr. Furnivall's Text* (New York: Duffield and Co.).

Chapter 2

1. The current state of the brasses can be seen in a photograph on the Church's website, available online: http://www.wrothamchurch.org/St_George/Tour/Floor_Brasses.html (accessed 25 April 2017).

Chapter 4

1. Only two goldsmiths' inventories survive, the other for James Grundy, d. 1578.
2. On banqueting houses, see Mark Girouard, *Life in the English Country House* (New Haven, CT, and London: Yale University Press, 1978), 106.

3. For the material measure of comfort in a Dutch context, see Dawn Hoskin 'Are You Sitting Comfortably? – Or, Plumping Up a 17th-Century Dutch Cushion', Victoria and Albert Museum Blog (2014), available online: http://www.vam.ac.uk/blog/creating-new-europe-1600-1800-galleries/are-you-sitting-comfortably-or-plumping-up-a-17th-century-dutch-cushion (accessed 8 April 2017).
4. The elite, with more space, retained a full-height hall, as did some individuals with prominent civic roles, to whom their gravitas apparently proved useful.
5. See also Brenda Preyer, 'The Florentine Casa', and Patricia Fortini Brown, 'The Venetian *Casa*', both in Marta Ajmar-Wollheim and Flora Dennis (eds.), *At Home in Renaissance Italy* (London: V&A Publications, 2006), 34–49 and 50–65, respectively.
6. For other 'great kitchens' set up for dining and sleeping, rather more like the English parlour, see Inneke Baatsen, Bruno Blondé and Julie De Groot, 'The Kitchen between Representation and Everyday Experience: The Case of Sixteenth-Century Antwerp', in Christine Göttler, Bart Ramakers and Joanna Woodall (eds.), *Trading Values in Early Modern Antwerp* (Leiden: Brill, 2014), 170.
7. Here, as in England, 'As one moves up the social scale, kitchens were less frequently used for sleeping purposes,' ibid., 173. The authors suggest that: 'pressure on domestic space seems to have determined the extent to which household functions were distributed across different rooms'.
8. *OED* 26 a. Something permanent; something that has lasted a long time. In *pl.*, permanent or necessary furniture or apparatus (of a household, etc.).
9. The majority of gifts, treated statistically, were of money (39.5 percent), clothing and leather (32 percent) and metal and trinkets (20.8 percent).
10. T.N. Brushfield has traced the family back to 1353 in Exeter; the diarist's father, John Hayne the elder, was bailiff in 1609 and sheriff in 1635, Thomas N. Brushfield, 'The Financial Diary of a Citizen of Exeter, 1631–43', *Transactions of the Devonshire Association for the Advancement of Science, Literature, and Art*, 33 (1901): 187–269. Account book: DRO Z19/36/14.
11. For purchase of matching sets of furniture, see Mark Merry and Catherine Richardson, *The Household Account Book of Sir Thomas Puckering of Warwick, 1620: Living in London and the Midlands with his Probate Inventory, 1637* (Stratford-upon-Avon: Dugdale Society in association with Shakespeare Birthplace Trust, 2012); Chinnery, 2012. For second-hand goods in Italy, see Ann Matchette, 'Credit and Credibility: Used Goods and Social Relations in Sixteenth-Century Florence', Michelle O'Malley and Evelyn Welch (eds.), *The Material Renaissance* (Manchester: Manchester University Press, 2007), 225–41.
12. See Paula Hohti's argument, however, that 'The houses of Sienese artisans and shopkeepers were often relatively well furnished and contained a number of household utensils as well as decorative furnishings,' and the example she gives of Vincenzo di Matteo, who 'owned notable quantities of linen, bedding and clothing', in addition to 'elaborate furniture and furnishings, including an expensive leather hanging, a gilded mirror, four paintings ... twenty-three chests ... as well as three elaborate posted beds', in '"Conspicuous" Consumption and Popular Consumers: Material Culture and Social Status in Sixteenth-Century Siena', *Renaissance Studies*, 24: 5 (2010), 654–70.
13. For more on the development of the season, see F.J. Fisher, 'The Development of London as a Centre of Conspicuous Consumption in the Sixteenth and Seventeenth Centuries', *Transactions of the Royal Historical Society*, 4th Series, 30 (1948), 37–50;

on new shopping practices, Linda Levy Peck, *Consuming Splendor: Society and Culture in Seventeenth-Century England* (Cambridge: Cambridge University Press, 2005).
14. Receptacle into which the table is cleared after a meal.
15. For more on old and new luxuries, see Richard A. Goldthwaite, *Wealth and the Demand for Art in Italy, 1300–1600* (London and Baltimore, MD: Johns Hopkins University Press, 1989). A very similar argument was consistently made by Chandra Mukerji in *From Graven Images: Patterns of Modern Materialism* (New York: Columbia University Press, 1983); Richard A. Goldthwaite, 'The Economic and Social World of Italian Renaissance Maiolica', *Renaissance Quarterly*, 42 (1), 20, 28–9. The second-hand market in Antwerp became less economically significant as the quality and then the value of new goods fell, Ilja van Damme, 'Changing Consumer Preferences and Evolutions in Retailing: Buying and Selling Consumer Durables in Antwerp (*c.* 1648–*c.* 1748)', in Bruno Blondé, Peter Stabel, Jon Stobart and Ilja van Damme (eds.), *Buyers and Sellers: Retail Circuits and Practices in Medieval and Early Modern Europe* (Turnhout: Brepols, 2006), *passim*.

Chapter 8

This chapter incorporates material published in the context of the (German-language) publication; 'Die Gestaltung des frommen Hauses im protestantischen Europa' in J. Eibach and I. Schmidt-Voges (eds), *Das Haus in De Geschichte Europas: Ein Handbuch* (De Gruyter, 2015), pp.195–214.
1. The term 'long reformation' recognizes that religious change was a long process, not a single event of 'Reformation', and allows consideration of the reforms of the early-mid-sixteenth century within a much longer perspective. See Nicholas Tyacke, ed., *England's Long Reformation 1500–1800* (London: Routledge, 2003).
2. The geographical range is therefore limited to Protestant areas, with a particular focus on England. The rich devotional life of Catholic households between 1450 and 1600 is established by Abigail Brundin, Deborah Howard and Mary Laven, eds., *The Sacred Home in Renaissance Italy* (Oxford: Oxford University Press, 2018).
3. Teellinck's Housebook (Huysboek ofte Eenvoudige verclaringhe ende toeeygheninghe van de voornaemste Vraegh-stucken des Nederlandtschen Christelijcken Catechism) is a commentary on the Compendium of the Catechism, showing how he viewed the Heidelberg Catechism as a worthy centre of family worship.
4. See, for example, Andrew Cambers, *Godly Reading: Print, Manuscript and Puritanism in England, 1580–1720* (Cambridge: Cambridge University Press, 2011).
5. Portable Antiquities Scheme Database: ID: NLM-AE4663, available online: https://finds.org.uk/database: (accessed 12 April 2018).
6. Historic England Red Box Archive, available online: https://historicengland.org.uk/images-books/photos/englands-places/ (accessed 10 April 2018).
7. Also discussed by the same author in 'Protestant Pots: Morality and Social Ritual in the Early Modern Home', *Journal of Design History*, 15 (4), 269.
8. The full text is provided by Andrew Morrall, 'Inscriptional Wisdom and the Domestic Arts in Early Modern Northern Europe', in Natalia Filatkina, Birgit Ulrike Münch and Ane Kleine-Engel (eds.), *Formelhaftigkeit in Text und Bild* (Wiesbaden: Reichert Verlag, 2012), 127.

9. Notes from Sotheby's auction catalogue, painting sold at auction, 5 December 2012, available online: http://www.sothebys.com/en/auctions/ecatalogue/2012/old-master-british-paintings-evening-l12036/lot.9.html (accessed 31 July 2014).
10. Following the King James Authorized Bible, so the paintings must post-date 1611 and may be as late as *c.* 1700. The property is owned by the Landmark Trust.
11. Illustrated in Tara Hamling, *Decorating the 'Godly' Household: Religious Art in Post-Reformation Britain* (New Haven, CT, and London: Yale University Press), 132–3, figs 80–1.
12. A useful comparison is provided by the display in the V&A British Galleries. The English cushion cover of *c.* 1600–10 (T.1-1933) copies the pictorial design of the Flemish cushion cover of *c.* 1575 (T.278-1913).
13. Museum of London, Accession No. 6333.
14. Illustrated in Francis Reader, 'Tudor Domestic Wall Paintings, Part II', *Archaeological Journal*, 93 (1936), 220–62, facing 251, pl. 24.
15. The jug is discussed by Victoria Jackson, 'Shakespeare's World in 100 Objects' (2012), available online: http://findingshakespeare.co.uk/shakespeares-world-in-100-objects-number-5-german-panel-jug (accessed 7 February 2013).
16. Accession No. 27.224.4.
17. As, for example, with two dishes in the V&A: a sixteenth-century example made in Flanders or Nuremburg (Museum No. 7842-1861) and a later-seventeenth-century Dutch version (Museum No. 162-1891).
18. Julie De Groot, 'Devotion on Display: Decorative and Devotional Objects in the 16th-Century Bruges Home', paper presented at the 11th International Conference on Urban History, Prague, 29 August–1 September 2012.
19. Rafael Valls Gallery, London. Image viewable on Bridgeman Images, available online: http://www.bridgemanimages.com (accessed 10 April 2018).
20. Pieter de Hooch, *Interior with Women beside a Linen Cupboard*, 1663, Rijksmuseum.
21. See, for example, Henry Ainsworth, *Annotations upon the first book of Moses, called Genesis* (London, 1616); Gervase Babington, *Certain plaine briefe, and comfortable notes upon everie chapter of Genesis* (London, 1592); Robert Aylett, *Joseph, or Pharoah's favourite* (London 1623).

BIBLIOGRAPHY

ARCHIVAL MATERIALS

British Library (BL), London

BL/Add MS 33058: Vol. I, 1581–1759. County of Sussex: Papers relating to local affairs in: 1581–1814.

BL/Add MS 33084: 34, Correspondence of the family of Pelham, of Sussex, consisting of official, business, and private and domestic letters; 1543–1722., Thomas Pelham: Letter to, from E. Pelham: seventeenth cent.

Clothworkers' Company Archive (CL), London

CL/G/7/1: 31r, West Smithfield and Cow Lane, surveyed by Ralph Treswell, 1612.
CL/G/7/1: 15v–16r, Fenchurch and Billiter Streets, surveyed by Ralph Treswell, 1612.

Curia del Placito (CDP), Siena

Inventories of the Sienese Office of the Wards

CDP/682/38, 1531.
CDP/684/10, 1532.
CDP/699/40, 1537.
CDP/712/233, 1544.
CDP/722/3, 1546.
CDP/722/10, 1546.
CDP/722/13, 1546.
CDP/725/70, 1547.
CDP/733/215, 1549.
CDP/733/240, 1550.
CDP/733/273, 1549.
CDP/746/457, 1551.

Devon Record Office (DRO), Exeter

DRO/Z19/36/14, Account book of household expenses of John Hayne of Exeter (1605–1643), 1631–1643.

Essex Record Office (ERO), Chelmsford

ERO/Ass 35/12/4, Calendar of Essex Assize File 1570.
ERO/D/ABD 1–8, depositions, 1618–42, Bishop of London's Commissary in Essex and Hertfordshire.
ERO/DB5 Sb2/2–9, 1573–1687, Colchester Borough Records, Books of Examinations and Recognizances.
ERO/Q/SBa 2: main series, 1621–89, Quarter Sessions Records, Quarter Sessions Bundles.
ERO/Q/SR 5–560, 1580–1714, Quarter Sessions Records, Quarter Sessions Rolls.

Ipswich Record Office (IRO), Ipswich

IRO/C/4/3/1/1: 269, Plan for a new lobby-entry house at Holbrook, Suffolk, 1577, showing three ground-floor rooms, a 'buttery', a 'parlour' and a 'hall'.

Kent History and Library Centre (KHLC), Maidstone

KHLC/PRC/10/1, Register of Inventories, 1565–1566.

London, Metropolitan Archive (LMA)

LMA/DL/C/211–258, Depositions, 1586–1740, Bishop of London's Consistory Court.

The National Archives (TNA), Richmond

TNA/PROB 2/5, Salle, Thomas, citizen and draper of London [regd copy of will: PROB 11/5, sig 25] 1468 [or 1501].
TNA/PROB 2/825, Wilcox, Richard, [citizen and] haberdasher, of St Magnus the Martyr, London [regd copy of will: PROB11/145, sig 30] [1625].
TNA/SP 16/305/87, Letters and papers Dec 23–31, 1635.
TNA/SP 16/345/92, Letters and papers Jan 27–31, 1637.
TNA/SP 16/370/80, Letters and papers Oct 19–31, 1637.

West Sussex Record Office (WSRO), Chichester

WSRO/Cap I/23/1, Statutes, rentals, accounts, sixteenth–nineteenth cent.
WSRO/Cap I/30/1, Survey of Chapter and prebendal lands, Jan 1650–Nov 1651.
WSRO/Cap I/30/2, Survey of Chapter, prebendal and Vicars Choral lands, June 1649–Oct 1650.
WSRO/ChiCity/K/2, Court Leet and View of Frankpledge, October 1574.
WSRO/ChiCity/K/3, Court Leet and View of Frankpledge, May 1604.
WSRO/ChiCity/K/6, Court Leet and View of Frankpledge, April 1628.
WSRO/EP/I/29/042/2, Probate inventory of William Moore, 1582.

WSRO/EP/I/29/189/4, Probate inventory of Richard Pullengen, 1622.
WSRO/EP/I/29/215/35, Probate inventory of Nicholas Austen, 1697.
WSRO/EP/III/5/1, Deposition book, Dean of Chichester's Peculiar, Mar 1607–Jun 1623.
WSRO/EP/III/5/2, Deposition book, Dean of Chichester's Peculiar, July 1623–March 1634.
WSRO/QR/W19, Quarter Sessions rolls, Place unknown, 1626 or 1627.
WSRO/QR/W21, Quarter Sessions rolls, Chichester, Oct 1627.
WSRO/QR/W43, Quarter Sessions rolls, Chichester, May 1641.
WSRO/QR/W53, Quarter Sessions rolls, Arundel, Apr 1645.
WSRO/QR/W71, Quarter Sessions rolls, Chichester, Oct 1651.

WORCESTERSHIRE ARCHIVES AND ARCHAEOLOGY SERVICE (WAAS), WORCESTER

WAAS, Inventories, 008.7, fol. 61C.

PRINTED PRIMARY SOURCES

Ainsworth, Henry (1616), *Annotations upon the first book of Moses, called Genesis*, London.
Alberti, Leon Battista ([1443–52] 1988), *On the Art of Building in Ten Books*, Joseph Rykwert, trans. Robert Tavernor and Neil Leach, Cambridge, MA: MIT Press.
'An act against erecting and maintaining cottages', 31 Eliz. C. 7 (1589), cl. 1–5, *The Statutes of the Realm* (1819), IV (ii), 804–5.
Aubrey, John ([17th c.] 1949), *Brief Lives and Other Selected Writings*, ed. Anthony Powell, London: Cresset Press.
Austen, Jane ([1814] 2003), *Mansfield Park*, ed. James Kinsley, Oxford: Oxford University Press.
Aylett, Robert (1623), *Joseph, or Pharoah's favourite*, London.
Babington, Gervase (1592), *Certain plaine briefe, and comfortable notes upon everie chapter of Genesis*, London.
Bachelard, Gaston ([1958] 1969), *The Poetics of Space*, trans. Maria Jolas, Boston, MA: Beacon Press.
Bacon, Francis ([1625] 1985), 'Of Building', Essay XLV, *The Essayes or Counsels, Civill and Morall*, ed. Michael Kiernan, Oxford: Clarendon Press.
Baldwin, William ([1533, 1570] 1988), *Beware the Cat*, eds. William A. Ringler, Jr. and Michael Flachmann, San Marino, CA: Huntington Library.
Bargagli, Girolamo (1572), *Dialogo de' giochi che nelle vegglie sansei si usano di fare*, Siena: Luca Bonetti.
Barlow, Edward ([1659–1703] 1934) *Barlow's Journal of His Life at Sea in King's Ships: East & West Indiamen & Other Merchantmen from 1659 to 1703*, ed. Alfred Basil Lubbock, 2 vols, London: Hurst & Blackett Ltd.
Bayly, Lewis (1613), *The practise of pietie directing a Christian how to walke that he may please God*, 3rd edn, London: John Hogets.
Belmonte, Piero (1587), *Istituzione della sposa*, Rome: Per gl'Heredi di G. O. Gigliotto.
Booy, David, ed. (2007), *The Notebooks of Nehemiah Wallington 1618–1654*, London: Routledge Taylor & Francis.

Boynton, Lindsay, ed. (1971), *The Hardwick Hall Inventories of 1601*, London: Furniture History Society.
Brahe, Per ([1585] 1971), *Oeconmia eller Hushållsbok för ungt adelsfolk. Utg. Med inledning, kommentar och ordförklaringar av John Granlund och Gösta Holm*, Nordiska museets handlingar, 78, Stockholm: Nordiska museet.
Breton, Nicholas ([1580] 1929), 'The Miseries of Mavillia', in ed. Ursula Kentish-Wright, *A Mad World My Masters and Other Prose Works by Nicholas Breton*, 2 vols, vol. 2, 111–66, London: Cresset Press.
Brushfield, Thomas N. (1901), 'The Financial Diary of a Citizen of Exeter, 1631–43', *Transactions of the Devonshire Association for the Advancement of Science, Literature, and Art*, 33: 187–269.
Byng, John (Torrington) (1934), *The Torrington Diaries, Containing the Tours through England and Wales of the Hon. John Byng (later 5th Viscount Torrington) between the Years 1781 and 1794*, ed. C. Bruyn Andrews, 4 vols, London: Eyre & Spottiswoode.
Clarke, Samuel (1683), *The Lives of Sundry Eminent Persons in this Later Age, Book II*, London.
Coke, Sir Edward ([1628] 1832), *The First Part of the Institutes of the Laws of England, or, A Commentary on Littleton*, Third Institute, 19th edn, eds. F. Hargrave and C. Butler, London: J. and W.T. Clarke.
Coke, Sir Edward (1651), *An Exact Abridgment in English, of the Eleven Books of Reports of the Learned Sir Edward Coke*, London: M. Simmons, for Matthew Walbancke.
Comenius, Johannes Amos ([1658] 1672), *Orbis Sensualium Pictus*, 3rd edn, ed. Charles Hoole, London: T. R. for S. Mearne.
Croce, Giulio Cesare (1620), *Veglia carnevalesca del Croce, Nella quale s'introducono un bellissimo drappello di Cavallieri et di Dame a danzare, Et si sentono varij linguaggi, et canzoni. Et in ultimo una bella Mascherata d'Ortolane che vendono del latte. Opera nova, bella e di grandissimo spasso*, Per Bartolomeo Cochi, Bologna: Al pozzo rosso.
Crocker, Janine, ed. (2016), *Elizabethan Inventories and Wills of the Exeter Orphans' Court*, vol. 1, Exeter: Devon and Cornwall Record Society.
da Castiglione, Sabba (1554), *Ricordi overo ammaestramenti di Monsignor Saba da Castiglione cavalier Gierosolimitano, ne quali con prudenti, e Christiani discorsi si ragiona di tutte le materie honorate, che si ricercano a un vero gentil'huomo. Con la tavola per alphabeto di tutte le cose notabili*, Venice: Paolo Gherardo.
Daniel-Tyssen, J.R. (1871), 'The Parliamentary Surveys of the County of Sussex, 1649–1653', *Sussex Archaeological Collections*, 23: 217–313.
Daye, Richard (1578), *A Booke of Christian Prayers, Collected Out of the Ancient Writers, and Best Learned in Our Tyme, Worthy to Be Read with an Earnest Mynde of all Christians*, London.
Deloney, Thomas ([1597] 1859), *The History of John Winchcomb, Usually Called Jack of Newbury, the Famous Clothier*, ed. James O. Halliwell, London: Thomas Richards.
Dod, John and Robert Cleaver (1612), *A Godly Form of Householde Government: For the Ordering of Private Families*, London: R. Field for Thomas Man.
Emmison, F.G. (1973), *Elizabethan Life: Morals and the Church Courts*, Chelmsford: Chelmsford Records Office.
Erasmus, Desiderius ([1518] 1997), 'The Godly Feast,' in *The Colloquies of Erasmus*, Craig R. Thomson (trans. and ed.), 171–243, Toronto and London: University of Toronto Press.

[Éstienne, Charles] (1616), *Maison rustique, or The countrey farme· Compyled in the French tongue by Charles Steuens, and Iohn Liebault, Doctors of Physicke. And translated into English by Richard Surflet, practitioner in physicke. Now newly reuiewed, corrected, and augmented, with diuers large additions, out of the works of Serres his Agriculture, Vinet his Maison champestre, French. Albyterio in Spanish, Grilli in Italian; and other authors. And the husbandrie of France, Italie, and Spaine, reconciled and made to agree with ours here in England: by Geruase Markham*, London: Printed by Adam Islip for Iohn Bill.

Éstienne, Henri (1581), *The stage of popish toyes conteining both tragicall and comicall partes: played by the Romishe roysters of former age: notably describing them by degrees in their colours. Collected out of H. Stephanus in his Apologie vpon Herodot. With a friendlie forewarning to our Catelin Catholikes: and a brief admonition, of the sundrie benefites we receiue by hir Ma: blessed gouernement ouer vs. Compyled by G.N.*, 1531–1598, London: Henry Binneman.

Evelyn, John (1659), *A Character of England as It was Lately Presented in a Letter to a Noble Man of France*, London: John Crooke (London: Printed for Jo. Crooke).

Fielding, John, ed. (2012), *Diary of Robert Woodford*, Cambridge: Cambridge University Press for the Royal Historical Society.

Frere, Walter Howard, ed. (1910), *Visitation Articles and Injunctions of the Period of the Reformation*, 3 vols, London: Longmans, Green and Co.

Fuller, Thomas (1642), *The Holy State and the Profane State*, Cambridge.

Fuller, Thomas ([1662] 1987), *Fuller's Worthies: Selected from The Worthies of England by Thomas Fuller*, ed. Richard Barber, London: Folio Society.

Furnivall, Frederick J., ed. (1868), *The Babees Book, Aristotle's ABC, Urbanitatis, Stans Puer ad Mensam, The Lytille Childrens' Lytil Boke, The Bokes of Nurture*, The Early English Text Society, London: N. Trübner.

Furnivall, Frederick J. and Edith Rickert, eds. (1923), *The Babees' Book: Medieval Manners for the Young: Done into Modern English from Dr. Furnivall's Texts*, London: Chatto & Windus.

Fussell, G.E., ed. (1936), *Robert Loder's Farm Accounts 1610–1620*, London: Royal Historical Society.

Gardiner, Samuel (1599), *The Portraitur of the prodigal sonne livelie set forth in a three-fold discourse*, London.

Gataker, Thomas (1620), *Marriage duties briefely couched together out of Colossians, 3, 18, 19*, London: William Iones, for William Bladen.

Geater, Jacqueline B., ed. (2016), *Birmingham Wills and Inventories 1512–1603*, Stratford-upon-Avon: Dugdale Society.

Gilbert, W.S. and Arthur Sullivan ([1878] 2006), *HMS Pinafore; or, The Lass That Loved a Sailor*, in Ed Glinert (ed.), *The Complete Gilbert & Sullivan*, London: Penguin.

Gouge, William (1622), *Of Domesticall Duties: Eight Treatises*, London: Iohn Haviland for William Bladen.

Harrison, William ([1577] 1877), *Harrison's Description of England in Shakspere's Youth. Being the Second and Third Books of His Description of Britaine and England*, ed. Frederick J. Furnivall, London: N. Trübner & Co.

Harrison, William ([1577] 1698, 1994), *The Description of England: The Classic Contemporary Account of Tudor Social Life*, ed. Georges Edelen, Washington, DC: Folger Shakespeare Library and New York: Dover Publications.

Havinden, M.A. ed. (1965), *Household and Farm Inventories from Oxfordshire, 1550–1590*, London: Her Majesty's Stationery Office.

Hentzner, Paul ([1612] 1797), *Paul Hentzner's Travels in England, During the Reign of Queen Elizabeth, Translated by Horace, Late Earl of Orford, and First Printed by Him at Strawberry Hill*, London: Edward Jeffery.

Herbert, George (1640), *Ovtlandish Proverbs, Selected by Mr. G. H.*, London: T.P. for Humphrey Blunden.

Herbert, George ([1652] 1671), *A Priest to the Temple. Or the Country Parson His Character, and Rule of Holy Life*, 2nd edn, London: T. Roycroft for Benj. Tooke.

Herrick, Robert (1648), 'A Country Life: To his Brother, M. Tho: Herrick', in *Hesperides: Or, The Works Both Humane & Divine*, London: John Williams and Francis Eglesfield.

Heywood, John (1555), *Two Hundred Epigrammes, Upon Two Hundred Prouerbes, With a Thyrde Hundred Newely Added*, London: n.i.

Hill, Thomas (1568), *The Profitable Arte of Gardening*, London: T. Marshe.

Hinde, William (1641), *A faithfull remonstrance of the holy life and happy death of John Bruen of Bruen-Stapleford, in the county of Cheshire, Esquire*, London.

Hunnisett, R.F., ed. (1996), *Sussex Coroners' Inquests 1558–1603*, Kew: Public Record Office Publications.

Jones, Jeanne, ed. (2002), *Stratford-upon-Avon Inventories 1538–1699*, Vol. 1: *1538–1625*, Stratford-upon-Avon: Dugdale Society.

Jonson, Ben ([1616] 1947), 'To Penshurst', *The Forrest*, in C. H. Herford and Percy and Evelyn Simpson (eds.), *Ben Jonson*, 11 vols, vol. 8, 93–6, Oxford: Clarendon Press.

Josselin, Ralph (1976), *The Diary of Ralph Josselin, 1616–1683*, ed. Alan Macfarlane, Oxford: Oxford University Press.

Knafla, Louis, ed. (1994), *Kent at Law 1602: The County Jurisdiction: Assizes and Sessions of the Peace*, London: HMSO.

Latham, Robert C. and William Matthews, eds. (1970–83), *The Diary of Samuel Pepys*, 11 vols, London: G. Bell and Sons.

León, Fray Luis de ([1583] 1999), *La Perfecta Casada*, ed. and trans. John A. Jones and Javier San José Lera, Lewiston, NY: Edwin Millin Press.

Lewis, M.G. (1798), *The Castle Spectre: A Drama. In Five Acts*, London: J. Bell.

Mayer, John (1619), *A Pattern for Women setting forth the most Christian life and comfortable death of Mrs Lucy, late wife to the Worshipfull Roger Thornton*, London.

Merry, Mark and Catherine Richardson (2012), *The Household Account Book of Sir Thomas Puckering of Warwick, 1620: Living in London and the Midlands with his Probate Inventory, 1637*, Stratford-upon-Avon: Dugdale Society in association with Shakespeare Birthplace Trust.

Middleton, Thomas ([1630] 1969), *A Chast Mayd in Cheapeside. A Pleasant Conceited Comedy Neuer Before Printed. As it hath been often acted at the Swan on the Banke-side, by the Lady* ELIZABETH *her Seruents*, London: Francis Constable and Menston: The Scolar Press.

Moody, Joanna, ed. (1998), *The Private Life of an Elizabethan Lady: The Diary of Lady Margaret Hoby 1599–1605*, Stroud: Sutton Publishing.

Mulcaster, Richard (1581), *Positions Wherein Those Primitive Circumstances be Examined, Which are Necessarie for the Training Up of Children, Either for Skill in Their Booke, or Health in Their Bodie, etc.*, London: T. Vautrollier.

Norden, John (1607), *The Surveior's Dialogue*, London.

Olaus, Magnus ([1555] 1996–8), Historia de Gentibus Septentrionalbis Romaae *History of the Northern Peoples: Description of the Northern Peoples Rome 1555*, ed. Peter Foote and trans. Peter Fisher and Humphrey Higgens, London: Hakluyt Society.

Parkinson, Richard, ed. (1845), *The Life of Adam Martindale*, Chetham Society, 4, Manchester: Charles Simms.

Paston family ([15th c.] 1983), *The Paston Letters*, ed. James Gairdner, 6 vols, Gloucester: Alan Sutton.

Perkins, William (1609), *Christian oeconomie: or, A short survey of the right manner of erecting and ordering a familie according to the scriptures*, [London].

Pitt, William, 1st Earl of Chatham ([1763] 1839), Speech on the Excise Bill in the House of Commons, in ed. Lord Brougham, *Historical Sketches of Statesmen Who Flourished in the Time of George III*, First Series, 3 vols, vol. 1, 41–2, London: Charles Knight.

Pontano, Giovanni and Francesco Tateo, ed. ([1498] 1999), *I Trattati Delle Virtù Sociali de Liberalitate, de Beneficentia, de Magnificentia, de Splendore, de Conviventia*, Rome: Bulzoni Editori.

Ray, John ([1670] 1678), *A Collection of English Proverbs Digested into a convenient Method for the speedy finding any one upon occasion; with Short Annotations*, 2nd edn, Cambridge: John Hayes for W. Morden.

Repton, Humphry (1805), *Observations on the Theory and Practice of Landscape Gardening*, London: T. Bensley and Son for J. Taylor.

Repton, Humphry (1816), *Fragments on the Theory and Practice of Landscape Gardening, Including some remarks on Grecian and Gothic Architecture*, London: T. Bensley and Son for J. Taylor.

Rickerts, Edith (1908), *The Babees' Book: Medieval Manners for the Young: Done into Modern English from Dr. Furnivall's Text*, New York: Duffield and Co.

Sachse, W., ed. (1938), *The Diary of Roger Lowe of Ashton-in-Makefield, Lancashire 1663–74*, New Haven, CT, and London: Yale University Press.

Sansovino, Francesco ([1581] 1663), *Venetia citta nobilissima et singolare, Descritta in XIIII. Libri*, Venice: Steffano Curti.

Schofield, Barbara, ed. (1949), *The Knyvett Letters, 1620–1644*, vol. 20, Norwich: Norfolk Record Society.

Schofield, John, ed. (1987), *The London Surveys of Ralph Treswell*, London: London Topographical Society.

Sermini, Gentile (1975), *Le Novelle*, eds. Giuseppe G. Ferrero and Maria Luisa Doglio, Turin, Novella XXV, 295–6.

Shakespeare, William (1593), *The Taming of the Shrew*. Available online: www.opensourceshakespeare.org/views/plays/play_view.php?WorkID=tamingshrew&Act=5&Scene=2&Scope=scene (accessed 3 August 2017).

Shakespeare, William (1623a), *The Comedy of Errors*, ed. Matthew Steggle, at Internet Shakespeare. Available online: http://internetshakespeare.uvic.ca/doc/Err_F1/scene/2.1/ (accessed 5 June 2017).

Shakespeare, William (1623b), *King John*, ed. Michael Best, at Internet Shakespeare. Available online: http://internetshakespeare.uvic.ca/doc/Jn_F1/scene/2.1/ (accessed 5 June 2017).

Shakespeare, William (1623c), *The Merry Wives of Windsor*, ed. Helen Ostovich, at Internet Shakespeare. Available online: http://internetshakespeare.uvic.ca/doc/Wiv_F1/scene/1.4 (accessed 5 June 2017).

Shakespeare, William ([1623d]), *Two Gentlemen of Verona*, ed. Melissa Walter, at Internet Shakespeare. Available online: http://internetshakespeare.uvic.ca/Library/Texts/TGV/ (accessed 5 June 2017).

Smith, Henry (1591), *A Preparative to Marriage*, London: T. Orwin for T. Man.

Spenser, Edmund (1595), *Colin Clout's Come Home Again*, London: William Ponsonby.

Southall, John E., ed. (1899), *Leaves from the History of Welsh Nonconformity in the Seventeenth Century: Being Chiefly the Autobiography of Richard Davies of Welshpool Quaker (1636–1708)*, Newport, CT: J.E. Southall.

Stout, William ([1665–1752] 1967), *Autobiography of William Stout, of Lancaster, Wholesale and Retail Grocer and Ironmonger, a Member of the Society of Friends. A.D. 1665–1752*, ed. J.D. Marshall, Manchester: Chetham Society.

Stow, John ([1598] 1994), *A Survey of London Written in the Year 1598 by John Stow*, ed. Henry Morley, Stroud: Alan Sutton Publishing.

Stow, John ([1598] 1633), *The Survey of London: Contayning the Originall, Increase, Modern Estate, and Government of that City*, 4th edn, London: Elizabeth Purslow.

Strachey, Lytton ([1922] 1971), 'Lancaster Gate', in Michael Holroyd (ed.), *Lytton Strachey by Himself: A Self-Portrait*, 16–28, London: Heinemann.

Teellinck, Willem (1639), *Huysboek ofte eenvoudige verclaringhe ende toeeygheninghe van de voornaemste Vraegh-stucken des Nederlandtschen Christelijcken Catechism*, Middelburg: Hans van der Hellen.

Travers, Anita, ed. (2010), *Robert Furse: A Devon Family Memoir of 1593*, Exeter: Devon and Cornwall Record Society.

[Trevisano, Andrea] ([1500] 1847), *A Relation, or Rather a True Account of the Island of England; With Sundry Particulars of the Customs of These People, and of the Royal Revenues under King Henry the Seventh, about the year 1500*, trans. Charlotte Augusta Sneyd, London: Camden Society.

Tusser, Thomas ([1573] 2013), *Five Hundred Points of Good Husbandry, Together with a Book of Huswifery*, ed. William Fordyce Mavor, Cambridge: Cambridge University Press.

Twain, Mark (1869), *The Innocents Abroad, or the New Pilgrims' Progress*, Hartford, CT: American Publishing Co.

Weever, John (1631), *Ancient Funerall Monuments within the United Monarchie of Great Britain*, London.

Whitford, Richard (1530), *A Werke for Housholders*, London.

Woodward, Donald, ed. (1984), *The Farming and Memorandum Books of Henry Best of Elmswell 1642*, London: The British Academy.

Wotton, Henry (1624), *The Elements of Architecture*, London: Iohn Bill.

Wotton, Henry ([1624] 1903), *The Elements of Architecture, collected by Henry Wotton from the best Authors and Examples*, Part II: *Of the Elements of Architecture*, London: Chiswick Press.

Wyatt, P., ed. (1997), *The Uffculme wills and Inventories 16th to 18th Centuries*, Exeter: Devon and Cornwall Record Society.

SECONDARY SOURCES

Unpublished

De Groot, Julie (2012), 'Devotion on Display: Decorative and Devotional Objects in the 16th-Century Bruges Home', paper presented at the 11th International Conference on Urban History, Prague, 29 August–1 September.

Osborne, Kate (2016), 'Illuminating the Chorus in the Shadows: Elizabethan and Jacobean Exeter 1550–1610', PhD thesis, University of Exeter.

Vilkuna, Anna-Maria (1998), 'Kruunun taloudenpito Hämeen linnassa 1500-luvun puolivälissä (Financial Management at Häme Castle in the Mid-Sixteenth Century, from 1539 to about 1570)', PhD dissertation, *Bibliotheca Historica*, 31, University of Jyväskylä.

Published

Online

Bridgeman Images. Available online: http://www.bridgemanimages.com (accessed 10 April 2018).

Historic England Red Box Archive. Available online: https://historicengland.org.uk/images-books/photos/englands-places/ (accessed 10 April 2018).

Hoskin, Dawn (2014), 'Are You Sitting Comfortably? – Or, Plumping Up a 17th-Century Dutch Cushion', Victoria and Albert Museum Blog. Available online: www.vam.ac.uk/blog/creating-new-europe-1600-1800-galleries/are-you-sitting-comfortably-or-plumping-up-a-17th-century-dutch-cushion (accessed 8 April 2017).

J.E.M. (1981), 'Pelham, Thomas (d. 1624), of Laughton; later Halland Place, Sussex', in ed. P. W. Hasler, *The History of Parliament: The House of Commons 1558–1603*. Available online: www.historyofparliamentonline.org/volume/1558-1603/member/pelham-thomas-1624 (accessed 28 April 2018).

Krausman Ben-Amos, Ilana (1997), 'Human Bonding: Parents and Their Offspring in Early Modern England', Oxford University, *Discussion Papers in Economic and Social History*, 17: 13–14. Available online: www.nuffield.ox.ac.uk/economics/history/paper17/17www.pdf (accessed 15 May 2017).

Portable Antiquities Scheme Database. Available online: https://finds.org.uk/database (accessed 12 April 2018).

Sarti, Raffaella (2005a), 'Domestic Service in Europe (16th–21st Centuries): Introduction', in S. Pasleau and I. Schopp (eds.), with R. Sarti, *Proceedings of the Servant Project*, 5 vols, vol. 2, 3–59, Liège: Éditions de l'Université de Liège. Available online: www.uniurb.it/sarti/Raffaella%20Sarti-Who%20are%20Servants-Proceedings%20of%20the%20Servant%20Project.pdf, xv–xxx (accessed 20 July 2016).

Sarti, Raffaella (2005b), 'Who are Servants? Defining Domestic Service in Western Europe (16th–21st Centuries)', in S. Pasleau and I. Schopp (eds.), with R. Sarti, *Proceedings of the Servant Project*, 5 vols, vol. 2, 3–59, Liège: Éditions de l'Université de Liège.

Sarti, Raffaella (2005c), 'Conclusion: Domestic Service and European Identity', in S. Pasleau and I. Schopp (eds.), with R. Sarti, *Proceedings of the Servant Project*, 5 vols, vol. 5, 195–276, Liège: Éditions de l'Université de Liège.

St George's Church. Available online: www.wrothamchurch.org/St_George/Tour/Floor_Brasses.html (accessed 25 April 2017).

V&A Search the Collections website. Available online: https://collections.vam.ac.uk/ (accessed 18 August 2018).

Articles and Books

Adams, Tracy (2008), 'Fostering Girls in Early Modern France', in Susan Broomhall (ed.), *Emotions in the Household 1200–1900*, 103–18, Basingstoke: Palgrave Macmillan.

Ågren, Maria, ed. (2017), *Making a Living, Making a Difference: Gender and Work in Early Modern European Society*, Oxford: Oxford University Press.

Airs, Malcolm (1975), *The Making of the English Country House 1500–1640*, London: Architectural Press.

Ajmar-Wollheim, Marta (2006), 'Sociability', in Marta Ajmar-Wollheim and Flora Dennis (eds.), *At Home in Renaissance Italy*, 206–21, London: Victoria and Albert Museum.

Ajmar-Wollheim, Marta and Flora Dennis, eds. (2006), *At Home in Renaissance Italy*, London: Victoria and Albert Museum.

Alcock, Nat (2015), 'The Development of the Vernacular House in South-West England, 1500–1700', in John Allan, Nat Alcock and David Dawson (eds.), *West Country Households 1500–1700*, 9–33, Woodbridge: Boydell Press.

Allerston, Patricia (1998), 'Wedding Finery in Sixteenth-Century Venice', in Trevor Dean and Kate Lowe (eds.), *Marriage in Italy, 1300–1650*, 25–40, Cambridge: Cambridge University Press.

Amussen, Susan Dwyer (1988), *An Ordered Society: Gender and Class in Early Modern England*, Oxford: Basil Blackwell.

Aston, Margaret (1988), *England's Iconoclasts*, Vol. 1: *Laws Against Images*, Oxford: Clarendon Press.

Aston, Margaret (2003), 'The Use of Images', in Richard Marks and Paul Will (eds.), *Gothic: Art for England 1400–1547*, 68–75, London: V&A Publishing.

Aston, Margaret (2015), *Broken Idols of the English Reformation*, Cambridge: Cambridge University Press.

Aynsley, Jeremy and Charlotte Grant (2006), 'Introduction', in *Imagined Interiors: Representing the Domestic Interior Since the Renaissance*, London: V&A Publications.

Baatsen, Inneke, Bruno Blondé and Julie De Groot (2014), 'The Kitchen between Representation and Everyday Experience: The Case of Sixteenth-Century Antwerp', in Christine Göttler, Bart Ramakers and Joanna Woodall (eds.), *Trading Values in Early Modern Antwerp*, 162–85, Leiden: Brill.

Baatsen, Inneke, Bruno Blondé and Carolien De Staelen (2016), 'Antwerp and the "Material Renaissance": Exploring the Social and Economic Significance of Crystal Glass and Majolica in the Sixteenth Century', in Catherine Richardson, Tara Hamling and David Gaimster (eds.), *The Routledge Handbook of Material Culture in Early Modern Europe*, 436–51, London: Routledge.

Baer, William (2000), 'Housing the Poor and Mechanick Class in Seventeenth-Century London', *London Journal*, 25 (2): 13–39.

Baer, William (2008), 'Housing for the Lesser Sort in Stuart London: Findings from the Certificates and Returns of Divided Houses', *London Journal*, 33 (1): 61–88.

Bailey, Joanne and Loreen Giese (2013), 'Marital Cruelty: Reconsidering Lay Attitudes in England, c. 1580 to 1850', *History of the Family*, 18 (3): 289–305.

Barclay, Katie (2011) *Love, Intimacy and Power: Marriage and Patriarchy in Scotland, 1650–1850*, Manchester: Manchester University Press.

Barley, Maurice (1967), 'Rural Housing in England', in Joan Thirsk (ed.), *The Agrarian History of England and Wales*, Vol. 4: *1500–1640*, 696–766, Cambridge: Cambridge University Press.

Bastress-Dukehart, Erica (2008) 'Sibling Conflict within Early Modern German Noble Families', *Journal of Family History*, 33, (1): 61–80.

Bath, Michael (2003), 'Grave Sentences', in *Renaissance Decorative Painting in Scotland*, 169–84, Edinburgh: National Museums of Scotland Publishing.

Begiato (Bailey), Joanne (2016), 'Pregnancy and Childbirth', in Susan Broomhall (ed.), *Early Modern Emotions: An Introduction*, 211–13, London: Routledge, Taylor & Francis.

Begiato (Bailey), Joanne (2017) 'Breeding a "Little Stranger": Managing Uncertainty in Pregnancy in Later Georgian England', in Jen Evans and Ciara Meehan (eds.), *Perceptions of Pregnancy from the Seventeenth to Twentieth Century*, 13–33, Basingstoke, Hampshire: Palgrave.

Bennett, Judith and Amy Froide, eds. (1999), *Singlewomen in the European Past, 1250–1800*, Philadelphia, PA: University of Pennsylvania Press.

Bibring, Tovi (2008) 'Love Thy Chambermaid: Emotional and Physical Violence Against the Servant in Les Cent Nouvelles', in Susan Broomhall (ed.), *Emotions in the Household 1200–1900*, 53–68, Basingstoke: Palgrave Macmillan.

Braddick, Michael, J. (2009), 'Introduction: The Politics of Gesture', in *The Politics of Gesture: Historical Perspectives, Past and Present*, Supplement 4, Michael J. Braddick (ed.), 9–35, Oxford: Oxford University Press.

Brady, Andrea (2008) 'A Share of Sorrows: Death in the Early Modern English Household', in Susan Broomhall (ed.), *Emotions in the Household 1200–1900*, 185–202, Basingstoke: Palgrave Macmillan.

Brady, Thomas A., Heiko Oberman and James Tracy, eds. (1995), *Handbook of European History, 1400–1600: Late Middle Ages, Renaissance, and Reformation*, Leiden: Brill.

Bremmer, Jan and Herman Roodenurg, eds. (1991), *A Cultural History of Gesture*, Oxford: Polity.

Broomhall, Susan (2002) '"Women's Little Secrets": Defining the Boundaries of Reproductive Knowledge in Sixteenth-Century France', *Social History of Medicine*, 15 (1): 1–15.

Broomhall, Susan (2008), 'Emotions in the Household', in Susan Broomhall (ed.), *Emotions in the Household 1200–1900*, 1–37, Basingstoke: Palgrave Macmillan.

Brown, Carleton, ed. (1962), 'The Latemest Day', no. 29, in *English Lyrics of the XIIIth Century*, Oxford: Clarendon Press.

Brundin, Abigail, Deborah Howard and Mary Laven, eds. (2018), *The Sacred Home in Renaissance Italy*, Oxford: Oxford University Press.

Burke, Peter (2009), *Popular Culture in Early Modern Europe*, Aldershot: Ashgate Publishing.

Bushnell, Rebecca (2003), *Green Desire: Imagining Early Modern English Gardens*, Ithaca, NY, and London: Cornell University Press.

Cambers, Andrew (2011), *Godly Reading: Print, Manuscript and Puritanism in England, 1580–1720*, Cambridge: Cambridge University Press.

Capp, Bernard (2003), *When Gossips Meet: Women, Family, and Neighbourhood in Early Modern England*, Oxford: Oxford University Press.

Carson, Neil (1988), *A Companion to Henslowe's Diary*, Cambridge: Cambridge University Press.

Casey, James (1999), *Early Modern Spain: A Social History*, London and New York: Routledge.

Casey, James (2007), *Family and Community in Early Modern Spain: The Citizens of Granada 1570–1739*, Cambridge: Cambridge University Press.

Cathcart, Alison (2008), '"Inressying of kyndnes, and renewing off thair blud": The Family, Kinship and Clan Policy in Sixteenth-Century Scottish Gaeldom', in Elizabeth Ewen and Janay Nugent (eds.), *Finding the Family in Medieval and Early Modern Scotland*, 127–38, London and New York: Routledge.

Cavallo, Sandra (2006), 'The Artisan's Casa', in Marta Ajmar-Wollheim and Flora Dennis (eds.), *At Home in Renaissance Italy*, 66–75, London: V&A Publications.

Cavallo, Sandra (2010), 'Family Relationships', in Sandra Cavallo (ed.), *A Cultural History of Childhood and Family in the Early Modern Age*, Vol. 3: The Early Modern Age, 15–32, Oxford: Berg.

Cavallo, Sandra and Lyndon Warner, eds. (1999), *Widowhood in Medieval and Early Modern Europe*, New York: Longman.

Chapelot, Jean and Robert Fossier (1985), *The Village and House in the Middle Ages*, London: B.T. Batsford.

Chartier, Roger, ed. (1989), *A History of Private Life*, Vol. 3: *Passions of the Renaissance*, Cambridge: Harvard University Press.

Chavasse, Ruth (2008), 'Humanist Educational and Emotional Expectations of Teenagers in Late Fifteenth-Century Italy', in Susan Broomhall (ed.), *Emotions in the Household 1200–1900*, 69–84, Basingstoke: Palgrave Macmillan.

Chayanov, A.V. (1986), *The Theory of Peasant Economy*, Madison, WI: University of Wisconsin Press.

Chojnacka, Monica (2001), *Working Women of Early Modern Venice*, Baltimore, MD: Johns Hopkins University Press.

Clark, Alice ([1919] 1982), *The Working Life of Women in the Seventeenth Century*, London: Routledge.

Cohen, Elizabeth S. and Thomas V. Cohen (2001–2), 'Open and Shut: The Social Meanings of the Cinquecento Roman House', *Studies in the Decorative Arts*, 9 (1): 61–84.

Collins, James B. (1989), 'The Economic Role of Women in Seventeenth-Century France', *French Historical Studies*, 16 (2): 436–70.

Cooper, Nicholas (1999), *Houses of the Gentry, 1480–168*, New Haven, CT, and London: Yale University Press.

Corazzini, G.O., ed. (1906), *Ricordanze di Barolomeo Masi calderaio fiorentino dal 1478 al 1526*, Florence: G. C. Sansoni.

Cowan, Alexander (1998), *Urban Europe, 1500–1700*, London: Arnold.

Currie, Elizabeth (2006), 'Textiles and Clothing', in Marta Ajmar-Wollheim and Flora Dennis (eds.), *At Home in Renaissance Italy*, 342–51, London: V&A Publications.

Davies, Kathryn (2008), *Artisan Art: Vernacular Wall Paintings in the Welsh Marshes, 1550–1650*, Almeley: Logaston Press.

Davis, Natalie Zemon (1982), 'Women in the Crafts in Sixteenth-Century Lyon', *Feminist Studies*, 8 (1): 46–80.

de Vries, Jan (1974), *The Dutch Rural Economy in the Golden Age: 1500–1700*, New Haven, CT, and London: Yale University Press.

de Vries, Jan (2008), *The Industrious Revolution: Consumer Behaviour and the Household Economy, 1650 to the Present*, Cambridge: Cambridge University Press.

Dennis, Flora (2010), 'Scattered Knives and Dismembered Song: Cutlery, Music and the Rituals of Dining', *Renaissance Studies*, 24 (1): 156–84.

Dewald, Jonathan (2015), *Status, Power and Identity in Early Modern France: The Rohan Family 1550–1715*, University Park, PA: Pennsylvania State University Press.

Dolan, Frances E. (2002), 'Gender and the "Lost" Spaces of Catholicism', *Journal of Interdisciplinary History*, 32 (4): 641–65.

Douglas, Mary (1993), 'The Idea of Home: A Kind of Space', in Arien Mack (ed.), *Home: A Place in the World*, 261–81, New York: New York University Press.

Duffy, Eamon (1992), *The Stripping of the Altars: Traditional Religion in England 1400–1580*, New Haven, CT, and London: Yale University Press.

Duffy, Eamon (2011), *Marking the Hours: English People and their Prayers 1240–1570*, New Haven, CT, and London: Yale University Press.

Dyer, Christopher (2003), *Making a Living in the Middle Ages: The People of Britain 850–1520*, London: Penguin Books.

Earle, Peter (1989), *The Making of the English Middle Class: Business, Society and Family Life in London, 1660–1730*, Berkeley, CA: University of California Press.

Earle, Peter (1994), *A City Full of People: Men and Women of London, 1650–1750*, London: Methuen.

Emigh, Rebecca Jean (2000), 'The Gender Division of Labour: The Case of Tuscan Smallholders', *Continuity and Change*, 15 (1): 117–37.

Emigh, Rebecca Jean (2001), 'Theorizing Strategies: Households and Markets in 15th-Century Tuscany', *History of the Family*, 6 (4): 495–517.

Emmer, Pieter (2003), 'The Myth of Early Globalisation: The Atlantic Economy, 1500–1800', *European Review*, 11 (1): 37–47.

Erickson, Amy L. (1993), *Women and Property in Early Modern England*, London: Routledge.

Faini, Marco and Alessia Meneghin, eds. (2018), *Domestic Devotions in the Early Modern World*, Leiden and Boston, MA: Brill.

Fairchilds, Cissie (1984), *Domestic Enemies: Servants and Their Masters in Old Regime France*, Baltimore, MD: Johns Hopkins University Press.

Fairer, David (2006), 'Mary Leapor, "Crumble-Hall"', in Christine Gerrard (ed.), *A Companion to Eighteenth-Century Poetry*, 223–36, Oxford: Blackwell, 2006.

Fenlon, Jane (2011), 'Moving towards the Formal House: Room Usage in Early Modern Ireland', *Proceedings of the Royal Irish Academy: Archaeology, Culture, History, Literature, Special Issue: Domestic Life in Ireland*, 111C: 141–68.

Fernández, Mercedes Borrero (1998), 'Peasant and Aristocratic Women: Their Role in the Rural Economy of Seville at the End of the Middle Ages', in Marilyn Stone and Carmen Benito-Vessels (eds.), *Women at Work in Spain from the Middle Ages to Early Modern Times*, 11–32, New York: Peter Lang Publishing.

Fisher, F.J. (1948), 'The Development of London as a Centre of Conspicuous Consumption in the Sixteenth and Seventeenth Centuries', *Transactions of the Royal Historical Society*, 4th Series, 30: 37–50.

Flather, Amanda J. (2007), *Gender and Space in Early Modern England*, Woodbridge: Boydell Press.

Flather, Amanda J. (2011), 'Gender, Space, and Place: The Experience of Service in the Early Modern English Household c. 1580–1720', *Home Cultures*, 8 (2): 171–88.

Flather, Amanda J. (2013), 'Space, Place, and Gender: The Sexual and Spatial Division of Labor in the Early Modern Household', *History and Theory*, 52 (3): 344–60.

Fleming, Hannah (2014), 'At Home with Books: Resuscitating the History of Eighteenth-Century Reading and Readers at the Geffrye Museum', *Art Libraries Journal*, 39 (3): 5–9.

Fleming, Peter (2004), *Family and Household in Medieval England*, Basingstoke: Palgrave.

Fletcher, Anthony (1975), *Sussex 1600–1660: A County Community in Peace and War*, Chichester: Phillimore.

Fletcher, Anthony (1995), *Gender, Sex and Subordination in England 1500–1800*, New Haven, CT: Yale University Press.

Fletcher, Catherine (2015), *Diplomacy in Renaissance Rome: The Rise of the Resident Ambassador*, Cambridge: Cambridge University Press.

Foakes, R.A. (1968), 'Introduction', *The Comedy of Errors*, The Arden Edition of the Works of William Shakespeare, xli, London: Methuen and Cambridge, MA: Harvard University Press.

Foister, Susan (1981), 'Paintings and Other Works of Art in Sixteenth-Century English Inventories', *Burlington Magazine*, 123: 273–82.

Foister, Susan (2003), 'Private Devotion', in Richard Marks and Paul Williamson (eds.), *Gothic: Art for England 1400–1547*, 334–47, London: V&A Publications.

Fortini Brown, Patricia (2000), 'Behind the Walls: Material Culture of Venetian Elites', in John Martin and Dennis Romano (eds.), *Venice Reconsidered: The History and Civilization of an Italian City-State*, 295–338, Baltimore, MD: Johns Hopkins University Press.

Fortini Brown, Patricia (2006), 'The Venetian *Casa*', in Marta Ajmar-Wollheim and Flora Dennis (eds.), *At Home in Renaissance Italy*, 50–65, London: V&A Publications.

Foyster, Elizabeth (1999a), 'Boys will be Boys? Manhood and Aggression, 1660–1800', in Tim Hitchcock and Michelle Cohen (eds.), *English Masculinities*, 151–66, London: Longman.

Foyster, Elizabeth (1999b), *Manhood in England: Honour, Sex and Marriage*, London and New York: Longman.

Foyster, Elizabeth (2002), *Marital Violence: An English Family History, 1660–1857*, Cambridge: Cambridge University Press.

Fraiman, Susan (2017), *Extreme Domesticity: A View from the Margins*, New York: Columbia University Press.

Franits, Wayne (1986), 'The Family Saying Grace: A Theme in Dutch Art of the Seventeenth Century', *Simiolus: Netherlands Quarterly for the History of Art*, 16 (1): 36–49.

Friedman, Alice T. (1989), *House and Household in Elizabethan England: Wollaton Hall and the Willoughby Family*, Chicago, IL, and London: University of Chicago Press.

Frigo, Daniela (1985), *Il padre di famiglia: Governo della casa e governo civile nella tradizione dell' 'Economica' tra Cinque e Seicento*, Rome: Bulzoni.

Froide, Amy (2005), *Never Married: Singlewomen in Early Modern England*, Oxford: Oxford University Press.

Gager, Kristin Elizabeth (1996), *Blood Ties and Fictive Ties: Adoption and Family Life in Early Modern France*, Princeton, NJ: Princeton University Press.

Gaimster, David (1997), *German Stoneware 1200–1900: Archaeology and Cultural History*, London: British Museum Press.

Gaimster, David, Richenda Goffin and Lyn Blackmore (1990), 'The Continental Stove-Tile Fragments from St Mary Graces, London, in Their British and European Context', *Post-Medieval Archaeology*, 24 (1): 1–49.

Garrard, Rachel (1980), 'English Probate Inventories and Their Use in Studying the Significance of the Domestic Interior, 1500–1700', *AAG Bijdragen*, 23: 53–77.

Gilchrist, Roberta (2012), *Medieval Life: Archaeology and the Life Course*, Woodbridge: Boydell Press.

Girouard, Mark (1978), *Life in the English Country House*, New Haven, CT, and London: Yale University Press.

Goldberg, Jeremy (2010), 'Family Relationships', in Louise Wilkinson (ed.), *A Cultural History of Childhood and Family in the Middle Ages*, vol. 2, 21–39, Oxford: Berg.

Goldberg, P.J.P. (1992), *Women, Work and Life Cycle in a Medieval Economy: Women in York and Yorkshire c. 1300–1520*, Oxford: Oxford University Press.

Goldberg, P.J.P., ed. (1995), *Women in England c. 1275–1525: Documentary Sources*, Manchester: Manchester University Press.

Goldthwaite, Richard, A. (1987), 'The Empire of Things: Consumer Demand in Renaissance Italy', in F.W. Kent and Patricia Simons (eds.), *Patronage, Art and Society in Renaissance Italy*, 153–75, Oxford: Oxford University Press.

Goldthwaite, Richard, A. (1989), 'The Economic and Social World of Italian Renaissance Maiolica', *Renaissance Quarterly*, 42 (1): 1–32.

Goldthwaite, Richard, A. (1993), *Wealth and the Demand for Art in Italy, 1300–1600*, London and Baltimore, MD: Johns Hopkins University Press.

Goody, Jack (1982), *Cooking, Cuisine and Class: A Study in Comparative Sociology*, Cambridge: Cambridge University Press.

Gordon, Sarah (2008), 'Humour and Household Relationships: Servants in Late Medieval and Sixteenth Century French Farce', in Susan Broomhall (ed.), *Emotions in the Household 1200–1900*, 85–102, Basingstoke: Palgrave Macmillan.

Gowing, Laura (1996), *Domestic Dangers: Women, Words and Sex in Early Modern London*, Oxford: Oxford University Press.

Gowing, Laura (2003), *Common Bodies: Women, Touch and Power in Seventeenth-Century England*, New Haven, CT, and London: Yale University Press.

Gray, Marion W. (2000), *Productive Men and Reproductive Women: The Agrarian Household and the Emergence of Separate Spheres during the German Enlightenment*, New York: Berghahn Books.

Grieco, Allen (1999), 'Food and Social Classes in Late Medieval and Renaissance Italy', in Jean-Louis Flandrin and Massinori Montanari (eds.) and Albert Sonnerfeld (trans.), *Food: A Culinary History*, 302–12, New York: Columbia University Press.

Grieco, Allen (2006), 'Meals', in Marta Ajmar-Wollheim and Flora Dennis (eds.), *At Home in Renaissance Italy*, 244–53, London: Victoria and Albert Museum.

Griffin, Ralph (1915), *Kentish Items Wrotham*, London: John Bale, Sons & Danielsson, Ltd.

Guerzoni, Guido (2011), *Apollo and Vulcan: The Art Market in Italy, 1400–1700*, East Lansing, MI: Michigan State University Press; originally published in 2006 as *Apollo e Vulcano: I mercati artistici in Italia, 1400–1700*, Venice: Marsilio Editori S.p.A.

Haeger, Barbara (1986), 'The Prodigal Son in Sixteenth and Seventeenth-Century Netherlandish Art: Depictions of the Parable and the Evolution of a Catholic Image', *Simiolus*, 16: 128–38.

Haines, W. (1879), 'Spershott's Memoirs of Chichester (18th Century)', *Sussex Archaeological Collections*, 29: 219–31.

Hajnal, John (1965), 'European Marriage Pattern in Historical Perspective', in D.V. Glass and D.E.C. Eversley (eds.), *Population in History*, 101–43, London: Arnold.

Hallam, Elizabeth (1996), 'Turning the Hourglass: Gender Relations at the Deathbed in Early Modern Canterbury', *Mortality*, 1 (1): 61–82.

Hamling, Tara (2010), *Decorating the 'Godly' Household: Religious Art in Post-Reformation Britain*, New Haven, CT, and London: Yale University Press.

Hamling, Tara (2013), '"An Arelome To This Hous For Ever": Monumental Fixtures and Furnishings in the English Domestic Interior, *c.* 1560–*c.* 1660', in Andrew Gordon and Thomas Rist (eds.), *The Arts of Remembrance in Early Modern England: Memorial Cultures of the Post Reformation*, 59–88, Aldershot: Ashgate.

Hamling, Tara (2015), 'Seeing Salvation in the Domestic Hearth in Post-Reformation England', in Jonathan Willis (ed.), *Sin and Salvation in Reformation England*, 223–44, Aldershot: Routledge.

Hamling, Tara and Catherine Richardson (2017), *A Day at Home in Early Modern England: Material Culture and Domestic Life 1500–1700*, New Haven, CT, and London: Yale University Press.

Hanawalt, Barbara (1986), *The Ties that Bound: Peasant Families in Medieval England*, Oxford: Oxford University Press.

Hardwick, Julie (2006), 'Early Modern Perspectives on the Long History of Domestic Violence: The Case of Seventeenth-Century France', *Journal of Modern History*, 78 (1): 1–36.

Hardwick, Julie (2010), *The Practice of Patriarchy: Gender and the Politics of Household Authority in Early Modern France*, Philadelphia, PA: Pennsylvania University Press.

Harrington, Joel (2008), 'Child Circulation within the Early Modern Urban Community: Rejection and Support of Unwanted Children in Nuremberg', in Michael Halverson and Karen Spierling (eds.), *Defining Community in Early Modern Europe*, 103–20, London: Routledge.

Harris Sacks, David (2000), 'London's Dominion: The Metropolis, the Market Economy, and the State', in Lena Cowen Orlin (ed.), *Material London, ca. 1600*, 20–54, Philadelphia, PA: University of Pennsylvania Press.

Harvey, Karen (2012), *The Little Republic: Masculinity and Domestic Authority in Eighteenth-Century Britain*, Oxford: Oxford University Press.

Hatfield, Rab (1970), 'Some Unknown Descriptions of the Medici Palace in 1459', *Art Bulletin*, 52 (3): 232–49.

Hausen, Reinhold, ed. (1909), 'Förteckning öfver Hertig Johans af Finland och hans gemål Katarina Jagellonicas lösendom 1563', *Bidrag till Finlands historia*, 3, Helsinki: The National Archives of Finland.

Heal, Felicity (1990), *Hospitality in Early Modern England*, Oxford: Clarendon Press.

Hewitt, Margaret and Ivy Pinchbeck (1969), *Children in English Society*, Vol. 1: *From Tudor Times to the Eighteenth Century*, London: Routledge & Kegan Paul.

Hodgkinson, Jeremy (2010), *British Cast-Iron Firebacks of the 16th to Mid 18th Centuries*, Crawley: Hodgers Books.

Hohti, Paula (2010a), '"Conspicuous" Consumption and Popular Consumers: Material Culture and Social Status in Sixteenth-Century Siena', *Renaissance Studies*, 24 (5): 654–70.

Hohti, Paula (2010b), 'Domestic Space and Identity: Artisans, Shopkeepers and Traders in Sixteenth-Century Siena', in Fabrizio Nevola and Guido Rebecchini (eds.), *Journal of Urban History*, 37, Special Issue (3): 372–85.

Hollander, Melissa (2008), 'The Name of the Father: Baptism and the Social Construction of Fatherhood in Early Modern Edinburgh', in Elizabeth Ewen and Janay Nugent (eds.), *Finding the Family in Medieval and Early Modern Scotland*, 63–72, Farnham: Ashgate.

Hoskins, W.G. (1953), 'The Rebuilding of Rural England, 1570–1640', *Past and Present*, 4: 44–59.

Howard, Maurice and Edward Wilson (2003), *The Vyne: A Tudor House Revealed*, Manvers: The National Trust.

Howell, Martha (1986a), *Women, Production and Patriarchy in Late Medieval Cities*, Chicago, IL: University of Chicago Press.

Howell, Martha C. (1986b), 'Women, the Family Economy, and the Structures of Market Production in Cities of Northern Europe during the Late Middle Ages', in Barbara Hanawalt (ed.), *Women and Work in Pre-Industrial Europe*, 198–222, Bloomington, IN: University of Indiana Press.

Howell, Martha C. (1996), 'Fixing Movables: Gifts by Testament in Late Medieval Douai', *Past & Present*, 150 (1): 3–45.

Jackson, Anna and Amin Jaffer (2004), *Encounters: The Meeting of Asia and Europe, 1500–1800*, London: V & A Publications.

Jackson, Victoria (2012), 'Shakespeare's World in 100 Objects'. Available online: http://findingshakespeare.co.uk/shakespeares-world-in-100-objects-number-5-german-panel-jug (accessed 7 February 2013).

Jardine, Lisa (1996), *Worldly Goods: A New History of the Renaissance*, New York: Nan A. Talese.

Jenkins, David, ed. (2003), *The Cambridge History of Western Textiles*, Cambridge: Cambridge University Press.

Johnson, Matthew H. (1993a), 'Rethinking the Great Rebuilding', *Oxford Journal of Archaeology*, 12 (1): 117–25.

Johnson, Matthew H. (1993b), *Housing Culture: Traditional Architecture in an English Landscape*, London: University College London Press.

Johnson, Matthew (1996), *An Archaeology of Capitalism*, Oxford: Blackwell.

Johnson, Matthew (2010), *English Houses, 1300–1800: Vernacular Architecture, Social Life*, Harlow: Pearson Longman.

Kamen, Henry (2000), *Early Modern European Society*, London. Routledge.

Kent, F.W. (1987), 'Palaces, Politics and Society in Fifteenth-Century Florence', *I Tatti Studies: Essays in the Renaissance*, 2: 41–70.

Kent, F.W. et al. (1981), 'The Making of a Renaissance Patron of the Arts', in *Giovanni Rucellai ed il suo Zibaldone, II: A Florentine Patrician and His Palace*, 9–95, London: Warburg Institute.

King, Chris (2009), 'The Interpretation of Urban Buildings: Power, Memory and Appropriation in Norwich Merchants' Houses, *c.* 1400–1660', *World Archaeology*, 41 (3): 471–88.

Kingsley Kent, Susan (2012), *Gender and History*, Basingstoke: Palgrave MacMillan.

Kuehn, Thomas (2017), *Family and Gender in Renaissance Italy, 1300–1600*, Cambridge: Cambridge University Press.

Kümin, Beat, ed. (2018), *The European World 1500–1800: An Introduction to Early Modern History*, 3rd edn, London: Routledge.

Kussmaul, Anne (1981), *Servants in Husbandry in Early Modern England*, Cambridge: Cambridge University Press.

Lamberg, Marko (2008), 'Suspicion, Rivalry and Care: Mistresses and Maidservants in Early-Modern Stockholm', in Susan Broomhall (ed.), *Emotions in the Household 1200–1900*, 170–84, Basingstoke: Palgrave Macmillan.

Laslett, Peter (1965), *The World We Have Lost*, London: Methuen.

Laslett, Peter (1977), *Family Life and Illicit Love in Earlier Generations*, Cambridge: Cambridge University Press.

Laslett, Peter (1983), *The World We Have Lost Further Explored*, London: Routledge.

Laslett, Peter and Richard Wall (1972), *Household and Family in Past Times*, Cambridge: Cambridge University Press.

Laumonier, Lucie (2016), 'Grandparents in Urban and Rural Lower Languedoc at the End of the Middle Ages', *Journal of Family History*, 41(2): 103–17.

Leech, Roger (1996), 'The Prospect from Rugman's Row: The Row House in Late Sixteenth- and Early Seventeenth-Century London', *Archaeological Journal*, 153: 201–42.

Leech, Roger (2000), 'The Symbolic Hall: Historical Context and Merchant Culture in the Early Modern City', *Vernacular Architecture*, 31 (1): 1–10.

Lefebvre, Henri (1991), *The Production of Space*, trans. Donald Nicholson-Smith, Oxford: Blackwell.

Levy Peck, Linda (2005), *Consuming Splendor: Society and Culture in Seventeenth-Century England*, Cambridge: Cambridge University Press.

Liefkes, Reino (2006), 'Meals', in Marta Ajmar-Wollheim and Flora Dennis (eds.), *At Home in Renaissance Italy*, 254–65, London: Victoria and Albert Museum.

Lindow, James R. (2007), *The Renaissance Palace in Florence: Magnificence and Splendour in Fifteenth-Century Italy*, Aldershot: Ashgate.

Loomis, Catherine (2016), '"Now Began a New Miserie": The Performance of Pedagogy in Nicholas Breton's *The Miseries of Mavillia*', in Kathryn M. Moncrief (ed.), *Performing Pedagogy in Early Modern England: Gender, Instruction, and Performance*, 21–32, London: Routledge.

Lundberg, Erik (1948), *Byggnadskonsten i Sverige. Sengoti och renässans, 1400–1650*, Stockholm: Nordisk Rotogravyr.

Machin, Robert (1977), 'The Great Rebuilding: A Reassessment', *Past and Present*, 77: 33–56.

Mann, Catherine (2008), '"Whether Your Ladiship Will or Ne": Displeasure, Duty and Devotion in *The Lisle Letters*', in Susan Broomhall (ed.), *Emotions in the Household 1200–1900*, 119–34, Basingstoke: Palgrave Macmillan.

Martin, Jessica and Alec Ryrie, eds. (2012), *Domestic and Private Devotion in Early Modern Britain*, London & New York: Routledge.

Martin, David (2000), 'End Reversal during the Conversion of Medieval Houses in Sussex', *Vernacular Architecture*, 31 (1): 26–31.

Martin, David and Barbara (2006), *Farm Buildings of the Weald 1450–1750*, King's Lynn: Heritage Marketing and Publications.

Martin, David and Barbara, Jane Clubb and Gillian Draper (2009), *Rye Rebuilt: Regeneration and Decline within a Sussex Port Town, 1350–1660*, Burgess Hill: Domtom Publishing.

Martin, David and Barbara, Christopher Whittick and Jane Brisco (2017), *Rural Medieval and Transitional Housing in the Eastern High Weald 1250–c. 1570*, Burgess Hill: Domtom Publishing.

Massey, Doreen (1994), *Space, Place and Gender*, Cambridge: Polity.

Matchette, Ann (2007), 'Credit and Credibility: Used Goods and Social Relations in Sixteenth-Century Florence', in Michelle O'Malley and Evelyn Welch (eds.), *The Material Renaissance*, 225–41, Manchester: Manchester University Press.

Matthews-Grieco, Sarah F. (2006), 'Marriage and Sexuality', in Marta Ajmar-Wollheim and Flora Dennis (eds.), *At Home in Renaissance Italy*, 104–19, London: Victoria and Albert Museum.

McCarthy, Conor (2004), *Marriage in Medieval England: Law, Literature, and Practice*, Woodbridge: Boydell Press.

McGough, Laura J. (2010), *Gender, Sexuality and Syphilis in Early Modern Venice: The Disease that Came to Stay*, Basingstoke: Palgrave MacMillan.

McIntosh, Marjorie K. (2005), *Working Women in English Society, 1300–1620*, Cambridge: Cambridge University Press.

McKeon, Michael (2006), *The Secret History of Domesticity: Public, Private, and the Division of Knowledge*, Baltimore, MD: John Hopkins University Press.

Meldrum, Tim (2000), *Domestic Service and Gender 1660–1750*, Harlow: Longman.

Mendelson, Sara and Patricia Crawford (1998), *Women in Early Modern England*, Oxford: Oxford University Press.

Mennell, Stephen (1985), *All Manner of Foods: Eating and Taste in England and France from the Middle Ages to the Present*, Oxford: Oxford University Press.

Mercer, Henry C. (1914), *The Bible in Iron: Or the Pictured Stoves and Stove Plates of the Pennsylvanian Germans*, Doylestown, PA: [Published for the Bucks County Historical Society].

Morgan, Roy (1992), *Chichester: A Documentary History*, Chichester: Phillimore.

Morrall, Andrew (2002), 'Protestant Pots: Morality and Social Ritual in the Early Modern Home', *Journal of Design History*, 15 (4): 263–73.

Morrall, Andrew (2007), 'The Reformation of the Virtues in Sixteenth-Century German Art and Decoration', in Tara Hamling and Richard L. Williams (eds.), *Art Re-formed: Re-assessing the Impact of the Reformation on the Visual Arts*, 105–26, Newcastle: Cambridge Scholars Publishing.

Morrall, Andrew (2012), 'Inscriptional Wisdom and the Domestic Arts in Early Modern Northern Europe', in Natalia Filatkina, Birgit Ulrike Münch and Ane Kleine-Engel (eds.), *Formelhaftigkeit in Text und Bild*, 120–38, Wiesbaden: Reichert Verlag.

Mukerji, Chandra (1983), *From Graven Images: Patterns of Modern Materialism*, New York: Columbia University Press.

Muldrew, Craig (1998), *The Economy of Obligation: Culture of Credit and Social Relations in Early Modern England*, Basingstoke: Palgrave.

Musacchio, Jacqueline (1999), *The Art and Ritual of Childbirth in Renaissance Italy*, New Haven, CT, and London: Yale University Press.

Musacchio, Jacqueline (2008), *Art, Marriage and Family in the Florentine Renaissance Palace*, New Haven, CT, and London: Yale University Press.

Musgrave, Peter (1999), *The Early Modern European Economy*, Basingstoke: Macmillan.

Newton, Hannah (2012), *The Sick Child in Early Modern England 1580–1720*, Oxford: Oxford University Press.

Nicholas, David (2003), *Urban Europe, 1100–1700*, Basingstoke: Palgrave Macmillan.

Nuechterlein, Jeanne (2005), 'The Domesticity of Sacred Space in the Fifteenth-Century Netherlands', in Andrew Spicer and Sarah Hamilton (eds.), *Defining the Holy: Sacred Space in Medieval and Early Modern Europe*, 49–80, Aldershot: Ashgate.

O'Brien, Karen (2016), 'Intimate Worlds: Kinship Relations and Emotional Investment among Nantwich Women 1603–1685', *Journal of Family History*, 41 (2): 131–43.

O'Day, Rosemary (1994), *The Family and Family Relationships, 1500–1900: England, France and the United States of America*, Basingstoke: Macmillan.

Ogilvie, Sheila (2003), *A Bitter Living Women, Markets, and Social Capital in Early-Modern Germany*, Oxford: Oxford University Press.

Ogilvie, Sheila and Jeremy Edwards (2000), 'Women and the "Second Serfdom": Evidence from Early Modern Bohemia', *Journal of Economic History*, 60 (4): 961–94.

Ogilvie, Sheila and Markus Cerman, eds. (1996), *European Proto-Industrialization*, Cambridge: Cambridge University Press.

Oja, Linda (2015), 'Childcare and Gender in Sweden c. 1600–1800', *Gender and History*, 27 (1): 77–111.

Orlin, Lena (1994), *Private Matters and Public Culture in Post-Reformation England*, Ithaca, NY: Cornell University Press.

Orlin, Lena Cowen (2002), 'Things with Little Social Life (Henslowe's Theatrical Properties and Elizabethan Household Fittings)', in Jonathan Gil Harris and Natasha Korda (eds.), *Staged Properties in Early Modern English Drama*, 99–128, Cambridge: Cambridge University Press.

Orlin, Lena Cowen (2007), *Locating Privacy in Tudor London*, Oxford: Oxford University Press.

Orlin, Lena Cowen, ed. (1995), *Elizabethan Households: An Anthology*, Washington, DC: Folger Shakespeare Library.

Orlin, Lena Cowen, ed. (2000), *Material London ca. 1600*, Philadelphia, PA: University of Pennsylvania Press.

Overton, Mark, Jane Whittle, Darron Dean and Andrew Hann (2004), *Production and Consumption in English Households 1600–1750*, Abingdon: Routledge.

The Oxford English Dictionary (OED) (1989), Second Edition, ed. John Simpson and Edmund Weiner, Oxford: Clarendon Press,

Ozment, Steven (1986), *Magdalena and Balthasar: An Intimate Portrait of Life in 16th Century Europe Revealed in the Letters of a Nuremberg Husband and Wife*, New York: Simon and Schuster.

Ozment, Steven (1989), *Magdalena and Balthasar: An Intimate Portrait of Life in 16th Century Europe Revealed in the Letters of a Nuremberg Husband and Wife*, New Haven, CT, and London: Yale University Press.

Palumbo-Fossati, Isabella (1984), 'L'interno della casa dell'artigiano e dell'artenella Venezia del Cinquecento', *Studi Veneziani*, 8: 109–53.

Pardailhe-Galabrun, Annik (1991), *The Birth of Intimacy Privacy and Domestic Life in Early Modern Paris*, trans. Jocelyn Phelps, Oxford: Polity.

Pearson, Sarah (1994), *The Medieval Houses of Kent*, London: Royal Commission on Historical Monuments.

Peel, J.H.B. (1972), *An Englishman's Home*, London: Cassell.

Pennell, Sara (2016), *The Birth of the English Kitchen 1600–1850*, London: Bloomsbury Academic.

Penny, Nicholas (2006), 'Introduction: Toothpicks and Green Hangings', in Roberta Olson, Patricia L. Reilly and Rupert Shepherd (eds.), *The Biography of the Object*, 1–10, Oxford: Blackwell.

Peters, Christine (2003), *Women in Early Modern Britain, 1450–1640*, Basingstoke: Palgrave Macmillan.

Phillips, John (1974), *Reformation of Images: Destruction of Art in England, 1535–1660*, Berkeley, CA: University of California Press.

Piponnier, Francoise (1999), 'From Hearth to Table: Late Medieval Cooking Equipment', in Jean-Louis Flandrin and Massinori Montanari (eds.) and Albert Sonnerfeld (trans.), *Food: A Culinary History*, 339–46, New York: Columbia University Press.

Pollock, Linda (1989), '"Teach Her to Live under Obedience": The Making of Women in the Upper Ranks of Early Modern England', *Continuity and Change*, 4 (2): 231–58.

Pollock, Linda (1990), 'Embarking on a Rough Passage: The Experience of Pregnancy in Early-Modern Society', in V. Fildes (ed.), *Women as Mothers in Pre-Industrial England: Essays in Memory of Dorothy McLaren*, 39–67, London: Routledge.

Poos, L.R. (1991), *A Rural Society after the Black Death: Essex 1350–1525*, Cambridge: Cambridge University Press.

Poska, Allyson (2005), *Women and Authority in Early Modern Spain: The Peasants of Galicia*, Oxford: Oxford University Press.

Preyer, Brenda (1999), 'Planning for Visitors at Florentine Palaces', *Renaissance Studies*, 12 (3): 357–74.

Preyer, Brenda (2006), 'The Florentine Casa', in Marta Ajmar-Wollheim and Flora Dennis (eds.), *At Home in Renaissance Italy*, 34–49, London: V&A Publications.

Pylkkänen, Riitta (1956), *Renessanssin puku Suomessa 1550–1620*, Helsinki: WSOY.

Razi, Zvi (1981), 'Family, Land and the Village Community in Later Medieval England', *Past and Present*, 93 (1): 3–36.

Reader, Francis (1936), 'Tudor Domestic Wall Paintings, Part II', *Archaeological Journal*, 93: 220–62.

Rebel, Hermann (1983), *Peasant Classes: The Bureaucratization of Property and Family under Early Hapsburg Absolutism 1511–1636*, Princeton, NJ: Princeton University Press.

Reddy, William (2012), *The Making of Romantic Love: Longing and Sexuality in Europe, South Asia, and Japan, 900–1200 CE*, Chicago, IL: University of Chicago Press.

Reid, Margaret (1934), *Economics of Household Production*, New York: John Wiley and Sons.

Richardson, Catherine (2006a), *Domestic Life and Domestic Tragedy in Early Modern England: The Material Life of the Household*, Manchester: Manchester University Press.

Richardson, Catherine (2006b), 'Home, Household and Domesticity in Drama in Early Modern London', in Jeremy Aynsley and Charlotte Grant (eds.), *Imagined Interiors: Representing the Domestic Interior Since the Renaissance*, 50–67, London: V&A Publications.

Richardson, R.C. (2010), *Household Servants in Early Modern England*, Manchester: Manchester University Press.

Ricketts, Annabel (2007), *The English Country House Chapel: Building a Protestant Tradition*, Reading: Spire Books.

Riello, Giorgio (2017) 'Global Things: Europe's Early Modern Material Transformation', in Catherine Richardson, Tara Hamling and David Gaimster (eds.), *The Routledge Handbook of Material Culture in Early Modern Europe*, 29–45, London: Routledge.

Roberta, Olson, Patricia L. Reilly and Rupert Shepherd, eds. (2006), *The Biography of the Object*, Oxford: Blackwell.

Roberts, Michael (1979), 'Sickles and Scythes: Women's Work and Men's Work at Harvest Time', *History Workshop Journal*, 7: 3–28.

Roche, Daniel (2000), *A History of Everyday Things: The Birth of Consumption in France 1600–1800*, Cambridge: Cambridge University Press.

Rogers, Clifford J., ed. (1995), *The Military Revolution Debate: Readings on the Military Transformation of Early Modern Europe*, Oxford: Westview Press.

Romano, Dennis (1996), *Housecraft and Statecraft: Domestic Service in Renaissance Venice 1400–1600*, Baltimore, MD: John Hopkins University Press.

Rosenwein, Barbara A. (2006), *Emotional Communities in the Early Middle Ages*, Ithaca, NY: Cornell University Press.

Rothery, Mark and Henry French, eds. (2012), *Making Men: The Formation of Elite Male Identities in England, c.1660–1900: A Sourcebook*, Basingstoke: Palgrave.

Rowlands, Alison (1999), 'The Conditions of Life for the Masses', in Euan Cameron (ed.), *Early Modern Europe: An Oxford History*, 31–62, Oxford: Oxford University Press.

Rublack, Ulinke (1999), *The Crimes of Women in Early Modern Germany*, Oxford: Clarendon.

Rybczynski, Witold (2001), *Home: A Short History of an Idea*, London: Pocket Books.

Ryrie, Alec (2013), *Being Protestant in Reformation Britain*, Oxford: Oxford University Press.

Sabean, David (1984), *Power in the Blood: Popular Culture and Village Discourse in Early Modern Germany*, Cambridge: Cambridge University Press.

Sandvik, Hilde (2005), 'Decision-Making on Marital Property in Norway 1500–1800', in Maria Ågren and Amy Erickson (eds.), *The Marital Economy in Scandinavia and Britain 1400–1900*, 125–40, Aldershot: Ashgate.

Sarti, Raffaella (2002), *Europe at Home: Family and Material Culture 1500–1800*, trans. Allan Cameron, New Haven, CT, and London: Yale University Press.

Sarti, Raffaella (2014), 'Historians, Social Scientists, Servants, and Domestic Workers: Fifty Years of Research on Domestic and Care Work', *International Review of Social History*, 53: 279–314.

Schmidt, Ariadne (2011), 'Labour Ideologies and Women in the Northern Netherlands, *c.* 1500–1800', *International Review of Social History*, 56: 45–67.

Schofield, John (1984), *The Building of London from the Conquest to the Great Fire*, London: British Museum Press.

Scott, Tom, ed. (1998), *The Peasantries of Europe: From the Fourteenth to the Eighteenth Centuries*, London and New York: Longman.

Segalen, Martine (1984), *Love and Power in the Peasant Family*, trans. Sarah Matthews, Chicago, IL: University of Chicago Press.

Shepard, Alexandra (2003), *Meanings of Manhood in Early Modern England*, Oxford: Oxford University Press.

Shepard, Alexandra (2015), *Accounting for Oneself: Worth, Status and the Social Order in Early Modern England*, Oxford: Oxford University Press.

Sherman, Caroline (2008), 'Resentment and Rebellion in the Scholarly Household: Son and Amaneusis in the Godfrey Family', in Susan Broomhall (ed.), *Emotions in the Household 1200–1900*, 153–69, Basingstoke: Palgrave Macmillan.

Smith, William George, ed. (1948), *The Oxford Dictionary of English Proverbs*, intro. Janet E. Heseltine, rev. Sir Paul Harvey, 2nd edn, Oxford: Clarendon Press.

Sommerville, Margaret (1995), *Sex and Subjection: Attitudes to Women in Early Modern Society*, London: E. Arnold.

Spicer, Andrew and Sarah Hamilton, eds. (2005), *Defining the Holy: Sacred Space in Medieval and Early Modern Europe*, Aldershot: Ashgate.

Stone, Lawrence (1977), *The Family, Sex and Marriage in England 1500–1800*, London: Penguin.

Tadmor, Naomi (1996), 'The Concept of the Household-Family in Eighteenth-Century England', *Past and Present*, 151 (1): 111–40.

Tadmor, Naomi (2001), *Family and Friends in Eighteenth Century England*, Cambridge: Cambridge University Press.
Tankard, Danae (2011), 'The Regulation of Cottage Building in Seventeenth-Century Sussex', *Agricultural History Review*, 59 (1): 18–35.
Tankard, Danae (2012), *Houses of the Weald and Downland: People and Houses in South-East England c. 1300–1900*, Lancaster: Carnegie.
Tatton-Brown, Tim (1994), 'The Buildings of the Bishop's Palace and the Close', in Mary Hobbs (ed.), *Chichester Cathedral: An Historical Survey*, 225–46, Chichester: Phillimore.
Thomas, Keith (2009), *The Ends of Life: Roads to Fulfilment in Early Modern England*, Oxford: Oxford University.
Thomas-Stanford, Charles (1910), *Sussex in the Great War and the Interregnum*, London: Chiswick Press.
Thompson, Craig. R. (1965), *Desiderius Erasmus*, Chigago, IL: Chicago University Press.
Thornton, Dora and Luke Syson (2001), *Objects of Virtue: Art in Renaissance Italy*, London: British Museum Press.
Thornton, Peter (1991), *The Italian Renaissance Interior, 1400–1600*, New York: Harry N. Abrams.
Tilly, Louise and Joan Scott (1987), *Women, Work and Family*, New York: Routledge.
Tucker, M.J. ([1974] 2006) 'The Child as Beginning and End: Fifteenth and Sixteenth Century English Childhood', in Lloyd de Mause (ed.), *The History of Childhood*, 229–58, Lanham, MD: First Rowman and Littlefield Edition.
Tyacke, Nicholas, ed. (2003), *England's Long Reformation 1500–1800*, London: Routledge.
Ulrich, L.T. (1980), *Good Wives: Image and Reality in the Lives of Women in Northern New England, 1650–1750*, New York: Vintage.
Valenti, Cristina (1992), *Comici artigiani. Mestiere e forme dello spettacolo a Siena nella prima metà del Cinquecento*, Modena: Franco Cosimo Panini.
Van Damme, Ilja (2006), 'Changing Consumer Preferences and Evolutions in Retailing: Buying and Selling Consumer Durables in Antwerp (*c.* 1648–*c.* 1748)', in Bruno Blondé, Peter Stabel, Jon Stobart and Ilja Van Damme (eds.), *Buyers and Sellers: Retail Circuits and Practices in Medieval and Early Modern Europe*, 199–224, Turnhout: Brepols.
Van Gent, J. and S. Broomhall (2009), 'Corresponding Affections: Emotional Exchange among William the Silent's Children', *Journal of Family History*, 34 (2): 143–65.
Vickery, Amanda J. (1993) 'Golden Age to Separate Spheres: A Review of the Categories and Chronology of English Women's History', *Historical Journal*, 36 (2): 383–414.
Vickery, Amanda (2009), *Behind Closed Doors: At Home in Georgian England*, New Haven, CT, and London: Yale University Press.
Virgoe, Roger, ed. (1989), *The Illustrated Letters of the Paston Family*, London: Macmillan.
Waddy, Patricia (1990), *Seventeenth-Century Roman Palaces: Use and the Art of the Plan*, Cambridge, MA: MIT Press.
Wall, Cynthia (2006), *The Prose of Things: Transformations of Description in the Eighteenth Century*, Chicago, IL: University of Chicago Press.

Wall, Richard (1981), 'Women Alone in English Society', *Annales de Demographie Historique*, 18: 303–17.

Walter, John (2009), 'Gesturing at Authority: Deciphering the Gestural Code of Early Modern England', in Michael J. Braddick (ed.), *The Politics of Gesture: Historical Perspectives*, 96–127, Oxford: Oxford University Press.

Warner, Lyndon (2013), 'Before the Law', in Allyson M. Poska, Jane Couchman and Katherine A. McIver (eds.), *The Ashgate Research Companion to Women and Gender in Early Modern Europe*, 233–56, London and New York: Routledge.

Watt, Jeffrey R. (1992), *The Making of Modern Marriage: Matrimonial Control and the Rise of Sentiment in Neuchatel, 1550–1800*, Ithaca, NY: New York University Press.

Watt, Tessa (1991), *Cheap Print and Popular Piety, 1550–1640*, Cambridge: Cambridge University Press.

Weatherill, Lorna (1988), *Consumer Behaviour and Material Culture 1660–1715*, London: Routledge.

Weber, Max (1968), *Economy and Society: An Outline of Interpretive Sociology*, New York: Bedminster.

Welch, Evelyn (2002), 'Public Magnificence and Private Display: Giovanni Pontano's "De Splendore" (1498) and the Domestic Arts', *Journal of Design History*, 15 (4): 211–21.

Welch, Evelyn (2005), *Shopping in the Renaissance*, New Haven, CT, and London: Yale University Press.

Whittle, Jane (2000), *The Development of Agrarian Capitalism: Land and Labour in Norfolk 1440–1580*, Oxford: Oxford University Press.

Whittle, Jane (2005a), 'Housewives and Servants in Rural England, 1440–1650: Evidence of Women's Work from Probate Documents', *Transactions of the Royal Historical Society*, 6th Series, 15: 51–74.

Whittle, Jane (2005b), 'Servants in Rural England c. 1450–1650: Hired Work as a Means of Accumulating Wealth and Skills before Marriage', in Maria Ågren and Amy Erickson (eds.), *The Marital Economy in Scandinavia and Britain 1400–1900*, 89–107, Aldershot: Ashgate.

Whittle, Jane (2011), 'The House as a Place of Work in Early Modern Rural England', *Home Cultures*, 8 (2): 133–50.

Whittle, Jane (2014), 'Enterprising Widows and Active Wives: Women's Unpaid Work in the Household Economy of Early Modern England', *History of the Family*, 19 (3): 283–300.

Whittle, Jane, ed., (2017), *Servants in Rural Europe 1400–1900*, Woodbridge: Boydell Press.

Whittle, Jane and Elizabeth Griffiths (2012), *Consumption and Gender in the Early Seventeenth-Century Household, the World of Alice Le Strange*, Oxford: Oxford University Press.

Wiesner Hanks, Merry (2000), *Women in Early Modern Europe*, 2nd edn, Cambridge: Cambridge University Press.

Wiesner Hanks, Merry (2019), *Women in Early Modern Europe*, 4th edn, Cambridge: Cambridge University Press.

Wilson, Adrian (2013), *Ritual and Conflict, The Social Relations of Childbirth in Early Modern England*, London and New York: Routledge.

Wood, Cynthia (1997), 'The First World/Third Party Criterion: A Feminist Critique of Production Boundaries in Economics', *Feminist Economics*, 3 (3): 47–68.

Wooding, Lucy (2014), 'Richard Whitford's Werke for Housholders: Haminism, Monasticism and Tudor Household Piety', in John Doran, Charlotte Methuen and Alexandra Walsham (eds.), *Religion and the Household, Studies in Church History*, vol. 50, 161–73, Woodbridge: Boydell Press.

Wrightson, Keith (1982), *English Society, 1580–1640*, London: Hutchinson.

Wrightson, Keith (2002), *Earthly Necessities: Economic Lives in Early Modern Britain, 1470–1750*, London: Penguin Books.

Wrigley, E.A. (1987), *People, Cities, Wealth: The Transformation of Traditional Society*, Oxford: Blackwell.

CONTRIBUTORS

Joanne Begiato is Professor of History at Oxford Brookes University. She specializes in the history of emotions, material culture, masculinities, family, and marriage. She has published on subjects as diverse as tearful sailors, nostalgia, wife-beating, fatherhood, pregnancy, and married women's legal status. Her books include *Manliness in Britain 1760–1900: Bodies, Emotions and Material Culture* (Manchester University Press, 2020), *Sex and the Church in the Long Eighteenth Century: Religion, Enlightenment and the Sexual Revolution* (I.B. Tauris, 2017) with William Gibson, *Parenting in England 1760–1830: Emotions, Identity and Generation* (Oxford University Press, 2012) and *Unquiet Lives: Marriage and Marriage Breakdown in England 1660–1800* (Cambridge University Press, 2003).

Amanda Flather is Lecturer in History at the University of Essex. She has broad interests in the social and cultural history of early modern England and her research focuses principally on gender relations, with particular emphasis on the history of the organization of social space in England between the mid-sixteenth and eighteenth centuries. She is the author of *Gender and Space in Early Modern England* (Boydell Press for the Royal Historical Society, 2007) and a number of articles and essays on the influence of gender on the organization and use of social and sacred space.

Tara Hamling is Reader in Early Modern Studies in the History Department at the University of Birmingham. She has published widely on the visual arts and material culture of early modern Britain, with a particular interest in lived religion and the domestic household. She is the author of *Decorating the Godly Household: Religious Art in Post-Reformation Britain* (Yale University Press, 2010) and, with Catherine Richardson, *A Day at Home in Early Modern*

England: Material Culture and Domestic Life, 1500–1700 (Yale University Press, 2017).

Paula Hohti Erichsen is Professor of History of Art and Culture, and is a fashion and material culture historian at Aalto University. Her research focuses on the Italian Renaissance, with a special interest in the role and function of dress and decorative arts at the lower artisanal levels. Hohti has been a principal investigator in the UK-based 'The Material Renaissance' and 'Fashioning the Early Modern' projects. In 2016, she was awarded a European Research Council (ERC) consolidator grant of €2 million to study early modern popular dress and historical and digital reconstruction as a methodology in dress history.

Catherine Richardson is Professor of Early Modern Studies at the University of Kent. She studies the literature and history of early modern material culture, and has written books on *Domestic Life and Domestic Tragedy in Early Modern England* (Manchester University Press, 2006), *Shakespeare and Material Culture* (Oxford University Press, 2011) and, with Tara Hamling, *A Day at Home in Early Modern England: Material Culture and Domestic Life, 1500–1700* (Yale University Press, 2017). She is currently editing *Arden of Faversham* for Arden Early Modern Drama, and running a project on 'The Cultural Lives of the Middling Sort', available at: https://research.kent.ac.uk/middling-culture/.

Danae Tankard is Senior Lecturer in History at the University of Chichester. She is a social and cultural historian, mainly of the seventeenth century, and focuses her research on the county of Sussex. She is the author of *Houses of the Weald and Downland: People and Houses of South-East England, c. 1300–1900* (Carnegie Publishing, 2012) and *Clothing in 17th-Century Provincial England* (Bloomsbury Academic, 2019). She is currently working on a study of seventeenth-century Chichester, exploring the physical environment of the city, especially housing, its social structure, trade and government.

Cynthia Wall is the William R. Kenan, Jr. Professor of English at the University of Virginia. She is the author of *Grammars of Approach: Landscape, Narrative, and the Linguistic Picturesque* (University of Chicago Press, 2019), *The Prose of Things: Transformations of Description in the Eighteenth Century* (University of Chicago Press, 2006; Honorable Mention, James Russell Lowell Prize), and *The Literary and Cultural Spaces of Restoration London* (Cambridge University Press, 1998). She has edited Pope, Defoe and Bunyan, as well as various essay collections, including most recently, with David T. Gies, *The Eighteenth Centuries: Global Networks of Enlightenment* (University of Virginia Press, 2018).

Jane Whittle is Professor of Economic and Social History at the University of Exeter. She has written books on *The Development of Agrarian Capitalism* (Oxford University Press, 2000), and, with Elizabeth Griffiths, *Consumption* *and Gender in the Early Seventeenth-Century Household* (Oxford University Press, 2012), as well as an edited volume on *Servants in Rural Europe* (Boydell Press, 2017). Her recent research on women's work has been published in *Economic History Review* and *Past and Present.* She is currently starting a new research project on 'Forms of Labour: Gender, Freedom and Work in the Preindustrial Economy'.

INDEX

A Chaste Maid in Cheapside, 26
A Relation, or Rather a True Account of the Island of England, 16
Adams, Tracy, 43, 48
adultery, 46
advice books, 11, 110–1, 125, 150–1
agricultural buildings, 68
Aguilar, Don Fernando de, 128
Ajmar-Wollheim, Marta, 156
Alderson, Katherine, 119–20
Alessandri, Torquato, 148
Amsterdam, 99
animals, 26–8, **27**, **28**, 126
Antwerp, 97, 100–1
apprentices, 1, 32–3, 105, 118–9, 120, 137, 140, 142, 143, 144
approaches, 10
Arienti, Giovanni Sabadino degli, 152
Aristotle, 106
Askwith, Christopher, 75
Aubrey, John, 21
Austen', Jane, *Mansfield Park*, 29, 31, 33
Austen, Nicholas, 65
Austria, 114–5
Aynsley, Jeremy, 23

Baatsen, Inneke, 101
Babees Book, The, 30
Bachelard, Gaston, 13, 13–4, 34
Bacon, Francis, 13, 21, 34
bakehouses, 78

Baldwin, William, 27–8
ballads, 11
banqueting houses, 87
banquets, 160–3
Bargagli, Girolamo, 156
Barley, Maurice, 122, 123
Barlow, Edward, 142
Bartholomeo, Christofano di, 160
Bastress-Dukehart, Erica, 50–1
Bayleaf, 62–3, **63**
Bayly, Lewis, 176
bedchambers, 89–90
beds, 88, 89, 90, 92–3, 124, 143
Begiato, Joanne, 4, 5
bequests, 92–4
Bernard, Vincent, 143
Bernardino, St, 53
Best, Henry, 120, 158
Bibles, 177
Biddle, Joan, 116–7, 123
Biddle, Robert, 116–7
Bird, Thomas, 123
Bisticci, Vespasiano da, 160
Black Death, 6, 18
Blatcher, Thomas, 68, 69
Blaxton, Thomasine, 59–60
Blondé, Bruno, 101
boarding, 48, 57
Bodmer, Hans Conrad, 183–4, **183**, 184–5, 186, 187, 192
Bourdieu, Pierre, 10

Brady, Andrea, 54
Brahe, Peter, 152
Breton, Nicholas, 27, 31
brewing, 112, 123, 124
Broomhall, Susan, 40, 41, 42, 49–50, 52
Brueghel, Pieter, the Younger, *Visit to the Farm*, 103, **104**
Bruen, John, 173, 176
Bruges, 192
buffets, 192
Button, Richard, 117–8
Byng, John, Viscount Torrington, 34

Calico House, 181–2, **181**
Calle, Richard, 42
Camden, William, 18
Campbell, Duncan, 47
capitalist industry, 109
Carissimi, Niccolo' de, 151–2, 157
Carson, Neil, 22–3
Catholic Reformation, 5
Catholicism, 9, 167
Cavallo, Sandra, 38, 40, 92
cellars, 59, 73
chairs, 86
Chayanov, A.V., 108, 109
chests, 89, **90**
Chichester, 59–60, 68, 76–80, **77**, 81
childbirth, 52–4
childcare, 112–3
childhood and children, 29–31, 36, 43, 46–8, 48–50, 57, 137, 141, 144
chimney stacks, 64, 70, 77–8, 81, 122, 189–90
China, 98, 99
Chinese porcelain, 100–1
Christmas season, 158
Clare, Richard, 65
Clark, Alice, 109, 115
Cleaver, Robert, 172
clutter, 23–4
Cohen, Elizabeth and Thomas, 150, 154
Coke, Sir Edward, 2, 14
Collier, Mary, 31
Collins, James, 112–3
Collins, William, 131
Comenius, Johann, 26, **27**
comfort, 2, 8
commemorative objects, 94–6, **95**, 160
conduct literature, 11

consumption practices, 7–8
control
 apprentices, 137
 children, 137
 domestic power, 135–7
 patterns of, 130–9
 servants, 136–7, 137–8
cooking, 141
cottages, 18, 65
court records, 11
courtship gifts, 94–6
Croce, Giulio Cesare, 'Veglia carnevalesca', 147
Cromwell, Thomas, 20
cupboards, 192–4, **193**
curtains, 79
Cuypers, Sebastiaen, 91

Darcy, Sir Edward, 74–5
Davies, Richard, 137
Davis, Natalie Zemon, 115
Day, Richard, 169
De Groot, Julie, 192
de Vries, Jan, 114
death, 54
decoration, 18, 151–3
 religious, 180–2, **181**, 184–6
decorum, 157, 163–4
Deloney, Thomas, 29, 33
demographic change, 5–6, 69
Devon, 123–5, 126
devotional objects and tools, 9–10, 177–82, **178**, **179**, **181**
devotional spaces, 174–6, **175**
dining rooms, 86–7, 184–7
Dissolution of the Monasteries, 20, 70
domestic
 arrangements, 1
 industry, 109
 needs, and local skills, 96
 objects, 83–5, 91–2
 power, 138–9
 space, 8, 25–6
 sphere, 3
 violence, 44–5, 53, 142
domesticity, 134
Douglas, Mary, 14, 24, 30
dowry items, 94–6
Dutch East India Company, 99
Dysell, John, 125

East India Company, 98–9
East Sussex, 61
eating arrangements, 139–43, **140**
   dining rooms, 184–7
   and religion, 168, 182–94, **183, 189, 190, 191, 193**
   spiritual significance, 182
elderly, the, 145
Emigh, Rebecca Jean, 113–4
emotional relations, 5
emotions history, 36–7, 39–42, 58
England, 2, 6, 15–7, 129, 189–90
   hospitality, 148–9, 156, 158, 163
   kin density, 38
   parenting, 47
   patterns of control, 130–1
   vernacular houses, 121–5
entertaining, 86–7
Erasmus Desiderius, 2
Éstienne, Charles, 110–3
Éstienne, Henri, 2
Evelyn, John, 71

Fairer, David, 32
family and household, 4, 35–58, **39**, 127
   affective accounts, 37, 40
   bonds, 48–52, **49**
   connections, 40
   constituencies approach, 41–2
   definition, 37
   demographic analysis, 37
   emotions history, 39–42, 58
   hierarchical relationships, 41
   kin density, 37–8
   life-stage events, 52–4
   marital relationships, 42–5
   North-West European, 37
   power relations, 43
   reputation, 52, 150–1
   responsibilities and reciprocities, 46–8
   Scottish Highland clans, 42
   separate spheres, 3
   sexual relations, 45–6
   sibling rivalry, 50–1
   size, 38, 46
   structural accounts, 36
   structures and forms, 37–9
   trust, service and support, 55–7, **55**
   variety, 41
   see also households

family industry, 109
farmsteads, 62
feasts, 158, **159**, 160, 164–5, **164**
Finland, 152–3
fireplaces, 7, 64, 65, 71, 72, 73, 189
Fisher, Thomas, 35–6
Flanders, 7, 154
Flather, Amanda, 3, 4, 32
Fleming, Hannah, 23
flooring, 64, 78
Foakes, R.A., 17
Foister, Susan, 177
food-processing, 112
fosterage, 43, 47–8
Fraiman, Susan, 24
France, 6, 113
Franits, Wayne, 168
freedom, 4
French language, 15
Friedman, Alice T., 25
Fugger, Jakob, 55, **55**
Fuller, Thomas, 18, 149
funerals, 158, 161–2
furniture and furnishings, 8, 26, 75, 79, 83–102, 150, 153–4
   bequests, 92–4
   elite, 85–7, 97–8
   forms of purchase, 96–8
   and gender, 93–4
   global trade, 98–102, **100**
   and the household, 83–5
   influence, 102
   the middling sorts, 87–8
   and religion, 192–4, **193**
   ritual objects, 94–6, **95**
   second-hand, 97
   for sleeping, 88, 88–91
   smaller houses, 88
   and social status, 85–8, 89–91
Furse, Robert, 120–1

gardens, 21–2
Gardiner, Samuel, 186
Gataker, Thomas, 127–8
gender and gender relations, 3–4, 49, 127–46
   eating arrangements, 139–43, **140**
   and furniture and furnishings, 93–4
   hierarchies, 41
   'natural' characteristics of, 127

patterns of authority, 133
patterns of control, 128, 130–9
sleeping arrangements, 143–5
specialization of space, 128–9
and work, 138
gender roles, 104–5, 110–7, **113**, 125, 133–4
Germany, 2, 50–1, 141, 142, 168
global trade, 98–102
Godfrey, Theodore, 56
Goody, Jack, 140
Gouge, William, 133
Gowing, Laura, 54
Grafton, Richard, 170
Grant, Charlotte, 23
Great Rebuilding, the, 17, 18, 61, 89, 121–2
Gresham, Sir Thomas, 102
Grieco, Allen, 161
Griffin, Ralph, 35–6

halls, 61, 63, 64, 74, 78–9, 79, 197n4
Hamling, Tara, 9–10
Hampshire, 61
Hanawalt, Barbara, 126
Hardwick, Julie, 44–5
Hardwick Hall, 85–7, 87, 89–90, 92, **175**
Harrington, Joel, 48
Harrison, William, 18, 18–9, 22, 27, 121–2
Harrys, John, 48
Hassilden, Joan, 111–2
Hastings, Sir Hugh, 156
Hayne, John, 96–7
Heal, Felicity, 156, 158, 162
hearths, 77
Henslowe, Philip, 22–3
Hentzner, Paul, 16, 27
Herbert, George, 18, 21, 24, 34
Herrick, Robert, 20–1, 27
hierarchies, 41, 163–5
Hoby, Lady Margaret, 173, 176
Hohti, Paula, 4
Holland, 114
Hollander, Melissa, 47
home
 boundary, 2
 the building, 17–22, **19, 20**
 definition, 1, 2, 14–5, 15–6, 29, 34
 English concept, 15–7

 and hospitality, 150–1
 management, 24–9
 meaning of, 13–34
 representation of, 22–4
 as verb, 33–4
homelessness, 14
homeliness, 24
homemaking, 24
honour, and hospitality, 148–9, 151–4
Hoskins, W. G., 7, 17, 121–2
hospitality, 147–65
 banquets, 160–3
 feasts, 158, **159**, 160, 164–5, **164**
 forms of, 156–7
 and hierarchy, 163–5
 and the home, 150–1
 and honour, 148–9, 151–4
 and identity, 150–1
 importance of, 147–8, 165
 nobility and, 148
 rules of decorum, 157, 163–4
 significance of, 148–9
 and social entertainment, 154–5
 social function, 154
 and status, 150
house construction, 7, 8, 59–81
 architectural division, 9
 bipartite, 61, 63–4
 Chichester, 59–60, 76–80, **77**, 81
 cost, 61
 cottages, 65, 67–9, 81
 devotional spaces, 174–6, **175**
 division, 75–6
 dwellings, 76
 English vernacular, 121–5
 land requirement, 67–8
 lobby-entry, 64–5, **66**, **67**
 London, 69–76, **72**, **73**, 81
 prodigy houses, 61
 quality, 60
 rural, 60–9, **63**, **66**, **67**, 81
 tripartite, 61–3, **63**
 urban, 59–60, 69–80, **72**, **73**, **77**, 81
 and work, 103–4, 120–5, **122, 124**, 126
house pride, 19
household accounts, 105–6, 134–5, **135**, 156
household economy, 9, 104, 105–10, **107**, 125–6

household management, 1–2, 24–9
　empowering possibilities of, 24–5
　and work, 104, 105–10, **107**
households, 1–2
　composition, 37
　definition, 2, 37
　furniture and furnishings, 83–5
　head of, 4
　heads of, 131–2
　Mediterranean, 37
　members, 4
　multigenerational, 38
　patriarchal relations, 2–3
　size, 38
　structure, 4
　see also family and household
Howell, Martha C., 93, 115
human and animal waste, 79–80

identity, 4, 15–7, 150–1
incomes, 6
India, 98
industrial development, 6
Italy, 2, 7, 84, 91, 156–7, 160–1

Jack of Newbury, 14
Jackson, Anna, 99
Jaffer, Amin, 99
Japan, 99
jettying, 61–2, 71, 77
John Russell's Book of Nurture, 32
John the Baptist, cult of, 177, **178**
Johnson, Matthew, 8, 121
Jonson, Ben, 34
Josselin, Ralph, 158

Kent, 115, 125
keys, 25
kin density, 37–8
King's Lynn, 97
kitchens, 62, 65, 68, 72, 73, 75, 78, 79,
　91–2, 123, 141, 197n6, 197n7
Knyvett, Thomas, 136

Lamberg, Marko, 46
landholding, 5
landowners, 61
Languedoc, 47
Laumonier, Lucy, 47
laundry, 111–2

Le Strange family, 97–8, 105–6, 134
Leapor, Mary, 32
Lefebvre, Henri, 10
Lewis, Matthew, 23
life-stage events, 52–4
Lillington, Jane, 141
Lisle, Lord, 56–7
Lisle Letters, the, 41
living standards, 60
Loder, Robert, 120, 122, 138, 142
London, 15, 19–20, **20**, 126
　building restrictions, 70
　housing, 69–76, **72, 73**, 81
　population, 69–70, 81
　shopping, 97–8
　shops, 71–2
　streets, 71
　suburbs, 70
　Type 1 houses, 71
　Type 2 houses, 71–3
　Type 3 houses, 73
　Type 4 houses, 73–4
Loomis, Catherine, 31
love and affection, 42–4, **44**
Luis, Fray, 127
luxury goods, 6, 102
Lyon, 115

maids, 26, 46, 51–2, 54, 76, 96, 131, 136,
　138, **139**, 142, 143, 144–5
male authority, 132–4
Mandelslo, John Albert de, 99
marital affection, 42–4, **44**
Markham, Gervase, 111, 122–3, **122**
marriage and marital relationships, 3, 4,
　37, 38, 42–6, **44**, 46, 94–6, **95**,
　104–5, 129, 130–1, 133
Marshall, Thomas, 84
masculinity and masculine identity, 4, 44,
　129, 134
material culture, 7–8
Mead, Elizabeth, 59–60
Medici, Catherine de', 53
Medici, Cosimo de, 151–2
Medici, Piero de, 151, 160
memorial brasses, 35–6
men, 3
　single, 39
Mercer, Henry C., 188
methodology, 10–1

Mexia, Vicente, 133
Middle Ages, 17
Milton, John, 21
Miseries of Mavillia, The, 31
Moore, William, 79
Morrall, Andrew, 183, 184, 186
mortality rates, 4
mouse halls, 76
Mulcaster, Richard, 2, 30–1
multigenerational households, 38

Naples, 91
National Archive, The, 177
national identity, 15–7
Netherlands, the, 168
Neuchatel, 133
Newman, John, 59, 78
Newton, Hannah, 43
nobility, the, 5, 6, 17, 50–1, 56–7, 148
Norden, John, 149
Norfolk, 114
Northern European languages, 15
Norwich, 97
Nuechterlein, Jeanne, 177–8

Oja, Linda, 112–3
Orlin, Lena, 8, 18, 19, 23, 116, 126
overcrowding, 9

paid workers, 105, 117–20, **118**
parenting, 30, 36, 43, 46–7, 137
Paris, 144, 145
parlours, 74–5, 79, 87, 87–8
Parthenay-Larchevesque, Jean de, 136
Paston, Margaret, 25–6
Paston, Margery, 42
patriarchal authority, 2–3, 38, 146
patriarchal manhood, 44
patriarchy, 5, 35, 45, 132
patronage, 47
Paumgartner, Magdalena and Balthasar, 43, 134
Pearlie, Robert, 68
peasants, 5, 60
Peck, Linda Levy, 97–8
Peckham, Reynold, 35–6
Peel, J. B. H., 14, 17, 18
Peerson, Eleanor, 19
Pelham, Sir Thomas, 61, 68, 69
Pendean, 65, **67**, 81

Perigord, 129
Perkins, William, 172
Piccotts End, **182**
piety
    behaviour, 169–74
    devotional spaces, 174–6, **175**
    devotional texts, **170**, 171
    devotional tools, 9–10, 177–82, **178**, 179, 181
    focal points, **189, 190, 191**
    and furniture, 192–4, **193**
    iconographies, 189–91, **190**, 192–3
    and mealtimes, 168, 182–94, **183, 189, 190, 191, 193**
    patterns of, 168, 168–82
    prayer, 175–6, 177
Pitt, William, the Elder, 17–8
plays, 11
plunder, 99
political authority, 50
political stability, 3
Pontano, Giovanni, 84, 88, 148, 163
poor law legislation, 67–8
poor relief, 48
population, 5–6, 60
Portugal, 7
possession, sense of, 8
pottery, 8
poverty, 69–70, 80, 132
power relations, family and household, 43
prayer, 175–6, 177
pregnancy and birth, 52–4
prices, 6
printing, 5
privacy, 1, 8–9, 126
privies, 59–60, 75, 79
probate inventories, 64, 74, 78, 79, 83, 91–2, 114–5, 120, 123, 123–4, 153
prodigy houses, 61
property ownership laws, 93
Protestant Reformation, 5
Protestantism, 9–10, 104, 168, 175
public/private separation, 8
Puckering, Sir Thomas, 87, 101
Pullengen, Robert, 68–9

Raby Castle, 34
Ray, John, 21, 29, 34
Rebel, Hermann, 114–5
reception rooms, 154–5

Rede, John, 48
Reid, Margaret, 110
religion, 5, 9–10, 167–94
  behaviour, 169–74
  complexity, 167
  devotional spaces, 174–6
  devotional texts, 169–72, **170**
  devotional tools, 9–10, 177–82, **178, 179, 181**
  focal points, 187–91, **189, 190, 191**
  and furniture, 192–4, **193**
  iconoclasm, 180
  iconographies, 189–91, **190**, 192–3
  idolatry, 179–80
  and mealtimes, 168, 182–94, **183, 189, 190, 191, 193**
  patterns of piety, 168, 168–82
  private devotion, 167
religious texts, 184–5
Repton, Humphry, 31–2
reputation, 52
Richardson, Catherine, 7–8, 17, 22, 23, 25
Ricketts, Annabel, 174
Riello, Giorgio, 100
Ripe, 69
Roberts, Richard, 78
Robinson, Robert, 161–2
rooms, 9, 18–9, **19**, 59, 63, 64, 65, 91
  service, 122–3
  specialized, 7
Rouen, 116
Rucellaio, Giovanni, 148, 150
rural housing, 60–9, **63, 66, 67**, 81
Rush, Benjamin, 15–6
Ruth Cottage, 64
Rybczynski, Witold, 17

Sabellico, Marcantonio, 55–6
Salle, Thomas, 75
Sarti, Raffaella, 155
Scandinavia, 152–3
Schofield, John, 70, 71
Scotland, 42, 47
security, 2
separate spheres, 3–4
Sermini, Gentile, 165
Serres, Oliver, 133
servants, 1, 31–3, 38, 46, 51–2, 105, 117–20, 136–7, 137–8, **139**
  eating arrangements, 141–2
  sleeping arrangements, 143–4, 145
  vulnerability, 145
service rooms, 122–3
sex and sexual relations, 29, 45–6, 52
Sforza, Francesco, 151–2
Sforza, Galeazzo Maria, 151–2
Shakespeare, William
  A Comedy of Errors, 16–7
  King John, 17
  The Merry Wives of Windsor, 22
  The Taming of the Shrew, 2
  Two Gentlemen of Verona, 17
Shepard, Alexandra, 4, 116
shops, 9, 71–2
sibling rivalry, 50–1
sickness, 54
Silverden, 64
sleeping arrangements, 143–5
Smith, Henry, 127
social entertainment, 154–5
social hierarchy, 3
social status, 7–8
  and furniture and furnishings, 85–8, 89–91
  and hospitality, 150
socioeconomic transformation, 5–6
sources, 10–1
space, specialization of, 128–9
Spain, 7
spatial practice, 10
Speed, John, 18
Spenser, Edmund, 17
splendour, social virtue of, 84, 88
Stephens, Jane, 54
Stone, Lawrence, 42
Stout, William, 134–5, 144
stoves and stove plates, 187–8, **189**
Stow, John, 19–20, 70
Strachey, Lytton, 29, 31, 33, 34
sumptuary laws, 161, 163
supernatural threats, 2
Sweden, 112

tables, 85, 86–7, 88, 192
tablewares, 101, 186–7, 191, **191**
Tankard, Danae, 7
Teellinck, Willem, 172
tenure, types of, 5, 132
Thakeham, 67–8
Thompson, Sarah, 120

Treswell, Ralph, 70–1, 72, **73**, 74, 75–6
Trevisano, Andrea, 16, 30, 32–3
Tucker, Barnard, 123–5
Tuscany, 113–4
Tusser, Thomas, 24–5, 29, 33
Twain, Mark, 15

urban housing, 59–60, 69, 81
  Chichester, 59–60, 76–80, **77**, 81
  London, 69–76, **72**, **73**, 81
urbanization, 7
Urbino, 94

Valois, Elisabeth de, 53
Van Gent, Jacqueline, 41, 49–50
van Spilbergen, Joris, 100
Venice, 46, 97, 119, 153, 161
Vickery, Amanda, 3
Vrins, Francesco, 153
Vyne, The, 174

wages, 6–7, 106, 109
wainscot panelling, 79, 85, 86
Wall, Cynthia, 2
Waller, J.G., 36
Wallington, Nehemiah, 173, 177
Wars of the Roses, 18
water house, 75
water supply, 79, 111
Watson, Elizabeth, 57
Weald and Downland Living Museum, 62, 65
Wealden house, 62–3, **63**
weavers, 123–5
Weber, Max, 108–9, 109
wedding feasts, 158, **159**, 160, 162, 164–5, **164**
Weller, John, 120
Wells, Thomas, 62
Wheeler, William, 131
Whitford, Richard, 169, 175–6
Whittle, Jane, 1–2, 3, 9, 138
Wilcox, Richard, 74
William the Silent, 49–50
Willoughby family, 25
Wilson, Edmond, 83–4, 88, 89
windows, 7, 8, 61, 79, 121, 122
witch-bottles, 2
Wix, Anne, 106

Wix, Richard, 106
Wollaton Hall, 25
women
  acceptance of husbands' authority, 43
  accounts management, 134–5, **135**
  agency, 43, 50–1
  authority, 53
  domestic power, 135–7
  domestic violence, 44–5, 53, 142
  eating arrangements, 141, 142
  empowerment, 24–5
  as heads of households, 4
  inheritance rights, 130–1
  legal position, 130–1
  out-of-house activities, 112
  separate spheres, 3
  single, 39, 57, 131–2
  subordination, 133–4, 137
  widows, 115–6, 131–2
  work, 109, 110, 110–3, 115–7
Woodford, Robert, 173
Woods, William, 80
work, 4, 9, 103–26
  activities, 103, **104**
  advice books, 110–1, 125
  capitalist industry, 109
  definition, 106
  domestic industry, 109
  family industry, 109
  and gender and gender relations, 138
  gender roles, 104–5, 110–7, **113**, 125
  and house construction, 103–4, 105, 120–5, **122**, **124**, 126
  and household economy, 125–6
  and household management, 104, 105–10, **107**
  occupations, 114–5
  paid, 105, 117–20, **118**
  unpaid, 110
  urban households, 115–6
  widows, 115–6
  women's, 109, 110, 110–3, 115–7
Wotton, Henry, 13–4, 151

Xenophon, 106, 108

York, 154
Young Children's Book, The, 30